"The Information Science papers on Sexology included in this volume, as well as the Author's Preface, are intended as essential additions to all present day Gender Studies high school and college curricula."

Gordon Fifer, Ph.D., D. Ed.,
Head of Educational Foundations
HUNTER COLLEGE OF THE CITY UNIVERSITY
OF NEW YORK 1973

"Artemis Smith a/k/a ArtemisSmith Morpurgo, was a prominent strategist of the 1950-60's Rainbow civil rights coalition movements and author of the pulp fiction best sellers *Odd Girl* and *This Bed We Made,* and principal co-author of 'Joan of Washington Square' a/k/a *The Third Sex.*

"Now also fondly referred to as *'the GrandmaMoseX of the GLBT Activist Community,'* ArtemisSmith is a contemporary of Andy Warhol and a still-living Metaphysical Poet, Playwright, Futurist and Digital-media Artist. Besides operating her own successful off-off-Broadway workshop that gave rise to many of today's vintage Film and Television celebrities, in the 1950-60's she was the first Invited Speaker to tell the Gay Community at pre-Stonewall 1960's ECHO Conferences to look toward the Advertising Industry to change the Gay Image, and to hurry up and 'Come out of the Closet' or get left out of the civil rights movement."

E. Sidney Porcelain
THE SAVANT GARDE INSTITUTE 1989

Billie Taulman in Rome, 1954.

ArtemisSmith's
THE THIRD SEX

by Annselm L.N.V. Morpurgo and Billie Taulman

The 2013 Color Library Edition with Appendix containing *ArtemisSmith's* ATHEIST MANIFESTO and the suppressed 1970's academic papers in the Philosophy of Sex and Love.

Sag Harbor . New York . U.S.A.

ArtemisSmith : The Third Sex

A Monograph of

THE SAVANT GARDE INSTITUTE

© 1958. 1959, 1972 and 2013 by ArtemisSmith. All rights reserved.
© 2013 by The Savant Garde Institute. All rights reserved.

Academic Library Color Edition: ISBN 978-1-878998-05-7
LIBRARY OF CONGRESS CONTROL NO: 2013901601

'the savant garde workshop' publishers
P.O.B. 1650 . SAG HARBOR . NEW YORK . 11963 . USA
Tel: 1.631.725.1414

Dear Colleagues:

I think it had to have been 1964 when best-selling phenomenologist and sexologist R.E.L. Masters—then researching the developmental stages of the libido in subjects with very high creativity—sought me out to include me in his study.

Masters' list of experimental subjects was drawn from a multinational selection of prominent persons in the arts and I was flattered to be recruited, although I was pretty turned off by then on the entire subject of human sexuality. Having coined and stylized the Unisex Movement in the early 1950's, and having penned three activist works which became underground pulp fiction best-sellers, and having become a featured speaker at various 1960's Rainbow civil rights conventions, I felt I had already done my part for the sexual liberation movements and was ready to dump sexology and pulp fiction altogether and go back to my more central avant garde experimental work in the literary and visual arts.

But Masters, always on the lookout for a new best-selling book idea, jumped on my *Unisex* bandwagon. After taking a special interest in all of my work in the arts, he hinted to me that transgender millionaire Reid Erickson might put up money for plastic surgeon Harry Benjamin to give me a free sex change if I wanted one. *Did* I want one, he then asked me point blank.

I was taken aback by the question and it took me a while to answer. How could Masters have misread my feminist anti-Gender stance as an endorsement of a *transgender* agenda? The two were axial opposites. Was he simply testing me? True, my second social novel, *The Third* Sex, had by now become an underground best seller and the gay rights community was pressing me to take a leadership position in their cause.

Apparently the novel was now providing a political platform for *all* the loosely-organized agendas of the budding sexual freedom movements—even those entirely different from what Taulman and I had intended when we co-wrote and sold our covert sexual freedom manifesto to Beacon Books back in 1959.

As neo-renaissance artists identifying ourselves as political lesbians, both Taulman and I admittedly had been miserably unhappy about being forced to live as women in a man's world - but not because either of us had any problem accepting our anatomical selves—but because the whole world was askew on the subject of gender-identity. Just as it was askew on the subject of race (i.e., how many black persons in those days would have jumped at the chance to pass for white for the same socially deplorable reason?) *and* also askew on the subject of all so-called handicapped persons then politically segregated from equal access to the social world.

After my return from Europe in 1963, grief-stricken over Taulman's illness and our forced separation,[1] I threw myself into producing, acting and directing off-off-Broadway with many budding talents in my theater workshop—many of whom quickly became Oscar and Emmy and Tony winners after they left me—but for my own career it was always an uphill battle. Not only was I being socially reviled and blacklisted for having penned three best-selling activist novels, I was also getting a lot of chauvinist flack as a "lady-poet" and "lady-playwright-producer-director" testing the limits of my comedic powers for anger management.

The overt rage against feminists in the professions had become stronger than ever, and seemed to be coming almost entirely from multiple rival cliques each with local critics in their pockets, all competing for the same artistic turf in both the West

---

[1] cf. my 1950's Memoir, *ArtemisSmith's ODD GIRL Revisited: an autobiographical correlate,* ISBN 978-1-878998-35-4.

and East Village. (It was actually mostly coming from a third group, an infiltrating mob element subtly ensconced among them that increasingly controlled a large part of the arts media and was shafting some of the most worthy while wrapping its protective arms around only those they could enlist to further the growing drug and porn industry lining its ever-deepening pockets.)

The mob had all the money and the illicit manpower and therefore the upper hand. The good guys in the arts didn't stand a chance against the swelling tide—but at least where we were, then based at The Community Church of New York whose Pastor, Donald Harrington, also chaired the Liberal Party, there was some measure of political protection.

Throughout the NYC art scene, the sexist harassment directed against me everywhere I turned was strong enough to make me despise being trapped in my own body, much like black persons were despising being trapped in their own skin, and had I been tall and thin and wiry-looking, I might easily have turned transvestite like some of my feminist forebears, just to be treated as an artistic equal. But being short and too full of curves, I was trapped in my socially-defined female persona like it or not. So I decided instead to publicly declare myself gender-free and demanded that the whole world follow me in putting thumbs-down on the 'Gender-line' as being any more viable a socio-political category than the 'Color-line'. "Relegate it entirely to Medicine and Physiology, but keep it out of the rest of my life!"

How sick our puritanical culture was! In those days, not only was there flagrant sex and race segregation, but also the slightest imperfection—the slightest deviation from the socially-established norm—was looked upon as reason enough to exclude an otherwise-capable person from a job promotion or a romantic introduction. The Help Wanted pages were firmly split between Male and Female and executive employment agencies simply hung up on women who dared to apply.

The job bias didn't stop there or even at the color line. Despite F.D.R.'s example, multiple Polio victims with a shortened arm or leg were still being pitied and patronized and hired only as handicapped. And when singer Johnny Ray dared to appear on stage wearing a hearing aid, it prompted a sudden burst of applause at the close of his song from an audience that had been sitting in utter cultural shock.

Did I want a sex change?
A part of me did, but not the sexual side of me.
To answer Masters' question, it was one thing to be doggedly appearing in unisex pant-suits forty years before *Ellen,* and with hair barber-clipped like Bergman or Seberg as Saint Joan.[2] As a woman, tiny as I am, that made me look tomboy hot—but as a man? I cringed at the thought of turning myself into the next Toulouse Lautrec! In what way would that get me more respect? (My apologies to all the 'little people' who rightly take offense to this!) And how would both the men and women in my life react to me in my surgically-altered body? Wouldn't it be easier and more effective and reversible simply to strap on prosthesis for all the times a woman in my life might want a penis, and leave me free to go back to being fully female whenever and with whomever I wanted to be?

"Check back with me after menopause," I finally politely told Masters to tell Benjamin—and my diplomatic reply made all the underground grapevine gossip columns.

Nevertheless, thanks to Masters, I did get to interview Erickson for *Science & Mechanics Magazine.*[3] B.G. Davis Publications eventually suppressed that story along with a bunch of other far-out articles, including my memorable visit to a nudist colony for *Income Opportunities* while flanked by nude *Playboy*

---

[2] At Uptown bars and Hamptons celebrity bashes I also sometimes wore my great-grandmother's tuxedo. I'm told she belonged to a multinational multi-generational literary circle of feminist cross-dressers that included Georges Sand, George Eliot, perhaps Rachel Morpurgo, and probably also Emma Lazarus.

[3] Editor Lawrence Sanders couldn't convince our publisher, B.G. Davis, that such topics were now mainstream and no longer taboo. He finally quit to write a plethora of best sellers including *The Anderson Tapes.*

and *Esquire* paparazzi that my editor was paying me for but not printing.[4]

But thanks to Masters and wife, New Age theologian Jean Houston,[5] both of whom were now Uptown friends and neighbors of mine, I interviewed transgender Erickson in 1964 when he was still living in Sutton Place.

Erickson was happily married and already planning a child (by artificial insemination) which happened a year later. He eventually moved his family to Mexico where life was more affordable, and as far as I can tell the transgender decision was right for him—despite the fact that most women would have found no attraction to him as a medium-sized goateed male but would have certainly been turned on to him if he had remained a sexy blonde butch!

But even for the USA, that was another time and place. Sexual politics have sufficiently improved for metro-feminists now, making it more tolerable to put gender-identity issues aside and simply live our lives as we choose. However, still today in many parts of the world there are women who must either change their sex, or pretend to, simply because—being wealthy enough and physically fit enough, they can get away with it—because living as women under those political climates, regardless of true sexual orientation, is *intolerable*!

But in our part of the world, for most lesbians or political lesbians, as well as most gay men, that's a procrustean alternative that I strongly advise against, especially since there is no romantic advantage to having the surgery—it's more often than not a total turn off. Why treat the symptom rather than the disease? Why alter the person rather than the sick social climate that is genuinely in need of repair?

Society places altogether too much emphasis on dividing

---

[4] At that memorable outdoor occasion I ran into Barbara Gittings and Wife, and came to be graciously hosted and interviewed by none other than Nancy Reagan - thanks to my literary agent, Jeanne Hale!
[5] Later a Hillary mentor.

the world into the Male and the Female when it is obvious that there are, chromosomally, far more combinations than XX and XY at natural play.[6] Why not simply teach society to dump the male/female dichotomy altogether and just give people buttons to wear on their *WHATEVER* tee shirts advertising their sexual preference? Why not simply have everyone dress as they feel and get rid of the tyranny of fashion altogether?

When I took all this up with Drs. Masters and Benjamin in 1964, they assured me that the persons undergoing transgender procedures were not permitted to do so quickly or irresponsibly; that to qualify for the surgery they had to be adjudicated long-term hopeless cases facing severe psychological impairment if forced to remain in their present state. Yes, a sex change was merely treating the symptoms rather than providing a cure—but the cure— the repair of the oppressive social climate at the root of the disorder, was not likely to occur anytime soon.

But times they are changing in the USA and I strongly urge all persons now contemplating surgical procedures not to take such final and irreversible steps just because they have become more fashionable. At least in our own society, the world is finally moving fast-forward toward a new ethic of inclusion for all.[7]

But let's turn the clock back now to 1958 and the star of *this* show—the activist documentary disguised as a lesbian pulp

---

[6] Gender *identity*, in contrast to sexual *deviance*, is fully socially instilled and need not march in step with the hand we are dealt with at birth

[7] To make this Authors' Re-Issue more academic worthy, in the Appendix I have also included key papers I wrote and presented to colleagues I knew to be active in the Gay Community back in 1965-1973. The first today seems somewhat dated to me, since the progress of my thought on Gender-Identity has gone way beyond that, moving ever further away from Clinical Psychology and toward an Information Science concept of Mind; but the second is more current. A sanitized version of it, keyed specifically to the aesthetics of Dance rather than of Sex, was published in CORD's prestigious 1979 Dance Research Annual X. Look for both papers and more in the back pages of this volume.

novel co-written by me and Taulman, which happily became one of the key manifestos of the pre-Stonewall gay rights movement.

Our original title, *Joan of Washington Square*, would never have sold a million or more copies!. Lucky thing our sleazy publishers chose to dub it *The Third Sex* which, in addition to its earlier connection with the landmark work by Radcliffe Hall, was also now being used in fringe science psychological trash literature hotly competing with us for the same dime-store shelf space.

Titles, not protected by copyright laws, were regularly snatched and recycled at pulp editors' whim with impunity, and this one was a canny choice. But contrary to its editorial marketing strategy, there was nothing that Taulman and I claimed to be scientific about *The Third Sex*. Rather, we meant the work as purely activist and entirely journalistic, and limited in its scope to only a small, visible sector of the gay community of that era—emerging from the "gay bars" skirting the NYU collegiate community around Washington Square.

But by 1964, the socio-political effect of the so-called *sleaze* novel's publication apparently had stretched worldwide. Persons everywhere had now become increasingly sensitized to the possibility that the couple, or couples, living next door to them might secretly be other than *straight!* And with increasing public awareness came open conflict. The privacy rights of heretofore comfortably-closeted gays were suddenly being challenged and political activism was being forced upon them like it or not.

Those of us who were already in the Rainbow movement saw that this was a silent but very populous minority—when including *all* of the GLBT categories perhaps even a majority!—that immediately needed to stand up and be counted or risk being left out of the civil rights *putsch*. But just as with the closeted Jews in *Weimar* Germany, centuries-old fear of reprisal still held back those comfortably situated, those not trapped in the Ghettos, to wallow in self-deprecating denial.

During this period, circa 1963-'65, as an activist author I was asked to address two successive ECHO (East Coast

Homophile Organizations) Conferences. At the first of these, I spoke on the subject of improving the Gay image in the media, not only within pulp fiction but also through the advertising media—something that Taulman and I had brought up at a 1950's formative meeting of New York Mattachine—which must have included Marshall McLuhan—as a viable political strategy. After all, most of the creative staff in the advertising industry was already peopled by closet gays —why not tap into that massive voters' block for positive social change?

My address was well received and two years later, emboldened by the success of my Rainbow anti-war morality-play/happening, *Brother Thanatos*,[8] at the Unitarian-Universalist Park Avenue community center that doubled as the C.O.R.E./Liberal Party recruitment site for the MLK freedom marches—I followed up my earlier speech at the second ECHO Conference, telling everyone that it was time to "Come out of the closet."[9]

My spontaneous addition to the abstract of what was to be my speech took everyone by surprise—I had not cleared that part of my message with the leadership and their legal staff which was always on the lookout for too radical a stance. No one was prepared for that kind of statement. There was fear of anything that might prompt swift vice squad reprisal. It had already been difficult enough for the ECHO volunteers just to find a convention hall and hotel that wouldn't cancel out, would dare book our meeting. We were still only calling ourselves *Homophile* in order to avoid the legally inflammatory terms

---

[8] The final version, as performed in Fall 1965, is to be reprinted and included in the Appendix of the upcoming final volume of the GLBT Pulp Fiction Triad, *THIS BED WE MADE* (originally titled: FOR IMMEDIATE DEMOLITION).

[9] I think I must have added something like "Come out *Now*— because like the Jews in Germany you can't hide anymore! People like me in the arts are making you too visible! Either stand up and be counted or be scapegoated again and lose all the ground you've gained here today!"

Homosexual and *Bisexual*. Were we ready to assert our real identities and human rights so militantly?

In fact, it took about four years for the message to really sink in, and not until Stonewall for "Come out of the Closet" to become a standard GLBT battle cry. Meanwhile, on Memorial Day Weekend of 1966, just as the elders of The Community Church of New York—fired by the sustained heavy public attendance at my *Brother Thanatos* organizational human rights play- happenings—were voting to establish my off-off-Broadway workshop in our own theater—I came to be badly injured and nearly killed in a car accident in the Hamptons that I to this day maintain was no accident.

I know you will want to know more about this period, but you'll have to wait until my 1960's Memoir, included in the re-issue of the last pulp novel of my GLBT Triad, *This Bed We Made* (originally titled: For Immediate Demolition) for the rest.

Meanwhile, *Enjoy!*

Annselm LNVM 2013

FRAGMENT FROM *THE LEAGUE FOR SEXUAL FREEDEOM*'S FIRST 1965 NEWSLETTER:

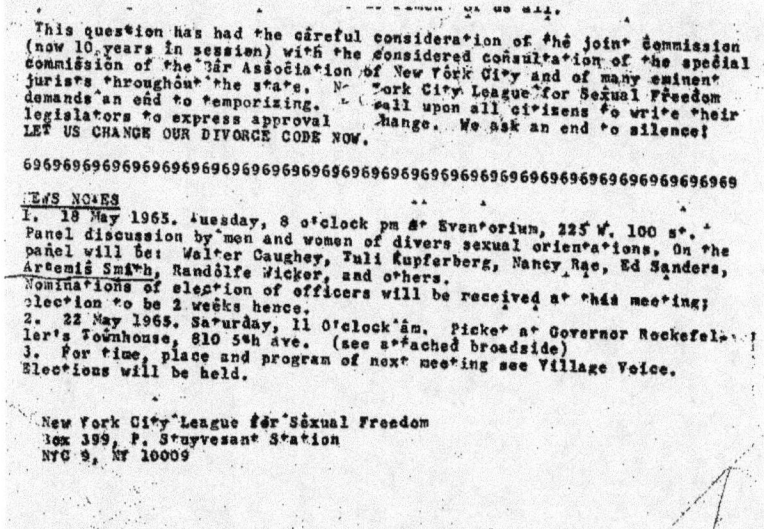

ArtemisSmith : The Third Sex

**PROGRAM FRAGMENT from the first
ECHO Conference c. 1963 ?**

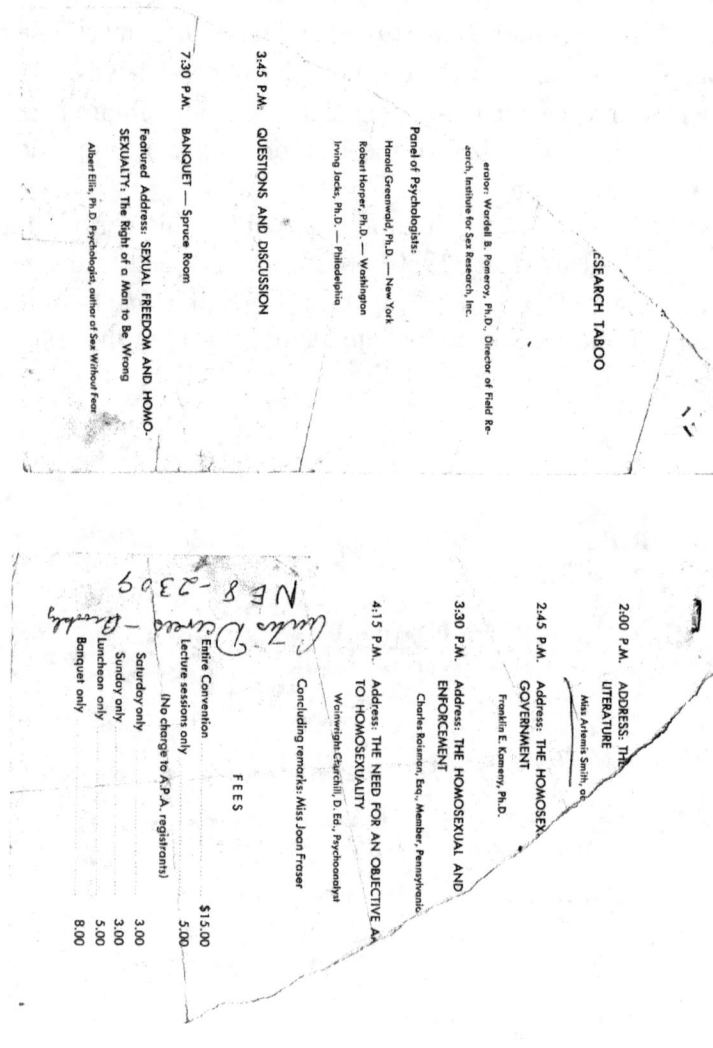

ArtemisSmith's
THE THIRD SEX

By Annselm L.N.V. Morpurgo and Billie Taulman

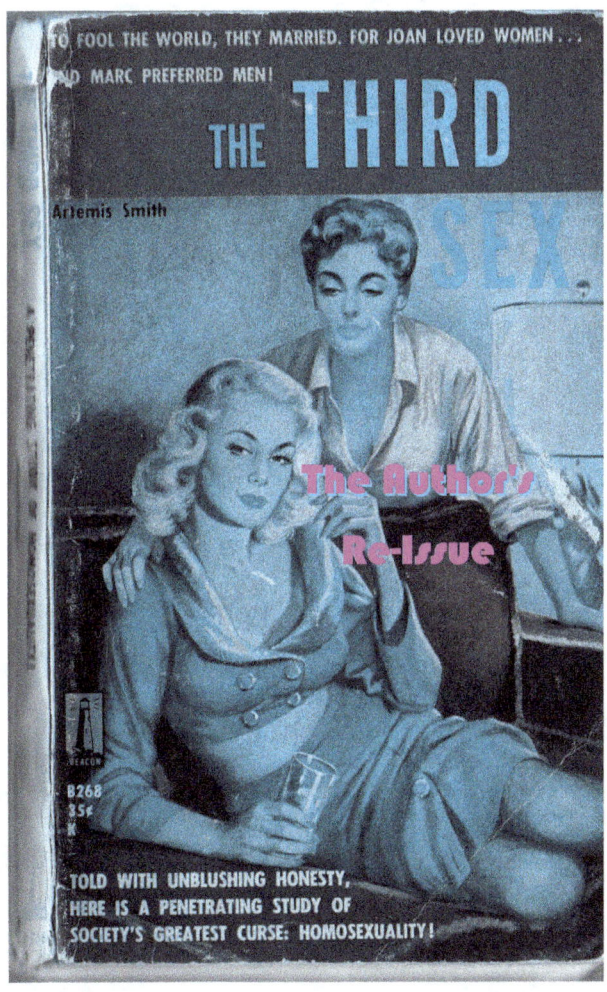

Joan of Washington Square (The Third Sex)
© 1958 by Artemis Smith. All rights reserved.*

---

* The 1959 publication of this work by Beacon Books (Universal Publishing and Distributing Corp.), retitled THE THIRD SEX, omitted our original copyright notice and was in breach of contract. This opened the way for pirated new editions in the late 1960's also infringing on our copyright. It took constant policing to force our publishers to pay royalties on new printings until they finally dissolved the corporation in order to avoid mounting lawsuits from their authors. It should be noted that the managing staff and covert owners of Universal Publishing, shielded as stockholders, simply went on to doing business as usual under new corporate names.

1.

JOAN looked out from her window toward MacDougal Street, the heart of Greenwich Village. A fire escape hampered her view and made her little furnished room seem all the more dark and depressing. Joan had chosen to live alone this way; she had refused to share a large light apartment with a friend. Because Joan was afraid that living with someone her own age might arouse the desires she tried so hard to ignore; living with a pretty girl might awaken the sleeping dog within her breast.

Joan walked away from the window and went to her mirror. She was scared, but she knew she would have to go through with tonight—or else wither in some ivory tower like the proverbial maiden lady, having only one unconsummated love to treasure for the rest of her days. In reality, Joan was much the maiden lady; but her need to live, to know all the pleasures of life—her need to satisfy the burning craving in her body for David—that need was taking away her fear and replacing it with a stoic, silent determination. Joan was going to find out about life—and about herself. And tonight was the start. She was going to find out why men did not attract her, find out why she had fallen in love with David, effeminate David, who wasn't really a man.

David had told her the reason, and somewhere within herself Joan whispered the truth. She was a Lesbian, and this was why

David had attracted her; he was so much like a woman. But Joan had decided to fight the truth. Before she became a Lesbian she wanted to be certain that normal men did repel her, that normal men could never please her.

She studied herself in the mirror, pulling her pony tail of light-red hair down to contrast against the pale skin of her neck. David had taught her to apply makeup—just a little rouge and deep orange lipstick. David had taught her to dress—a light fall sweater, white cashmere, with a long necklace of many-colored beads; a flair skirt in a Madras pattern made of rough linen; simple shoes with very high heels. She had been a tomboy before she had met David; now she was meticulously feminine.

Joan was ready to go out. She was going to a little club that showed old movies, followed by a dance. She had heard of the place from her friends in school. It was good hunting ground for the college crowd, a place where youth could find youth—and, for Joan, a place where she could find a young man to take home.

To take home a young man, to make love—this still seemed strange and unreal to her, but Joan knew she must do it. Her past two years longing for David must stop. She had to realize that she could never hope to marry David or have him at all; because David did not want her, found it impossible to consider her more than just his friend.

So much had happened in these past two years since she had entered college and met David—a merry-go-round of following him about, of having the happiest time of her life—for her life at home had been meaningless, bleak, foreign, never as real as these two years by herself and with David in the city. And she had gradually fallen in love, shutting herself away from all her other friends, making David an obsession.

The last six months had been hell. Hell had begun one day in David's apartment: Joan had rehearsed in her mind for several days what she wanted to say to him---that she loved him, desired him, was ready to do anything for him. And now that they were studying together, Joan sitting in a deep chair across from where he sat on the couch, as handsome as any movie star—now she decided to tell him.

"I love you," she said, and her voice sounded uncertain, trembled, cut through the thick air and faded. David pretended not to hear her. But Joan had waited too long to give up so easily. She spoke again, this time with a louder voice. "I love you, David," she said.

David didn't look up. His velvet voice, so much like a woman's, coughed slightly. "I'm sorry, Joan," he said. His hands were trembling as he put down his pen, and then he forced himself to look at her. "You mustn't love me, because I don't love you," he said.

The words shattered her, pinned her down in a waking faint, demolishing her dream, the dream of youth that all true love is returned. She was left trembling in her chair, unable to speak, while David continued reading to her as if nothing had been said at all in an effort to spare her the humiliation of being rejected by him.

Nothing more happened that afternoon. When Joan was able to leave, she left, and they were friends; she halted an urge to take his hand, to embrace him, to kiss his sensitive mouth—an urge that had repulsion coupled with attraction—repulsion at his maleness, attraction to his femininity.

But when David's door shut behind her, the trembling began again. And so did a wild stream of though and desperation, for she went over in her mind all the things that had been said about David in school—that he was effeminate, that he wasn't interested in women, that he was homo-sexual.

But this wasn't the end, it was only the beginning of hell. The next six months, months of being obsessed with only one thought, to make David love her---those months were hell, were what Joan consciously called her adolescent breakdown.

The final scene had come three days ago, over the telephone. David refused to see her and finally told Joan what she already knew—that he was different, couldn't possibly like women. And then he added that Joan was attracted to him primarily because she was different, because she was a latent homosexual herself. He told her to fight it, to seek help, said that he could not help her, had to stay out of it. Since then, every time Joan called him, he refused to speak to her.

Only Joan's much battered pride pulled her out of it. She forced herself to turn elsewhere. But this yielded only frustration because there was no one to whom she could go for help. Although she was studying to be a psychologist, she had a dread fear of what her personality might suffer under an analyst's scalpel; she did not want to cease loving David or to change in any way at all. So she decided to solve her own problem, to take her own drastic steps, and tonight was the night she had chosen. She was determined to find someone to replace David.

Like a sleepwalker, Joan picked up her raincoat and left the room. She did not even notice the tough-looking Lesbian who brushed by her as she walked down the stairs. She was too absorbed in her purpose, too afraid. Tonight felt like a kind of dying; tonight she was going to change herself.

The Flicker Club was dark. The movie had begun. She paid for her ticket at the entrance and went in, picking a chair to the side. They were playing a Mae West film—*My Little Chickadee*. Joan had never seen Mae West. She let herself be lost in the plot of the picture, trying her best to enjoy it.

"Hello," a voice whispered to her from the seat beside her.

Joan turned. She had thought the seat was empty but now a young man had sat down, a handsome, blonde young man, quite tall.

"Can I bring you some pop corn?" he smiled.

He was friendly and nice and took away Joan's fear. She knew it was permissible for him to talk to her here because that was how the club was run, making it easy for young people to meet.

"Yes, thanks," she nodded shyly and tried to smile in return. In her mind she thought, I wonder if he'll do. He seems nice enough.

When he came back the picture was about to end. She accepted the pop corn and waited, slightly embarrassed, for him to speak.

"Do you like Mae West?" he asked when the lights went on.

"Yes, very much," Joan said. She was lying. She could not see what it was that made Mae West such a legend.

"We're playing another one of her films next week," he said. "I hope you're going to be a regular here."

"I've been thinking of it," Joan said.

The chairs were being cleared away from the middle of the floor so that the dancing could begin.

"Let's go to the bar," the young man said.

Joan nodded and they got up, walking toward the small bar, tucked in a corner, that served beer and soda pop.

"My name's Paul," he said when they reached it. "May I buy you a beer?"

Joan nodded, wondering whether she should give him her real name. Then she decided that she should and said "I'm Joan Barnes."

She found it difficult to pay attention to Paul. Her mind wanted to be elsewhere. She found him permissible and not entirely repulsive, perhaps because of his light, almost girlish skin, but she could not be attracted to him. She looked around the room. No man here attracted her. But the blonde girl with the short haircut and fluffy sweater dancing past them with a rather plain partner—the blonde girl attracted Joan. A great feeling of panic brought Joan back to Paul. She would force herself to like him.

"You're a strange girl, Joan," Paul laughed pleasantly. "You don't seem to be really listening to me. Where are you from?"

"My home is in White Plains," she said, "but I'm going to college here and I'm staying in a furnished room not far from here." She felt she had to talk in large lumps or else she would forget to talk at all. "Where are you from?" she asked.

"Staten Island," he said, "I'm staying with my folks and I come here on weekends." He stopped now and looked at her. "Perhaps we can meet for lunch tomorrow and go to the museum or something."

Joan paused a moment. Tomorrow was Saturday; she had nothing to do but sit in her room and try to study. "That will be very nice," she said, feeling at once a great relief. Paul would be taking up some of her time—some of the time she was now spending in brooding over David.

He handed her a can of beer and a glass and she put down her pop corn and took a long swallow. The evening was becoming more pleasant, less desperate.

"Shall we dance?" Paul said, now that the juke box was playing a slow tune.

Joan left the bar and went to the middle of the floor with him. She had learned how to dance in high school but this was her first dance. She had avoided dances; she had avoided everything else which girls her age do. Only now did she realize how alone she had been, how very remote from the rest of the world.

She followed Paul awkwardly, not used to being held, used to leading herself. Paul held her at arm's length for a moment and then pressed her close, bringing his body next to hers.

Joan felt awkward; Paul's body felt only foreign to her. She allowed herself to press against him, but felt only puzzlement at why men and women enjoyed dancing.

"What are you majoring in?" he asked, trying to bring her back from her remoteness.

"English," she said. "I'm going to be a teacher." She looked up at him, towering over her, as they danced, "And you?"

"Engineering," he said. "I graduated last year. I may go overseas in September."

"How nice," Joan said, returning her head to his shoulder. "I've always wanted to go overseas. I was hoping that I could teach English somewhere like Paris."

"Paris? Somehow that doesn't seem like you at all." He was laughing and the corners of his eyes crinkled a little. Joan decided that he was likable. Perhaps she could play his game the way he wanted it, she thought. Perhaps tonight her life would begin to fall neatly into place. But she was unprepared for the wave of anger that inflamed her body as Paul drew her close. She felt his body, hard and aggressive in every part, and knew that he was attracted to her, as women, she supposed, have always known. His suit, of a light spring wool, fit him closely and she saw the long curve of his chest. She let her face rub against the rough wool, passively following his every movement. She felt as though she were drugged. When the music stopped he led her back to the bar as though she were a child.

Picking his way between the tables on the way to the bar ahead of her he turned and put his hand caressingly on her shoulder, as though inspired with an idea. "How about seeing some of the Bohemian places tonight?"

Joan reached his side, relieved that he did not intend to corner her or to turn elsewhere. Suddenly she liked the idea of spending the evening with him—perhaps she could speak freely to him, a stranger, as she had not been able even to David. They walked arm-in-arm back to the bar and Joan confessed, "I really want to see the inside of the Daisy. I live across the street, and it fascinates me."

"Well," Paul smiled, holding up his fingers to the bartender for another two beers, "you won't be fascinated after you've once been inside. I'll take you. With me, you won't have to be worried about those dough dikes."

"Dikes?" Joan laughed. "Please explain."

He put his hand on his head as if to think deeply. "They're Lesbians."

Joan said, "Oh."

"I mean," he said, explaining it slowly, "that those women are not only homosexuals—you know that word, don't you," he joked, "but they are aggressive and try to pretend that they own the world and all the women in it."

"In other words," Joan summed up, "they act like men."

Paul groaned. Joan decided he was becoming a bit discouraged. She finished her beer quickly and stood, taking his large hand in hers.

"Anyway," she said, "I'm sure that you're not like a dike." The words coming out of her own mouth surprised her. She was leading him on. Within her, she felt guilty. The women coming in and out of the Daisy had attracted her deeply in a way that she felt Paul could not ever attract her. Nonsense, she told herself quietly. You haven't given him a chance. She watched him to see if her words had shocked him or if he sensed the lie somewhere behind them. He seemed rather to be enjoying her last remark smugly.

"No," he said wickedly, "I'm not even a little bit that way—except sometimes." Watching him, Joan was sure that he felt like a naughty little boy. He paid the bill with an air of abandon and they walked out together, out the long flight of stairs and into the street.

A wave of fear rose to her throat as they reached the door of the Daisy. The hard-faced men at the door stared appraisingly at her body as she entered. Joan took Paul's arm and allowed him to lead her toward the back, where they might observe but not be too well seen.

He sat down next to her behind the table, his leg pressing close against hers. Joan forced herself to raise her eyes from the table; she looked curiously at the vulgar murals on the wall—paintings of strange women in men's clothing pressing close to large-breasted girls. Then she saw Paul looking at her, a strange smile on his face. She wondered briefly how well he understood.

"You're blushing," he said, pleased.

"What do you suppose is doing that?" she answered primly.

His hands dropped and his right hand rested on her leg under the table. She felt as though it were some strange, foreign object dropped on her flesh. She strained for a glimpse of the other women in the bar, which seemed strangely uninhabited.

"Don't be nervous," he said. "There's hardly anyone here. No one will see us."

She took his hand and began to massage the palm gently with her fingertips. She knew that her touch was like fire to him. "When will people start showing up?" she asked casually. He folded his fingers around hers.

"The dikes usually start showing up around now, but the femmes don't come in until a little later. Around midnight the place is loaded. Frankly, though, if it weren't for taking you here, I'd stay away. These women are dynamite, if they have the yen—but even the ones that have the yen aren't steady."

Paul ordered brandies, explaining that it was always a good

idea to switch drinks in the middle of the evening. Joan like him for his frankly sexual approach to women. She felt that his sophistication was much beyond his years, and then she wondered how she knew. She supposed that she must have learned a great deal from David. She felt that David would have liked this man, would have tried to sleep with him. She smiled to herself. She was succeeding where David would have failed. She caught herself up—succeeding? There's many a slip twixt the cup and the lip, she said to herself firmly, already a bit dazed from the beers and the brandy.

The bartender came around again, and Joan waved him over. "I'd like a Johnny Walker," she said.

Paul looked up in surprise, "Hey, I was only joking. You're not supposed to mix your drinks—at least, not that much. I really was joking."

"You might be joking," she said, "but I'm serious."

"A Johnny Walker for the lady," he said to the bartender, and turned toward Joan. "Now what is the problem here? Am I such a nebbish that you have to get drunk before you can bear me?" He furrowed his forehead and leaned his head on his hand, tilting his face close to her face. She put her cheek close to his, smiling his aftershave lotion.

"Oh . . ." was all she could say. He drew closer to her. Joan felt his hands stroking the back of her neck and tension began to flow away into his fingers. She felt again that she could talk to a stranger as she could not to a friend. Her loneliness showed on her face.

"You haven't said a thing about yourself," he pointed out, seeming to divine her thoughts. He handed her the Johnny Walker. "I'm not so stupid about women, you know. I understand that you may have your reasons for coming to places like the Flicker. You may have other reasons for asking me to bring you here. I don't worry about those reasons. I take it as it comes, do my best and that's all that counts. But one thing I can tell you." He paused impressively.

Joan, amused, fed him the line. "What?" she asked.

He smiled broadly. "You don't belong in a place like this."

Joan looked about them. A group of girls had entered, most of them in pairs. They seemed to be tourists---but tourists with a difference. They were all women, and all obvious Lesbians. Several of them were very attractive. One blonde girl had the face of an eagle, with an aquiline nose and high cheekbones, her curly hair short-cropped against her head. Joan's arms and legs grew cold with desire. She did not understand her feelings, but they were so intense she wanted to faint. She felt that she shouldn't hide anymore, that she should be honest, that she should try, somehow, to join the women who were to her so compellingly beautiful---the Lesbians.

"You're wrong," she burst out, almost desperately. "I think that I do." Tears filled her eyes. She felt a desperate need to convince him that she was a Lesbian.

"Do you mean that you sleep with girls like these?" he asked bluntly, toying with his glass. Joan sensed that he was not annoyed, but patient with her as one might be with a child of retarded intelligence. Perhaps she was retarded, she thought. Then she felt her spirit returning.

"No," she answered his question. "But I don't think it would be such a terrible fate. After all, haven't you slept with them?"

He nodded, seeing her reasoning. "Yes, but the ones I have made love to aren't really Lesbians. Something bad happens to them, or too many good things, sometimes," he paused, looking at her meaningfully, "and they become prostitutes, to be perfectly frank, and hang out in bars like this. The Lesbians are attracted to some of the more intelligent girls, but they have even less success in winning their love than I do. And that's not much."

Joan nodded, understanding that he was sincerely concerned with the girls here---a rarity, she decided, among men. She felt warmer toward him.

"I know that I may seem strange to you," she stated, "with all my interest in homosexuals. But I am also interested in male homosexuals, in a sense."

She saw that her statement piqued him. He sat back and looked into her eyes and said, "Tell me about it."

Joan told him about David. They had another drink—Paul a

brandy and she another Johnny Walker, and the evening wore on as they talked. He told her of the prostitute he had met when he was very young and very impressionable. Joan was shocked, but she could tell that confessing his affair made him feel better, helped him understand himself. As they spoke, his fingers caressed her arm, ran up and down the inside of her forearm. Joan began to identify him with David as she told of David, of the love she thought she had wanted but had never felt. She was unashamed, as though they were in a confessional.

She looked up once during a pause and saw a dark, mysterious girl stop at the Lesbian's table to chat with the masculine blonde who looked like an eagle. The beautiful girl with the dark hair wore no makeup; she had a strange half-smile; yet her beautifully molded body was classic in its proportions, and showed plainly through her simple dress.

Joan wanted to possess her body, to press close to the other woman, to—

And then her mind refused to go further. She felt Paul's hand on her knee again; she felt him pressing closer to her, whispering into her ear, "Let's go somewhere else. Where do you suggest?"

Joan was like a dreamer as she left the Daisy, and her dream was of the girl with the half-smile. She felt as though she herself smiled just such a smile, as though she herself were very much like the girl she had seen. She realized that for the first time she had seen another woman like herself—a Lesbian—yet this woman might not feel the immense difference Joan felt between herself and the rest of the world. She knew as she opened the door of the apartment house for Paul that she felt that immense difference between herself and him, that there was no way of resolving it or of making it less harsh, making what they could have together less barren. She was bringing him home to her apartment, but not as a lover, not as a mate—as an animal who might perform the acts an animal might.

She opened the door to her apartment and forced herself against him after the door closed.

"Hey," he exclaimed, surprised at her action, "do you want to be kissed good-night? I mean, shall I go?" He was nervous, aware that her passion was playing along tightened nerves.

She put his arms around her neck and pressed closer, innocent but determined, feeling his body grow taut.

"No, don't go," she said, scarcely hearing her own voice through a tide of flame that seemed to bathe her body. "But kiss me."

He smiled and bent his head down, to take her lips. How many men David has kissed like this, she thought, how many times he has submitted to their embraces, taken them to his apartment . . . And then Paul's lips were gone. The kiss was over. His lips were sweet, yet there was no sensation.

She walked away, across the room, and said, "How about some coffee?" He stood awkwardly at the doorway until she remembered and asked him to sit down, motioning toward the couch. She busied herself in the kitchen, filled with a strange excitement.

I'm feeling the thrill of the hunt, she realized. She walked into the front room as the coffee percolated, and saw that he was involved in the sports page. "Sports page?" she asked. "At this hour?"

"In a beautiful girl's apartment, at this hour?" he countered, imitating her tone, smiling at her. "I'm surprised that you trust me."

Joan could see that he felt flattered that she trusted him. She smiled. "Yes, I trust you."

He looked up in some surprise. Joan smiled impishly and turned the lights down. Then she walked across the room and put on a long-playing record of soft, romantic music. She had played this record over and over again while she thought of David, while her love for David tortured her physically. She served the coffee and sat across the room rather than on the couch.

She saw Paul look at her for a long moment and knew that his hunger for her was deepening.

He finished his coffee quickly then rose, determined to leave. Joan got up from her chair and slowly walked over to him, her face raised, expecting a kiss. Paul kissed her again, this time allowing his hands to play over her breasts. His whole body was stiff and tense.

A great embarrassment began to fill Joan, but she forced herself to press closer to him, pretending to respond to his searching mouth which was only a wet and foreign thing to her. Then Paul tore way and turned toward the chair where he had put his hat and coat. But Joan caught him by the hand and made him turn back.

"I want you to stay," she said hoarsely.

Paul grasped her tightly and kissed the nape of her neck. Excitement seared Joan for a moment and she thought joyously--- perhaps I am normal. Now Paul was fumbling with the buttons on her blouse and she felt his hands on her breast. They were rough, male hands---all of Paul was lacking in softness. A great and sudden desire possessed Joan, but not for Paul—for David, for someone soft and lovely; for a woman.

As he began to undress her she wondered if she should tell him she was a virgin. But it wasn't necessary. He knew. He had known all evening. That was why he had tried to leave before.

She lay on the bed and watched him prepare her, feeling detached, almost cynical. There was something very unimportant about what they were doing—except for its novelty, it was like watching a B-movie re-digested on television.

2.

JOAN saw Paul almost every night after that. He was patient and understanding with her. He tried to bring some meaning into their relationship, perhaps more out of guilt and conscience than from a real feeling for Joan. For his feelings were not allowed to grow; Joan's thoughts were with David. Paul sat, night after night, in the Flicker or in the Open Room—or, once in a while, in the Daisy—listening to Joan talk about David. He began to feel what was true—that he was an experiment, a means to David. Joan treated Paul as some men treat women—as a thing to go to bed with, from whom to feel alien and detached.

One evening, as they sat in the Daisy, the girl with the strange smile approached Joan as she sat with Paul.

"Won't you sit down," Joan asked, "and join us in a drink?" Paul looked sharply at her, surprised.

"Where did you get the habit of ordering drinks for other girls on my money?" he asked. Joan was annoyed.

"I'll pay for her drinks," she snapped. The dark girl seemed upset.

"I'm sorry, I hadn't meant to cause an argument." She walked off, smiling. "Perhaps another day."

"Maybe," Joan said, angrily turning to Paul, "I wanted her to sit down and talk to us. I'm becoming annoyed with you. If you don't mind, I'll choose my own friends."

Paul knew what was coming. He knew that Joan would begin to blame him, as she had so often before---for his inadequacies, for his shallowness and possessiveness—for not being David. He picked up the check and slammed out the door.

"Good riddance," Joan told herself. She had not felt as women said they did with men; she had not loved him; she had not found the relief she needed so desperately. She was glad that he was safely away. And yet, because he had not pleased her, she resented him. Resented him for having destroyed a precious dream. Resented him for having taken what was David's.

He called back several times after that, and she told him that her parents were in town. And then one night he did not call, nor did she hear from him again.

A parade of men followed, one more masculine than the other, and none very interesting. She made a science of finding men and then of rejecting them, hurting them as David had hurt her, she thought. Only after she had repeated the process many times did she realize that these men were not devastated as she had been—that they were not hurt, they were often amused.

She sat in front of her mirror, brushing her face with a large white powder-puff. The fur was soft against her face—soft as a woman's cheek. She wondered how it felt to kiss a woman.

Suddenly the pieces fell together. She knew that soon she would become fixed in her pattern, a thing to be used but not lived with. Many men had used her in these few months—used her but not loved her—and each man spoke of her to someone else. She had withdrawn from them, withdrawn into a more sophisticated dream of David. She saw her reflection in the glass, powdered and white and hard-looking. She saw herself and she realized that there was no David. If David existed, it was she. The realization brought agony to her face. She stared at herself crying in the mirror and, with an expression of rage, picked up a perfume bottle and broke the glass. Her reflection shattered, and pieces of glass fell out of the frame before her. She picked up a piece and looked at its sharp edge for a long moment. Then she knew that she wanted to live. She wanted to live.

She was free of David but she wanted to live. She did not know where to start, how to find the life she hoped to find, but she thought that she might start in the Village.

She got up and removed her dressing-gown. It was Saturday, and there was sunshine, the clatter of busy grocers and the noise of playing children in the street outside her window. She walked nude to the drapes and looked outside.

"My world," she said. Down the street she saw the Prospect Playhouse. She had avoided the theater because she felt that she could not enter that world, and uncomplicated life of happy make-believe. "Perhaps," she thought, "I'm not so very different from some of them."

She picked out a casual skirt and a brilliant red cotton blouse and dressed herself for the street. She felt adventurous, as though it were spring.

She turned and eyed the broken mirror. Replacing it would eat into her savings. She had quite a hoard now, she told herself, and chided herself for her miserliness.

She supposed that her concern with money was linked with her wish for independence. Now she knew why the Lesbian tourist at the Daisy had looked like an eagle---her face was serene in its fearlessness and in its independence. Her eyes looked about her as though the world were hers as well as anyone else's. Joan knew that she herself had been beaten down. She felt defeated by the men who had used her. A determination to live, to be herself---even, she hoped, someday to be happy—filled her like the cool summer air.

She watered the plants in her window box. They were dying from the foul air outside. Soot and dust were taking their toll. She wiped the tender leaves. Mankind destroys beautiful things as soon as they are formed, she thought; buds are too soon plucked from the bush, trees are cut as they stand, and the very earth itself is ripped apart by greed for precious metals. She knew now why she was confused. The world---the whole world was in her way. She was indeed a Lesbian; but there was no way for her to find herself within the society she knew.

She left the apartment, carefully locking the door behind her. The neighborhood was full of thieves and criminals of all sorts—including, she reminded herself, Lesbians. The act of Lesbianism is criminal, she said to herself, under the law.

She felt her hair blow backward into the air and lifted her face to meet the light wind. She ran down MacDougal Street, hardly caring where she was going. Brushing past a dignified man on the street who looked after her with amusement, she dashed into the Positano.

David had first taken her to the Positano, and she had decided that she liked it. After than she often went herself to sit alone at a table until others would join her.

The place had a classical atmosphere, and the statues on the walls reminded Joan of dead civilizations; but she liked the warmth and the simplicity of the wooden paneling. The room was decorated in 16th century Italian style, and modern paintings by a Village artist hung on the walls. Music was played in the evening and some afternoons; today it was Cesar Franck sounding very serious for a happy, giddy Saturday. Joan sat in a corner, away from the rest, and began to be part of another dream. She often sat in the Positano for hours like this, sipping coffee, with no excuse but her love of music, listening to the concert.

Many tourists came to the Positano every week, but the beatniks came daily and stayed all day. Mail was even sent to them at the coffee chop; many left their belongings with the management, sometimes for several days. Mostly dancers and actors, they seldom cared how they dressed or who heard their inner-most secrets. They were all one family, a family of children, all without mothers and fathers to go home to—all with ambitions, and all very lazy.

The man who had brushed by Joan on the street came in. She noticed that he joined the people on the other side of the room, many of whom she knew. She was surprised to see him with them, for she had felt instinctively that this man was a homosexual. Something about him reminded her of David. She saw him look up and stare at her.

She lowered her eyes and sipped her coffee. She was startled when she saw the man beside her table, about to address her.

"Don't be startled," he said, noticing her reaction. "Some of your friends said they thought you might be willing to join us for a cup of coffee."

"I am surprised," she said, "because you don't seem like the sort of man I associate with my friends over there. Why don't you join me here?"

Immediately she regretted her invitation, but he sat down, eager to talk to her, leaning forward in an interested way.

"I'm Marc," he said, smiling a beautiful smile. "Who are you?"

"I'm Joan," she admitted, ready to be amused.

"I'm gay." His remark took Joan by surprise. She said nothing for a moment.

Suddenly a spontaneous desire filled her, and she spoke out quite loudly, "So am I."

"Oh?" He smiled again. "A fellow-conspirator."

Suddenly Joan felt as though she were indeed a Lesbian, suave and experienced. She knew that it was a fantasy, but she felt the need for fantasy.

"That's why I asked you to join me rather than going back to see our friends there." she said. "I could tell that you were gay too and I decided to set up a queer corner on this side of the room." *Gay* was a term Paul had taught Joan. It meant homosexual and pertained to both sexes. She liked the word. It seemed to characterize the individuals she had observed at the bar---filled with *joie de vivre*, free, and just a little bit pagan.

She swerved back toward reality. "What are your great all-consuming passions in life, Marc?"

She felt that would hold him for a while. He began to talk about himself and she, too, was held by his accounts. His life had been spent in traveling, for the most part, but his experiences in the South were very perplexing to Joan. She saw that he described what was a primitive culture at some levels, but that he was able to pretend to fit in as one of them. She was surprised. He told of lynchings, of knifings and of rapes with an apparent unconcern which almost disguised his deep hatred of ignorance and hypocrisy.

"Tell me about some of your friends," she said when he had done. "Or is there one particular, special friend?"

Joan saw from his smile that there was not. "No."

"Still," she urged, "there must be someone or several someone's for you in the big city of New York."

"Aside from gatherings in the Village and a few great nights at the bars . . ." he shrugged, "I feel emotionally flat, somehow, about anyone." His thin fingers ran through a crop of wavy light brown hair as he talked. He looked much like David.

Joan commiserated. "I have that problem, myself. When did you begin to feel this way?"

Marc looked at her, turning his head sharply. "I've always been this way. What you mean is—" He had been trying to avoid her questions. Now he gave up and faced her squarely. "I don't really know whether I can talk about it. I know, though, that I've really been looking for someone to talk to for weeks, and that somehow you seemed like the right one. I think the whole thing began to grow when I was in the South. I guess I saw too much of man's inhumanity to man. I was fool enough to care a little bit about humanity in the first place, and naturally enough, I'm suffering for it. You can't watch one man beating another with the assistance of a group of your friends and not care at all that he suffers. At least, I cant. I was angry, but there was absolutely nothing I could do. I tried to stop it, but my next-door neighbor slugged me."

He interrupted himself, realizing that he had been talking to himself, not noticing Joan's reactions. He saw that she had been listening with interest. "I'm sorry to go on like this, but there was one particular incident where a Negro was beaten up for nothing, that really got me. A lot of white men are treated badly, too, but they accept it as part of a kind of prison-like life."

The waitress stood at the table, and Marc looked up, "Oh yes," he murmured, "this is a coffee-shop, to be sure, and not a confessional. We would, would we not, like two coffees and some sort of pastry with nuts?" Joan nodded yes. The waitress walked off and Marc continued. "The prison in the South seems to stretch out until its walls are the boundaries of the South itself, and the righteous citizens are the inmates. I don't mean that I was in prison, but that freedom is not what it is here." He stopped. Joan knew that he had told her his story, or as much of it as he was about to tell her.

"In other words,' she interrupted his thoughts, "you were not among homosexuals in the South."

"Right. Except for my friend, who as jailed for something he hadn't done."

Joan was sorry for him. "Is there anything you can do?"

She knew he was telling the truth to her when he said, "No. Absolutely nothing. The man who did it manufactured an air-tight alibi. There is no evidence except what points to my poor friend."

He paused and then asked, "Is this what happens when a homosexual tries to make an adjustment and live in society as an adjusted human being?"

Marc was asking her a rather difficult question; she could see that he regarded her as a sophisticated Lesbian, concerned with social questions. Now that he mentioned it, she supposed that Lesbians should be concerned with such things. Marc's questions were apt to be rhetorical, so she decided not to answer this one.

"Why don't you come up to my place for dinner?" She felt that Marc was poor and probably needed a good dinner. Beyond that, her mind refused to function. She hoped, however, that she might find another clue to herself in knowing Marc.

When Marc left that night Joan walked him down to a boy's bar, the Over, and left him there. She had invited him to come over the next evening for drinks. She could see that he felt better after talking to her, and that he was beginning to get over being without his friend. She was surprised to find that it had been two years since his friend had been jailed.

The next night was more amusing for Joan. Marc seemed to be coming out of a long fog. Joan found him the handsomest and most considerate man she had met, and began to feel that he was a bit like David. He seemed to respect some unspoken code and did not touch her physically. He seemed not to mind, rather to enjoy, lack of consummation, and Joan began to feel that companionship she had felt with David.

One night Marc brought a boyfriend, Jay, to see her. Jay was effeminate but handsome. Joan liked the direct, friendly look in his eyes. She thought, "Soul mate."

Halfway through the evening, however, Marc left with Jay for a boys' party. She felt left out, but reconciled herself to studying that evening. It was nip-and-tuck with college. She was using every ounce of native wisdom in her classes, hoping to come out with B's and a few A's.

The next day Marc came over to help her with her French. She was using records he had given her as an auxiliary method of study, and he helped her perfect an accent her teacher admired. After dinner, sitting on the couch with him, she leaned back and rested on his arm. He hugged her and then got up to sit on the footstool facing her. "Let's get married," he said.

Joan was delighted. "Yes!" she answered.

The next morning Joan met him and they went to City Hall for the license. Joan was quite happy, although she knew that Marc had proposed a gay marriage. He did not intend to touch her. "Why do you want to marry me?" she asked.

He hesitated and she saw a strange look cross his face. He looked in a way dishonest. "I can't say that I'm marrying you for your sake, although I suppose it is a good thing if a girl has a husband she can point to. From my point of view, this is good for my job, for one thing. A married man has a better chance of getting ahead in my office. He gets the raises where another man is discouraged, kicked down the ladder. And a gay man is always open to blackmail. Perhaps being married will help rid me of that fear."

Joan felt that it was her turn to tell him why she wanted marriage. She knew that she wanted to marry and feel that she was doing the right thing, just for once. She felt that being a married woman might lessen the wrong of her past promiscuity. But she couldn't tell Marc any of this. She believed that his respect for her would diminish if she were as frank with him as he was with her.

"I want to marry you, Marc, because I feel that somewhere in the background you'll always be there, ready to protect me, in who-knows-what way." She knew that she did not ever want to call upon Marc, but she felt that having a husband was almost a charm; it was like a magic formula that seemed to work for everyone else, and would work for her—in a highly individual way.

Neither of them told their parents. Three days later they were married at City Hall. The man who said the word which united them seemed to have little faith in them, in marriage, or in life itself. He droned the words in a colorless monotone which was almost unbearable to Joan.

When they left the ceremony, Marc announced that he had to go to work, since they had only given him a half-day off. He left and Joan took the subway home.

The next night Marc returned—with Jay. They spent the evening drinking heavily. Joan decided that Marc drank too much, but she knew that there was no point in trying to reform him. She determined to see less of him. The wedding had made her feel degraded again, and she wanted to go off by herself—perhaps to the country. She could not leave town, however, because finals were approaching.

One night the two of them visited as Joan sat studying for an exam in elementary psych. She found the text dull and expurgated. Jay picked up the text. "So," he chortled, "stealing my thunder, eh?"

Joan looked up, surprised. "What do you mean, your thunder? This is Psychology 1.a and I'm afraid I'm going to flunk it. I've read Freud, but this is taught by a man who believes in psychological testing through divination, I think. You know—telling the future by feeling your skull or something."

"Watch your language," Jay muttered sternly. "I'm a psychological tester."

"Great guns!" Joan was delighted. "This course is all about it. Come over next weekend and help me study."

Jay looked at Marc sadly. "I guess I can't. Your husband is going to be out of town and I should stay home and mourn."

Marc laughed. "Joan really does need the help. I've done my best with her French, but she needs another A to keep her on the Dean's list."

Jay feigned ignorance. "You mean the Dean has a list, too?" He drew his address book from his pocket. "There's John and Henry and George and Agatha, and now," he grasped Joan's hands and danced around the room with her, "Joan!" He laughed, spinning around the room in a staggering circle, Joan in his arms. "The Dean's about to complete his list!"

Joan let go and dropped on the couch, exhausted. "Enough of this nonsense," she said. "You two are time wasters. You go off somewhere together. I don't want to see a soul except for you, Jay, this weekend. And then only to pick your brains."

The two stared at her for a moment, smiling. Then both of them tiptoed out, leaving Joan at her little desk, trying to find her place in *Fundamentals of Animal Psychology* by Maurice Taulman, Ph.D. In frustration she put it down, and decided instead to switch to her Classics assignment. There was so much to do, such a heavy credit load to carry.

Joan lost herself in study until the weekend. She had intended to go to the Daisy, but she hadn't the time. It was refreshing to discipline her mind as she did now. Studying Greek had opened new worlds for her. She was fortunate in having an excellent teacher, a humanist. As a consequence, the language was incredibly easy for her, since the basics were simple and the rest magic. She even had started a translation of some of Sappho's fragments and had come to the conclusion that it was indeed written by a Lesbian.

Friday night, two hours before Jay was expected, Joan closed her books. She could study no more. She had to divert her mind for a while before it died of exhaustion. Sappho's words seemed to reflect the longing Joan now felt, strong and definite—the longing for the arms of a beautiful woman.

She decided to visit the Daisy for a little while. She would at least expose herself to this new environment, alone, without Paul. It would be too early for anyone to be there—the Lesbians usually came in after eleven o'clock—but at least some of her nostalgia could be eased. She would come back in time for Jay, and talking to him would help. Perhaps Jay would know someone, a Lesbian she might meet.

She decided to wear slacks to the Daisy. With Paul she had always worn full skirts and much makeup, dressed in the way that David had taught; but now she was going back to the old Joan, the Joan of high school days, in slacks and men's shirts. She braided her hair tightly and cut her long nails, taking off the red polish, all traces of it, making her hands masculine again. A wonderful change began to take place in her. She felt as if she had lost herself for two years and now she was being Joan again. She had loved her name, because it was like Joan of Arc. But David had taken the warrior out of her personality for a while. Joan had stifled under the heavy makeup, under the brightly colored skirts and blouses. Now in slacks, she was back to her old and comfortable self. But all of David's efforts had not been lost. She was more attractive, poised and sure of herself, beautifully feminine despite the slacks and lack of nail polish. She was dressed like a boy with taste, not with the awful, truck-driver look of the butches at the Daisy, nor the strange, almost gay-boy daintiness of the femmes who wore gray streaks in their hair and horrid masks of rouge. Joan was Joan the warrior again, now Joan of Washington Square, simple and inspired, shining with the light of hope and inspiration, on a quest now for love.

3.

JOAN walked down the stairs of her apartment house, as she had done the night she had met Paul. But now she had become more aware of her surroundings. She knew, for instance, that the Daisy's bartender, a masculine woman who wore men's clothing, lived in the apartment directly below her with several other girls she had seen at the Daisy. Joan knew that her apartment house was a popular place with the Daisy crowd, perhaps because it had furnished apartments at low rent. She had heard the noise of the gay crowd often in the middle of the night, sometimes the racket of a terrible battle when one of the butches had lost her girl, or when the crowd was drunk—not only the Lesbians but the gay boys who lived down the hall. Joan wondered of all homosexuals were as coarse, as rough with each other. Her reaction to her neighbors was one of revulsion, even though she felt safe living near them—they seemed not to be concerned about anyone but themselves and their own troubles. Still, Joan was glad that her parents had not seen the apartment house, clean as it was in the hallways, for fear they might have caught a glimpse of her neighbors at a bad time.

And yet her neighbors were beginning to worry her. She was afraid that all Lesbians were horrible, even dangerous because of their violent tempers. The Daisy's beer bottle fights were infamous, and Joan had tossed in her bed uneasily every time she had heard a bottle break in the street outside her window. It did no good for her to tell herself that most of the fights at the Daisy had not involved women but men who got drunk and tried to beat off the bouncer. Still the air of violence was around the Lesbians, showing in their tough clothing and language—their language particularly. Joan had learned a whole new dictionary from the quarrels of her downstairs neighbors.

But Joan would not be frightened away from the Daisy and the Lesbians there. There could be no life for her with men. She was certain of that. Somewhere there would have to be a woman—perhaps like the women of Sappho's time, a soft, feminine woman, refined and beautiful; a woman for Joan.

Joan left the apartment house and entered the heat of summer. It was seven o'clock and the sun was still up, reluctant to leave MacDougal Street to the mercy of night—for night was vicious on MacDougal Street. Night filled the street with rowdy crowds, crowds that warned Joan of danger, danger from irresponsible and drunken men, crowds that warned her with whistles and vulgar voices.

But the day made her feel safe and she crossed the street carelessly and went up the steps to the Daisy, as if she too were a part of the Lesbian set. The cold aura of the air-conditioning splashed her and filled her with night, the cold night of the dark and now deserted Daisy. Only the bouncer was there—at the door, sleepily reading the funnies—and Bobo, the barmaid with the G.I. haircut, who was polishing whiskey glasses at the counter.

Joan went to the corner of the bar and sat on a stool, trying to appear tough and used to sitting at bars. She had drunk at the bar only once before, with Paul. She had always been taught that ladies do not sit at the bar alone. She felt awkward at breaking this rule she had always observed, but she forced herself to feel at ease, to like sitting at a bar.

"What'll it be?" Bobo said roughly, almost scornfully. She may not have liked strangers, or perhaps Joan did not seem the right type to be in here. Joan speculated for a moment that Bobo might be wary of her, might think her a policewoman.

"Beer," Joan said. She did not like beer, but it was a cold drink and could be made to last a long while.

Bobo opened a bottle at the other end of the bar and slid it toward Joan, followed it with a glass, then went back to her chores.

Joan poured the beer in the glass, feeling the cold hardness of the bottle. It gave her a feeling of security. The bottle was a weapon. She wondered if smashing it would give it just the right edge for slashing out. She pictured herself for a moment, slashing out with a broken beer bottle at a drunk who might accost her. She saw herself tough, her mouth turned up slightly in a twist of cruelty. It was almost a pleasant image—lashing out against someone who came toward her—but the drunk's face suddenly became Paul's. You're full of hatred, she told herself, and then decided it was frustration. She knew the bottle scene would only occur in her mind, but it was nice to get rid of hostilities that way when the world grew too tight around her.

The Daisy was painfully silent. Joan wanted to hear noise. She took out a quarter and got up, going to the next room to the juke box. She put on three rock-and-roll numbers, each composed for noise, and then went back to the bar.

The raucous music soon ended. Joan couldn't bear the emptiness, the silence. She decided to go home and return to the Daisy later in the evening after the crowd arrived.

She made her way stonily across the street and went upstairs again, feeling safe once the door of ther apartment was closed to the outside world. She went immediately to the kitchen and started to make coffee. She had bought a coffee ring earlier in anticipation of Jay.

She head his familiar ring now and buzzed in return.

"How are you, doll?" Jay said, kissing her cheek as he entered. He was carrying a briefcase and Joan took it from him, remembering that he had consented to bring his Rorschach cards. She was anxious to have him test her. It might throw some light on her psychological makeup, might explain why she wanted to be a Lesbian.

"I'm fine," she said, shaking off her previous mood. She put Jay's briefcase on the bed and hurried to turn the gas off under the percolating coffee. "Heard from Marc?" It was natural that Jay would have heard from Marc although Joan had not. Marc lived on the other side of the Village and Jay was closer to him than Joan in every way.

"No, not a word," Jay said bitterly. Joan returned to the living room with the coffee tray and looked at him. The mention of Marc had made him sour.

"Have you two broken up?" she asked.

"My dear, we never were that close," he said, shrugging a little and walking over to the window. The noise from the street brought him back to the middle of the room. "Why did you marry him, Joan?" he asked.

Joan put the tray down and smiled. "I don't know. I needed to marry someone, I guess."

Jay laughed, took the cup that she had poured for him and sat on the couch near her, taking out his test samples.

Joan watched him while he spoke. He was conscientious about helping her pass her psychology exam and told her all he knew and then said it again, patiently answering all her questions. He looked very much like David as he taught her, Joan thought. Yes, Jay was very much like David—wanting to be loved, to be admired, and yet afraid of anyone who might restrict him, might demand his love in return. Jay was not afraid of Joan. He thought of Joan as someone like himself, and this made her different from other women. He could not care for women because they expected him to be a man, but he could care for Joan. Joan was not a woman to him, she was a friend. He might go to bed with friends, but not with women. That had been the secret key to David, Joan suddenly understood. She could never win David, David was afraid of her now—but she was sure she could win Jay.

She made a resolution, a wild sort of thing. Now that Marc no longer cared for Jay, Joan would try her luck with him. She wanted to make love to Jay, to see what David would have been like in bed—only to prove to David that she could have someone like him.

At ten-thirty, Jay stopped talking for a minute. "We'd better start on the Rorschach's before it gets too late," he said.

Joan stretched and yawned, "Oh no, please, Jay. I think this has been enough for one evening. Could you possibly test me another night?"

"All right," he said, putting down the cards and sitting back. He looked at her a while and then said, "I'm concerned about you, Joan. You don't seem happy."

"I'm not," she said, wrinkling her brow a little. "I need to find a girl, Jay, before I go off some deep end. But I don't know where to start."

"Have you been to the bars?" he asked.

"No," she shook her head, "I haven't had time to find out where they are."

"Well, the Yellow Page and the Sun Dial are the best ones,"

he said.

"Could we go to one of them tonight?" Joan leaned forward anxiously. In a way she wanted to get Jay out of her apartment before she would decide to go through with her earlier mad resolution.

He thought a moment and then agreed. "The Yellow Page is nearest, so why don't we try there?" he said. "Besides, they seem to frown on male escorts at the Sun Dial."

She felt safe walking down MacDougal Street beside Jay; she took his arm for protection. The crowds of leering males kept away from her because she was with a tall, handsome man.

"The Village is too full of creeps," Jay commented as they walked on through the moving wall of people on the street. Joan was glad he said that. She had thought she was being overly sensitive about the neighborhood, but here was Jay agreeing with her.

"That's the Yellow Page," he said, stopping when they reached the corner of Third and Sullivan. "I hope their cover's not too high."

"I have enough money," Joan said. "Will you let me treat you?"

"Nonsense," he smiled embarrassedly. "I'm taking you."

"I at least insist on Dutch," Joan said firmly. She did not want Jay to spend all his money on her.

"All right," he said reluctantly, and took her across the street to the nightclub. It had a bright yellow canopy and there were pictures of strippers on each side of the door.

"I hope this isn't like the Daisy," Joan said warily. It looked like another tourist spot.

"I hear the entertainment's mad," Jay said.

It cost them three dollars each to get past the door and they found it was not yet crowded inside. "Most of these spots don't get lively until after midnight," Jay explained.

They found a table near the middle of the floor and watched the small orchestra with the girl drummer play an old tune. The drummer didn't look gay, Joan thought.

"What'll you have?" a rough but velvet voice asked behind

them. They turned and saw the waitress—at least, she was technically a waitress. She wore a skirt and a masculine shirt and her hair was short-cropped. She was a woman only from the waist down, the top was all male.

"A rum and coke," Joan said, and Jay ordered the same. They sat back and recovered from the shock. Joan was used to seeing Bobo and the girls who lived downstairs, but this one was even more masculine than they; she looked almost chemically different. It frightened Joan.

Jay whistled. "I could have sworn that was a boy in drag."

"I had my doubts too," Joan smiled, "but I think it's a girl."

"Whatever it was, I'm glad it's gone," Jay laughed. But he had spoken too soon. The waitress was returning with their drinks. She might have overheard him. She was smiling in great amusement.

"It's about time you got around to coming here," the waitress addressed Joan. "I've seen you several times at the Daisy."

Joan was startled that the girl had spoken to her directly. "Oh? But I've never seen you there."

"I stand mostly at the bar," the girl said. "You used to go there with a blonde guy."

"Yes," Joan blushed. Now that the girl was talking to her she seemed less frightening. "Won't you join us?" Joan motioned to an empty chair.

"Thanks," the girl said, treating the chair like a saddle with her legs. "My name's Gig. Yours?"

"Joan, and that's Jay," Joan motioned. Gig nodded to Jay then looked back at Joan. "Say, what's the bit? I thought you were femme, but now you're in slacks."

"I prefer slacks," Joan said, capriciously sipping her drink. "You don't look like you belong in a skirt."

"A rule of the management," Gig said. "I'm not supposed to be too obvious."

Jay laughed at that because he couldn't help himself.

"Don't get cute," Gig warned, but not threateningly. She was plainly embarrassed in a skirt.

"I'm sorry," Jay said.

The bank had begun to play a slow dance tune and two couples got up to dance. One of the couples was two women. Joan watched them with the same fascination she had felt so often in the Daisy.

"Want to dance?" Gig said to her, roughly shy.

"Sure," Joan said, getting up immediately. She was still a bit afraid of Gig, but she wanted to know what dancing with a woman was like. "Would you excuse us, Jay?"

"Of course, doll," he teased, and then sat back to watch them.

Joan let Gig lead and found herself pressed against Gig's body, a body slightly taller than hers and surprisingly soft, not like a man's at all. An odd awareness began to grow in Joan; she could scarcely control it. She found herself pressing closer to Gig, feeling trapped by desire, desire for Gig's body. Such impulses had never happened to her with a man. And it had nothing to do with Gig herself. It was the feel of Gig's body, completely detached from all that she was—the feel of a woman's body.

Gig sensed her awareness and led Joan to the far side of the dance floor. "Who's the queen with you?" she asked.

"A friend," Joan said, trying to fight the desire that was making her giddy.

Joan was certain now. Attracted to a woman as she had never been attracted to a man, not even to David—Joan knew she was a Lesbian.

"How about ditching him and coming back here later?" Gig said. "I don't live far."

"I live near here, too," Joan said, thinking of her empty apartment and letting the vivid picture of Gig fill the image, Gig making love to her tonight. The feeling was one of sheer animal pleasure. I've slept with strange men, Joan thought, why not a strange woman? I don't care what she'll look like in the morning. I want her tonight!

"Why don't you come over to my place after work?" Joan suggested.

"What's the address?" Gig said, stopping for a minute and taking out her pencil. She wrote it down on the back of her checkbook. Joan moved into her arms again and resumed dancing. It was torture to feel Gig's legs so close to her, Gig's hips pressing forward, leading her to the rhythm of the music.

Gig led her back to the table when the music stopped. Joan felt her insides quivering. Slowly, she sat down again next to Jay.

"I've got to get back to the customers," Gig winked at her, not sitting down again. "See you later."

"Mary, you're red as a lobster," Jay said. "What'd she do to you?"

"I don't know," Joan sighed, "but I'm sure about me now." She sat back and took a long gulp of her drink. "She may come over to the apartment after work."

"You're mad!" He looked at her, quickly concerned. "She looks like a rough cookie. Don't get involved with her."

"I'm involved already," Joan said, taking another sip. "I've got to have that girl." Hearing herself sound like some of the men she had slept with, Joan realized that she felt like a man now. She was full of the thrill of the chase, and it was infinitely more exciting than it had ever been before.

"Come on." Jay got up, pulled Joan up with him and put money down on the table for their drinks, "I'm taking you out of here before there's trouble."

"But I don't want to go yet," Joan protested.

"You're coming anyway," Jay said. "I don't like this setup."

Joan sighed, waved to Gig and followed Jay out. Gig would come up later anyway. There really wasn't much point to staying here.

"I'm staying over with you tonight," Jay said when they were outside. "I don't trust that girl."

"The hell you are," Joan said. "Why are you so worried about me? She was really very nice to me."

"She's too fast," Jay said, hurrying her down the street. "Girls don't operate that fast, unless there's something crooked going on. She may be pushing dope or something. Anyway, I don't like it and I'm staying over. You can put a blanket on the rug for me."

"You sound just like Paul," Joan said. "I'm sorry, Jay, my

mind's made up. I think I can take care of myself, really."

Jay sighed. "Well, at least I tried. I'll call you tomorrow morning and see if you're all right."

"Don't be surprised if I am," Joan laughed. "Somehow I feel I can trust women a whole lot farther than I can trust even the best men."

She said goodbye to him at the corner and then went into her house. Alone in her apartment, she began to straighten up and prepare for Gig.

In spite of herself, she began to wonder if Gig would show up after all. Gig might get drunk, or maybe meet another girl. Perhaps this was a routine she gave all the tourists. If Gig did come, it would be after three A.M.

Joan took a shower, feeling sensuous all the way to her toes; she would be in a miserable state if Gig didn't show up. She regretted having sent Jay away. At least there would have been Jay if Gig hadn't come. But Jay would be no substitute. She dried herself and spent a long time carefully perfuming her skin and hair, preparing herself for love, or something more close to that than she had known before.

Joan felt confused. She sensed the emotions of a man inside her, yet she was making herself a woman for Gig. Joan knew that Gig was attracted to her femininity, but she wondered what would happen after the first kiss—Joan did not want to be the woman, Joan wanted Gig to be the woman; she wondered how Gig would take to that.

Joan came out of the bathroom and put on her striped bathrobe, the man's robe she had bought for herself at Bloomingdale's; she sat down and waited, forcing herself to read a book.

At three her telephone rang.

"Joanie?" Gig's velvet voice, now very much like a man's, sounded shy.

Joan felt desire come up suddenly again. "Yes," she said curtly.

"You still want me up?" Gig asked.

"Yes," Joan said. "Five minutes?"

"Right," Gig said and hung up.

A panic now gripped Joan. Jay's warnings came to her mind—and she was also afraid of her own desire. It was not controlled as it had been with men; it was wild and helpless, at Gig's mercy. She buried her face in her hands and trembled, trying to control herself, trying to tell herself that everything would be all right.

Her doorbell rang, long and steadily, sending a sustained shock through her. She hesitated for a moment, then forced herself to get up and go to the buzzer.

"Hello, beautiful," Gig smiled. She had changed into slacks before coming up. They made her look less stark, more graceful. She stepped inside, past nervous Joan, obviously a little nervous herself. "I almost didn't call," she said. "I thought you might have just been teasing me about coming up."

"I always mean what I say," Joan said, relieved that Gig felt awkward too; it had brought innocence to Gig's strong face. Joan mentally kicked Jay for having planted suspicions in her mind.

"Won't you have a drink?" Joan asked.

"Thanks," Gig said, "you wouldn't have any coffee instead, would you?"

"A little." Joan smiled and moved to heat the coffee.

"This is quite a coincidence," Gig said, looking around the apartment. "You know, I have friends living right under you."

"You mean that Daisy set," Joan said. "I get the conversation sometimes."

"It must be a lulu," Gig laughed. She got up and went toward Joan in the kitchen. "Can I help you with anything?"

"No thanks." Joan blushed because of Gig's nearness. "Coffee'll be hot in a couple of seconds."

"So will I," Gig smiled and put her arms around Joan. It was a sudden but gentle embrace. Joan lost herself in it. The kiss did not come until a moment later. Joan waited for it, feeling her whole body lost to Gig's. It was a soft, tender kiss. Gig's mouth did not feel like a man's mouth, it was strangely sweet and familiar in a way that Joan had always known a woman's mouth and lips would be. The noise of perking coffee opened her eyes and brought her back.

"Turn it off," Gig said. "We won't need it."

Joan reached over and turned off the burner and let Gig lead her, almost as they had danced before, back into the living room. Joan felt completely passive for the first time. All her desire to make love to Gig was gone—she wanted Gig to make love to her. This was new; she had never been passive with men, but with Gig passivity and acceptance—femininity—seemed so natural, so inevitable and right.

As Joan watched Gig's gray shape bend over her, her mind worked separately from the scene, for a moment—as it had many times before. This is a stranger, she thought, and I'm not really attracted to her as a person, only as a woman. But the feeling lasted only for a moment. Gig's soft body met Joan's and there was nothing more to think about except pleasure, pleasure that splashed Joan's body like the waves of a violent sea against rocks, splashed again and again until Joan found herself taken with the tide, taken out to sea where only a remote peace under a warm sun lulled her to sleep.

Gig had poured herself a cup of cold black coffee and was sipping it, watching Joan. Her arm was under her head and her face looked distant, away in thought. Joan raised herself on one elbow and looked at Gig; she had not had time to study Gig before. Funny, she thought, I don't even know what she really looks like.

Joan had a wonderful feeling of belonging to Gig; her body had never belonged to anyone before, but now someone had claimed it in love-making. Joan didn't care any longer about the great wall of differences between them; they had one basic thing to share. They were women who had met physically; that one meeting was enough. They had grown together.

"What are you looking at?" Gig said, her velvet voice lower and more relaxed than before.

"You," Joan smiled, running her finger down to Gig's armpit.

"Hey, quit that!" Gig laughed and turned a little away to avoid

Joan's teasing finger.

Joan began to rub Gig's shoulder. Her hands were feeling very sensuous tonight. She tried to suppress a deep desire and longing to explore Gig's body. Gig's flesh was soft, not the hard muscular flesh that it had seemed when hidden under the hard lines of her clothes. Her breasts were large—there was no doubt about her body being a woman's. Joan wished Gig would never wear clothes; clothes hid her true beauty. And even Gig's face had taken on a look of beauty. It looked sculptured in the half light, strong with life and character but smooth and assured.

"You're funny," Gig said, enjoying her back rub.

"Why?" Joan asked, rubbing harder.

"You're so quiet. Most women talk my head off."

"Do they?" Joan said, a little guilty but for what she didn't know. She let her hand find Gig's thigh and remain there a moment. Gig's hand found hers and took it away, squeezing it tightly. Joan felt immediately excited and confused. Gig turned to face her and looked at her searchingly for a moment.

"Say, are you really femme?"

"I don't think so," Joan said, treating the question seriously. She knew from observation at the Daisy that these terms and the roles they represented were very important to Gig. She could not understand the importance, but she respected it, particularly now.

"What do you mean, you don't know?" Gig said, propping up to see her better.

"I mean you're the first woman I've slept with," Joan said. "You pleased me very much just a while ago, Gig, but somehow I feel the evening's not quite over." She tried to project the confusion she felt inside to her face, wrinkling her brows a little in worry.

Gig took another gulp of her coffee and sighed, looking away from Joan. "You should have told me this before." She lay back and looked at the ceiling, lost in thought.

Joan watched Gig's quiet, expressionless face, the face of a stoic, of a person who never cried with pain. But Joan felt a great urge to cry with pain. A burning sensation of frustrated desire was making it difficult for her to lie quietly, inches away from

Gig, inches away from what she needed now to be doing—making love to Gig.

"I guess I'd better be going," Gig said, not moving for a moment. Joan made no effort to keep her. It was better that Gig go; it made things easier for both of them.

"I'll call you tomorrow," Gig said, getting up. She stretched her lithe muscular body and began to put on her clothes. "Maybe we can have a drink or something and talk things over."

"Fine," Joan said, getting up and putting on her robe. She turned on the ceiling light and watched Gig. The brighter light made Gig look masculine again, not at all attractive. Joan was glad that nothing more had happened. The memory might have been repulsive to her in the morning.

Gig finished dressing now and looked as she had at the Yellow Page. She smiled and took Joan's hands in hers. "Still friends?" she asked.

Joan smiled too and nodded. "Friends." She knew what Gig meant. They were no longer lovers now—just pals. As a pal, Gig might be very useful, Joan thought absently, filing her away in the back of her mind for future reference e.

They didn't kiss goodnight—pals don't kiss—and Joan watched Gig go slowly downstairs.

She closed the door to her apartment, leaned against the jamb, and sighed. She tried in every way to see Gig's point of view, but it just wouldn't focus. She wanted both and, what was even more strange, she didn't want someone either masculine or feminine—she just wanted a Lesbian, an attractive Lesbian. But was there such a thing? Were there only butches and femmes, only the Daisy crowd to choose from? She wondered about the Sun Dial. Tomorrow she would look it up in the phone book and perhaps go there tomorrow night.

With this pleasant anticipation, Joan was able to sleep.

4.

JAY rang, awakening Joan at noon. "Are you still in one piece?"

His amused voice, slightly catty, sounded like the tinkle of a raucous alarm in her ear.

"Almost," she groaned and turned over, holding the receiver a little away. "I told you there was nothing to worry about."

"Well, I'm glad you were right," he said. "I suppose I'm inclined to be overly cautious. So many strange sidelines go on in the bars, you see."

"You're not telling me anything I don't already know," Joan said. She tried to raise herself out of bed but gave up. Her body was limp and tired, painful in every bone, almost as bad as it had been after Paul that first night.

"Shall I pick you up for breakfast?" Jay asked. "I'm going to be in the neighborhood."

"Fine," Joan yawned, "in one hour, at the Positano."

"Right," he said, and hung up.

Joan let the receiver drop back in its cradle heavily, then made another effort to get up. Slowly, painfully, she raised herself out of bed and plodded to the shower.

When Jay met her at the Positano she was fresh and awake again, wearing the same slacks as the night before.

She had decided to wear those slacks often, at least for the weekend and her visit to the Sun Dial. She would ask Gig about the Sun Dial later, when they perhaps might meet for a drink.

"Well, you certainly look fine," Jay said when he saw her.

"I feel wonderful," Joan said, taking him up on it.

"How's your F-small-c this morning?" Jay's words might have confused Joan, except that she remembered that "Fc" was a term used in the Rorschach tests.

"Great," she said. The term referred to the appreciation of furry substances, for one thing.

"As a matter of fact," she added, "I wish my F-small--c had gotten a better workout last night than actually was the case."

"What's wrong?" Jay teased her. "Inhibited?"

Joan smiled. "No. As a matter of fact, I'm happy to say that I am not. I think my psyche is in better shape this morning, speaking of psyches, than it has been for some years now."

Jay smiled sympathetically. Joan could see that he understood her feelings; moreover, he approved of her deliberately being an active Lesbian.

"For some women," he asserted, "repression of homosexual desires is a living hell which can lead them into all sorts of crazy mixed-up scenes. For other women," he emphasized, "these desires are fleeting—in terms of months or years—and disappear as would any other neurotic symptom when satisfied directly or indirectly. The problem with this sort of neurotic woman, of course," he went on, warming up on his subject, "is that her indirect satisfactions may take some mighty strange forms. I'm sure you've probably run into the rabid Lesbian-hater or homosexual hunter among married women you know—or even among some of the young career girls."

Joan felt that she had given him a false idea about herself. Now was the time, she decided, to tell him the truth. She was certain now, and the knowledge gave her a happiness and a feeling of wholeness which she knew would grow as time went on.

"Jay," she hunted for a way of telling him, "I'm afraid I've been giving everyone the wrong impression for a while now. You see, I told Marc that I was a Lesbian. Well, I am. I think I always have been. But I've only really felt strongly since I grew up and came off to college. Of course, the reason I left home was linked with my wanting to know more about myself. But still, I didn't really have anything to do with a woman until last night. She stopped flatly. She had said it. Now Jay and Marc would know that her front was false and that she was a pretender who had only recently worked into the role.

Jay laughed, but his laughter was unexpectedly soft. She hadn't expected such gentleness from a queen, from a mad camping fairy. He took her hand and held it gently.

"Now you listen to Uncle Jay. There's a first time for all things. I know that you are very experienced as far as men are concerned. This much you've told me. But I know that you are able to evaluate your experience last night in terms of its real values for you. So be it. I'm fairly sure that you are not one of the neurotic women I just mentioned. Professional opinion aside,

I think you are gay."

Joan smiled. "Thanks," she said, "I consider that a compliment."

"Good girl," Jay countered. "Most people have little or no insight into what makes them tick. Most of their desires are unconscious—makes for trouble later in life, when they're all wound up in their own knots."

"Are you free tonight?" Joan changed the subject; it was too nice a Saturday to talk shop.

Jay nodded. "Why?"

"I thought we might make a late stop at the Sun Dial," Joan said. "After you give me that Rorschach."

"Haven't had enough, I see," Jay smiled. "All right, it's a date."

Joan took out her books and they sat in the Positano studying together for a few hours. Later they had dinner and then Jay went upstairs with her to give her the psychological tests.

Spending the day with Jay was soothing for Joan. Jay was a good companion. Secretly, she almost wished that she hadn't married Marc, but had married Jay instead. Jay was much more like David.

They were seated side b y side on the bed. Joan was going over her last Rorschach card while Jay busily jotted down her impressions. Finally she stopped and Jay glanced quickly at his notes.

"I won't be able to tell you exactly until I score it," he smiled, "but offhand, you've one of the most creative Rorschach's I've seen. You're a fascinating creature, Joan." He turned to her and took her hand.

Joan wore a sphinxish expression. She was pleased to have charmed Jay; she had never been able to charm David that way. Impulsively, she brought her face forward and kissed Jay on the lips. She kissed him as a man might first kiss a woman, sweetly, but taking the lead. Jay let himself be kissed, responding like a woman, almost in fun.

"1/28/13o you still think I'm fascinating?" she asked when she stopped. She looked at him, teasing.

"What made you do that?" Jay laughed awkwardly. He was blushing now, taken by surprise.

"Kicks," she said with a sophistication that was only recent with her. She got up and walked around a bit, feeling the smallness of her apartment. "You know, lately I've been fighting a strange compulsion," she said. "It's as if I want to be a man—so much a man that I want to prove how much more I am a man than men—prove it to men, that is. I want to be a man with a man. Can you explain that?" She looked at him, concerned with her problem. She was fighting an attraction that she felt for Jay because she knew she could be masculine with him, could take the lead.

"That's odd," he smiled. "I don't know if I can explain it. It sounds as if you're terribly angry at someone."

"Perhaps that's it." She laughed embarrassedly. "Perhaps I'm just angry at David." This thought relieved her and she came to sit on the bed again. But Jay was handsome, sitting there so helplessly, and she decided to let herself do what she wanted to do—seduce him.

"Do gay men often sleep with women?" Joan asked.

"Some do," Jay said. "It depends—also, there's always a first and only time for some, before they decide they're gay."

"I suppose you know why I asked," Joan said. "Have you ever slept with a woman?" She was studying his face now, catching every change in his expression in an effort to understand him. Jay was fidgety, but he wasn't exactly running away from her stare.

"I'm not mixed up, Joan," he said, ignoring her question.

"I didn't think you were," she said. She sat back and stopped trying to be a vamp, conscious of Jay's discomfort. By retreating she succeeded in interesting Jay. He sat forward and took her hand.

"Joanie girl, you're a card!" he laughed. "God, what a triangle that would be—you, me and Marc."

"It might be fun," she smiled. "I've always wondered what a threesome was like."

"It doesn't work, Joan." Jay's face twisted in experienced

distaste. "There's always one of the three left out. I'd hate it to be you."

"That would be all right," she laughed embarrassedly. "I don't care for men for very long anyway." She looked at him seriously and took his head, brought it to her and kissed him again. This time her kiss was more forward; her hands ran over the pleats of his jacket and to his shirt, stopping finally when they reached his belt buckle. Joan felt the buckle with her fingers and began gently to open it, almost too gently for Jay to notice.

It was like undressing a girl. Jay made no effort to stop her. Patiently, she undid the buttons of his shirt, feeling his smooth hard chest beneath it. Jay's chest was sculptured, his entire body handsome and strong; for the first time Joan felt desire for a man. For the first time she really wanted to go on. But then the mood was broken. Jay had become aroused, and was responding now just like all the others, not allowing himself to be passive. He sat up and took Joan's arms with his strong hands and pressed his body to hers, finding her lips hungrily with his, and the same repulsion she had felt with other men, the same feeling of withdrawal began to take her. Detachedly, like so many times before, she waited for him to remove her clothes, allowing his mouth to find her breasts, allowing his hands to do what they wanted with her body, feeling nothing but a familiar sense of discomfort and distaste.

So that's what it would have been like with David, Joan thought again and again. Jay was lying next to her, a cigarette in his mouth, staring at the ceiling. She could not help admiring his body. In fact, she wished she had his body instead of her own. Her own body felt soiled with acrid sweat and her lungs were sick with cigarette smoke. It was nearly midnight and she wanted Jay to leave. She wanted to take a shower, and then find the Sun Dial, alone. Gig, with all her coarseness, had been a woman, had really pleased her; Joan wanted to find other women. Not even Jay would be a substitute.

"What are you thinking?" Jay asked, noticing her silence.

"I'm secretly trying to get rid of you," she smiled. She played with the hairs on his leg, her hands unable to keep still. "I was hoping to make the Sun Dial for an hour or so tonight."

"*Cherchez la femme*," Jay sighed with a slight bit of humor. "Doll, didn't I tell you you were gay?"

"What about you? You certainly weren't gay a while ago," Joan countered. "Are all homosexuals that good in bed with women?"

"We all have our ups and downs," Jay replied mockingly. He swung his legs off the bed. "I'm going to use your shower," he said, "then maybe I'll go cruise the bars. I'll walk you to the Sun Dial if you like."

"Thanks," Joan said.

It was odd, the way they were still friends on some other level, as if nothing had happened between them. She was glad, because she enjoyed Jay's friendship.

Jay sang in the shower and when he was through, Joan used it. And then they dressed, Joan in slacks and Jay in his smartly styled suit. They walked out into the street together like brother and sister, but a little more familiar than that now, as if their friendship had taken on a new dimension. Joan knew that at some time or other, for lack of something better to do, they would repeat that strange scene all over again, and it would mean just as little to both of them then.

Jay walked her to the Sun Dial, which was across the park, and left her at the door. Joan felt safe as soon as she walked in. The customers looked like part of a college sorority shindig, like healthy all-American girls in slacks or in skirts; not the way Gig had looked—not strange and grotesque like Gig.

The Sun Dial was noisy and smoke-filled, but with happy noise and properly vented smoke. A great feeling of relief came over Joan as she looked around. Not all Lesbians were like Gig. There were attractive women here like herself, some very feminine, and most of them her own age. The bartender and the waiters were men, clean cut and not seedy-looking like the ones at the Daisy. She felt secure as she walked to the bar. It was very crowded, but only with women.

She found a clear spot at the far end near a young couple who seemed happily involved with each other and deaf to the noise around them. Joan studied them for a moment. The more masculine girl wore a broad smile. She was wearing a college blazer and her hair was cut short, but not short enough to make her look like a boy. She had a large and interesting profile, not pretty, but appealing. Her partner was blonde and also wore a blazer, but her features were more feminine. They both were about twenty-two. Joan noticed that particularly. Unlike the Daisy, the crowd here was not in their teens. This was a clean bar. And then, as if to echo her thoughts, the bouncer walked toward her. He was small for a bouncer, but with the shapeless ears of a boxer. Joan wondered why he was approaching her; for a moment she felt afraid. Perhaps he wanted to throw her out because he had never seen her before.

"Hey, you," he motioned to her, "Yes, you, Miss."

Joan did not know what to make of his tone. She hoped it was just a natural coarseness. "Are you calling me?" she said.

"Yeah," he said, coming nearer. "Can you prove your age? I don't want any minors drinking in here," he growled.

Joan took out her birth certificate; she always carried it in her wallet, because she knew she looked too young to be drinking.

It satisfied him but he took hold of her arm briefly. "Who you looking for?" he said.

Joan, confused for a moment, mentioned Gig. It was the wrong name.

"Look, I want this place kept clean," he said. "I know you're new and you've been to them other places, but here it's different. Here we got rules. I want none of them characters in here—and no men! Now I tell all the girls when they first come in—no men, no characters. One slip, and you're out."

Joan held her temper, reminding herself that it was just his coarse manner that made her angry. Those rules were good ones; she wished they were applied at the Daisy and the Yellow Page. It was the prostitution and the other traffic that made those places unsafe, not the Lesbians.

She went back to the bar and ordered a beer. The customers were now massing and the place was becoming lively.

Joan looked about her more freely. The table directly opposite her was taken u by a jolly crowd of Irish-looking girls who might all have been student nurses. They reminded her of something Paul had said about most homosexuals being blonde. She had to laugh, because there were more than blondes here—all races seemed to be comfortable in this place, without any sort of segregation, black next to white, sometimes coupled and each shade attractive. On the whole, there were more attractive women here than one would find in an ordinary bar or at any of the Bohemian spots that Joan frequented.

She noticed especially one girl at the bar, a very blonde and small girl with sensitive eyes and lips. She was talking to a taller and more masculine woman, but they didn't seem to be together. Joan decided to wait until the two finished talking and then go over to the blonde. She had forced herself through necessity to be rid of her shyness—for she knew she would have to be aggressive if she wanted to be butch. But another girl had the same idea and before Joan could move, a tall and attractive butch had already asked the blonde to dance and escorted her out to the dance floor.

Joan sighed and sipped her beer. The juke box was playing a rock tune; as the beat blared, Joan went over in her mind what had happened a while ago with Gig. Half-memories of the night before kept repeating themselves—little images of lips and eyes and the feeling of soft breasts pressed against each other, and Gig's tender embraces that seemed to reach far beneath Joan's skin into the parts of her that needed most the feeling of being touched, of being caressed, of being ordered to and fro without the presence of a hungry, excited male partner who would leave her naked and degraded, corrupted and sore—like Paul's presence, and yes, even Jay's. Not even Jay, who was so much like David, had come near to Gig in tenderness—and Gig was by no means one of the most attractive Lesbians available.

As Joan thought about all this, she became aware that she was being watched. She raised her eyes and saw a mustache, and behind it, a bald-headed man who seemed about thirty, dressed in a sloppy brown suit.

"Hello." He smiled pathetically.

Joan turned around, ignoring him. She wondered why the bouncer had let him in at all. Most of all, she wondered why the man had wanted to come here—to a place filled with women who would have nothing to do with him.

She tolerated the mustached-man's stare for a while longer and then took her beer and moved to the other side of the bar, noticing a well-tailored girl sitting there with a drink in her hand. She seemed to be alone. Joan decided to practice at being butch.

"Would you like to dance?" Joan said, perhaps more awkwardly than she had intended.

The girl looked at Joan and smiled. It was an odd smile, one attractive with age and maturity; the woman seemed about thirty—not exactly feminine but not overly butch either.

"Why not?" the woman answered, putting her glass on the bar. "The name's Kim. What's yours?"

"Joan," Joan said. She smiled in return, feeling more confident.

They walked together to the back of the bar where the couples were dancing and fell into a fox trot despite the rock beat.

"What do you do, Joan?" Kim said as they danced. They were dancing closely but not the way Gig had danced, not with all their bodies.

"I'm a student," Joan said. "And you?"

"I'm a WAC," Kim replied reluctantly. They danced cheek to cheek for a while without speaking; then the record changed.

"Let's sit," Joan said. They found an empty table nearby and Kim went back for their drinks.

"God," Kim said when she returned, "what a bore —not you—I mean this dive."

"We could take a walk in a while," Joan suggested. The idea appealed to both of them.

"Are you on leave?" Joan asked.

Kim nodded. "Forty-eight hours—half spent already." She lit a cigarette and bobbed her head to the rhythm of the music. "You from New York?"

Joan nodded. There was something dreadfully restless about Kim and it was catching. They drank more beer and danced again and this time Kim held Joan tighter. There was something very strong about Kim, but it wasn't an unpleasant strength—like a man's strength was; it was an assurance and a protectiveness that seemed very natural and soothing to Joan. She closed her eyes and let her lungs fill themselves with the odor of Kim's cologne. Kim's cheek was very soft against hers and Kim's breasts were warm and comfortable. They danced without speaking until arousal grew too strong. Then the picked up their purses from the table and walked out of the bar into the fresh night air. It was drizzling slightly, cutting the heaviness of the warm night; holding hands, they walked slowly to the corner.

"Want some coffee?" Kim suggested, seeing the luncheonette still open.

Joan nodded and they went inside.

The quietness of the luncheonette was a relief after the noise of the 'Dial and in the stronger light Joan had a chance to study Kim's features more closely. Kim's face was beautiful, but in a hard, quiet way. Her eyes were colder than Gig's—they had a look of someone who had lost interest in people and things—yet their hardness was attractive. It was a hardness that went with a trim, muscular body and a self-sufficient personality. In Kim there was also a bitterness that can come with age, but also a rare wisdom and understanding. Joan reminded herself that she had just met Kim; she would hold off judgment until later. In the meantime, she wondered why Kim was so serious and distant.

"Just lost your friend?" she asked Kim. The counter man was far on the other side of the store and they could talk without his hearing them.

Kim gave a short laugh. "Months ago. And you?"

"No, just looking to find one," Joan said. This left them silent for a long time and they dank their coffee slowly.

"When do you have to be back on the base?" Joan asked finally.

"I have to leave by three o'clock tomorrow," Kim said. There was another long pause and Kim seemed to be thinking something over. At last she said, "I've got a room in the hotel across the street. Want to come upstairs for a while?"

Joan hesitated for a moment. The question had taken her by surprise. She hadn't been prepared for such a quick invitation. She almost didn't want to go—she had been with Jay not long ago and she didn't feel clean. She didn't want Kim to touch her tonight. But she did want to make love to Kim. In the bright light of the drugstore Kim was even more attractive than she had been at the 'Dial.

"All right—for a while," Joan said, rubbing her finger on the counter, tracing a line of water nervously with her hands.

Kim reached into her pocket and threw money on the counter and they both got up lazily and walked across the street. The lobby was dark and an old Negro porter who was at the desk got up and took them up in the elevator.

Joan knew the hotel. It wasn't a cheap hotel but it was shabby nonetheless, as the management found a certain pride in the tradition of old upholstery and threadbare rugs.

Kim had a double on the eighth floor with a private bath and a comfortable bed. They waited until the porter had left before Kim closed the door and latched it.

Joan threw her light jacket on a chair and looked around the room. The blinds were down, hiding the view across the courtyard to the other rooms, rooms just like this, where men or women, and men and women, were putting them to the same use. Joan had always hated hotels. For a moment she was sorry she had not brought Kim to her apartment, but laziness made her dismiss the thought.

Kim also threw her jacket down, reached into a drawer, took out a bottle of Scotch and two glasses and offered Joan a drink. Joan accepted the offer and stood, watching Kim pour. Kim seemed to be quite tired, using liquor to wake herself up. Joan too felt the strain of the evening and sat at the foot of the bed, waiting for Kim to speak. They both took a swallow of the Scotch before Kim broke the silence.

"I'm sorry there's no radio or anything," she said.

"I like the silence," Joan countered. She let her eyes meet Kim's. They were finally alone and she wanted very much to be kissed. Kim seemed to read her mind. She came nearer and put her mouth on Joan's. It was intended to be slow and casual, but they couldn't be casual. Joan felt as if she had been thirsty for months, and finally her mouth was being cooled by the refreshing sweetness of Kim's, finally her burning body was being soothed.

It turned into more than a kiss and they both lay back on the bed, each caressing the other simultaneously, lost in a hunger both had for the body of a woman. Joan felt that this wasn't the same as it had been with Gig. Kim was more her type, was even a potential lover, and so there was more than animal passion here, there was a beginning, a beginning of a good, clean feeling, a beginning of love. And Joan felt very butch. She forgot Jay, forgot about everything except making love to Kim.

Joan's lips and hands seemed to be electric with awareness as she gently opened Kim's blouse and slipped off her bra; and then she let Kim undo her own blouse and bra. They were both half naked on the bed and they paused for a word or two in order to establish some feeling of contact on another plane. They were both embarrassed at having skipped the preliminaries of love.

"Let's have more Scotch," Kim said. She broke away from Joan a little and poured some liquor in each glass. But Joan shook her head; she didn't want any. Kim drank hers down, looking at Joan from a distance. Her eyes seemed disturbed; they were still hard, as before, but they were uncomfortable now.

"What are you thinking?" Joan asked. She was sitting up by the side of the bed, herself upset by the suddenness of their contact. But mostly she was disturbed because Kim was bothered by it. She knew instinctively that this sort of thing was new for Kim—that Joan might have been the first girl Kim had kissed since months ago when she had lost her friend.

"I'm thinking there's a shower that goes with this room," Kim said, making a good recovery into a careless mood. She looked at Joan with an air of *What next?* as if the Scotch had reminded Kim that her standards were supposed to be those of men, not of women, and that a soldier couldn't turn down a beautiful girl who wanted to go to bed.

Kim moved suddenly and took her overnight bag with her. She was in the shower only a few minutes and she came out wearing pajamas. She tossed a towel to Joan and then got under the covers, preparing to read an old issue of *Life*.

The hot water relaxed Joan's muscles and awakened them at the same time; she was washing off Jay a second time. She had taken another shower earlier, but now she wanted to be cleaner than surface—for Kim.

When Joan came out, Kim was in bed blowing smoke rings up to the ceiling. Only the bed lamp was lit and Kim closed that also, moving over on the bed.

Joan put her clothes on the chair with the Jackets and lay down nude beside her. The only light came dimly through the which blinds on the window and the two lay there letting their eyes become accustomed to the near-darkness. Then Kim put out her cigarette. There was a long silence. There was only the feeling of apprehension and even slight repulsion that always comes when strange bodies prepare to meet.

And then Kim's hands took hold of Joan's, and there was Kim's warm breath as her lips touched Joan's—and then the hesitation and repulsion were gone. They became a strange familiarity and joy.

The maid's knock woke them early the next morning. "It's occupied!" Kim shouted through the door and the maid went away, apologizing, to another room. But it was too late. They were both awake now and didn't want to go back to sleep. Kim had only until three o'clock before the last train back to the base. She lit a cigarette, and came back to bed, fondly taking hold of Joan's hand. She bent down and kissed Joan sweetly on the lips.

"Ready for breakfast?"

Joan nodded, yawning one last time. She was very sleepy, but the beautiful Sunday morning kept her awake. She tightened her grasp on Kim's hand and brought it to her lips. They were not strangers this morning. They had become used to each other's presence and it was as if they had been living together a long time.

"I want a great big breakfast," Joan said, "and then let's walk together. We might go somewhere, like the zoo."

Kim laughed and bent over Joan once more, warming her cheek with her own. It reminded Joan of their love-making and she pressed Kim to her with both arms. It was almost too soon to say it, but that didn't matter now. Joan said—"I love you."

Kim laughed again and nibbled Joan's ear. Joan waited for her to say something in answer, but Kim did not. Instead, she sat beside Joan and said, "Do I see you again?"

"As often as you like," Joan answered. She felt happy. At least Kim liked her. "When are you coming back?"

"I can't get another leave for two weeks," Kim said. She seemed disturbed at this, as if she hated being in the Army. "There's a year left on my enlistment," she added, as if she wanted Joan to know all the disadvantages.

"And then what?" Joan asked.

"Then I can quit and go to school on the G.I. Bill," Kim said. That had been her reason for enlisting. That was the most usual reason in peacetime, not the fact that she was a Lesbian. There was no advantage to being a Lesbian in the Services.

Joan sat up and kissed Kim tenderly and they held the kiss a long time, almost starting all over again, their bodies beginning to remember the night before.

"Let's get dressed," Kim said finally, pulling herself away from Joan with great effort. They both felt that they needed some time simply to talk. Getting to know each other now was very important—important because it would carry the memory of this weekend along in the following awful days of separation.

They got up and dressed and groomed themselves and then left the room. Kim checked out and then they were free of the hotel, free of the stifling upholstery and tattered rugs, free to go out into the late May sun.

They walked with Kim's overnight bag between them, each with one hand on the handle and sharing the case's weight—almost like walking hand-in-hand. There was a large and modernly decorated restaurant on the corner, the kind that serves charcoal broiled hamburgers and eggs in the skillet. They stopped at the window and decided this was the place for breakfast. It was not crowded at this hour on a Sunday morning.

They took one of the large booths next to the wall-length window that let the sun shine directly on them, filling them with the warmth of a comfortable spring day. Their order was taken quickly and then they had nothing to do but sit and look at each other, sit and study each other's face.

Kim's face was beautiful, Joan noticed again. It had the inner glow of someone who liked the outdoors. Kim didn't look thirty in daylight. "How old are you," Joan asked.

"Twenty-eight," Kim said. "And you?"

"Just twenty," Joan said.

This came as a chock to Kim and for a moment she was plainly disturbed. "You mean I've been corrupting a minor?"

Joan smiled. "This minor was corrupted long ago and not by women." She touched Kim's hand. "It can't matter that much to you, can it?"

Kim squeezed Joan's hand for a moment and then let go. "I guess it's too late to worry about that now." She looked down and played with her fork. "I'm very glad we met."

"So am I," Joan said. She leaned forward. "Tell me about yourself. Where do you come from? I want to know all about you."

Kim smiled. "I'm from Chicago." Not freely, but under Joan's prying questions, she began to talk about herself—about her family and the Army and the friend she had lost six months ago. "It's hell in the Service," she finished. "You're always watched. Gay couples don't have a chance. If they can't get something on you, they transfer you to a different outfit. That's what happened with Bea and me. Bea's in Frisco now. They were close to kicking us out but they had no proof."

"And you don't even dare write her?" Joan had listened to Kim's story with horror. The Army's attitude toward homosexuals seemed close to Gestapo tactics, not at all what one expected in a free country. Why persecute two consenting adults for what they did in private?

"She has a new friend there," Kim finished. "I guess it's better for both of us that way."

"How can you say that?" Joan said, forgetting her own interest in Kim for the moment. "How can you let them beat you?"

"Time does things to people," Kim answered simply. She looked at Joan and smiled a little sadly. "That's why I'm somewhat cynical about last night. I don't dare hope that anything can last a year. It wouldn't be fair to expect you to wait that long just on the basis of a few weekends we can have together."

Joan thought about this for a moment. Seeing Kim briefly after long intervals would be difficult. Joan's body was young and alive and needed satisfaction—and her mind needed a friend, someone to share her daily life. It would be difficult to save herself for Kim. "We can give it a try," she said at last. And then she added, "I can't promise to be faithful, but at least we can keep on seeing each other."

Kim nodded and quietly finished her scrambled eggs.

After breakfast they walked to Washington Square and fed the pigeons. Suddenly, they realized how little time they had left before Kim's train.

"Let's go to my apartment," Joan said, and her words made them quicken their steps out of the park, made them anxious to return to each other's arms, anxious to spend the last hurried hours satisfying a need that would torture their bodies for two long and vacant weeks.

5.

JOAN did not accompany Kim to the station. She could not bear the thought of the train's taking Kim so far away. She went as far as the subway with her and then walked aimlessly down the street, not knowing where to go. She could not bear her lonely apartment just then, so she decided to go to the Positano. There she saw Marc and Jay.

"So, back together," she smiled, going to sit at their table. Her experience with Jay of the night before now seemed so remote, almost as though it had never happened.

"Did you have any luck at the 'Dial?" Jay asked.

Joan nodded, but said nothing.

"Your silence betrays you, young woman," Jay chided. "I'm glad you got here, though. I've been dying to tell Marc what happened last night, but I thought I should get your permission first. It's too funny to keep a secret."

"I don't mind your telling Marc," Joan answered. "But can we forget for now? Tell him sometime when you're alone."

"Tell me what?" Marc said, seeing the air of naughtiness around Jay.

"Later, doll," Jay said, feigning a swish.

Joan found them both annoying. In fact she suddenly found all men annoying, especially Marc and Jay because they were both so closely connected with her life. She didn't want to feel that men, any men, were a part of her life any longer. She looked desperately up and down the Positano for a woman's face, a lovely face that would give her some relief at this moment when her world somehow seemed composed only of men. The prospect of waiting two weeks for Kim was frightening.

As if in answer to her desperate wish, she saw Gig winking at her through the large café window. Joan waved for her to come join them. Gig quickly did so, coming in and pulling up a chair.

"Hi, beautiful," she said, then nodded to Jay.

"Hi," Joan smiled. "This is my husband, Marc. You know Jay." Gig nodded to Marc too and looked at the two men knowingly, guessing accurately their relationship with Joan.

"Doing anything tonight?" Gig then turned to Joan.

"Not very much," Joan said, and then she remembered that she really had to cram for exams. But perhaps she could take time out for one drink with Gig. She was feeling decidedly sentimental about Gig now.

"I had hoped we could all go to a movie," Marc said.

Joan looked at him sharply. His tone had been irritated and cold. Could it be that Marc felt possessive about her? She looked at Gig again. Gig was wearing a pair of old slacks and a wrinkled white shirt—housecleaning clothes. Marc was reacting to her appearance, Joan realized. She laughed to herself. Marc would never understand Lesbians; he liked neatness and makeup and femininity—he would never understand the "butch."

"Sorry, not tonight," Joan said to Marc. She turned to Gig. "But I do have time for one beer. Shall we?"

"A pleasure!" Gig grinned. She stood up and waited for Joan to do the same.

Joan rose and smiled at the two men. "I'll be around here tomorrow evening sometime, after I study for a while. Maybe we can all eat out." She felt she had to be warm to Marc and Jay.

"All right, doll," Jay waved. Marc was too peeved to answer.

Gig frowned when they left the Positano. "How long have you been married?" she asked.

"A few weeks," Joan answered. "I'm already beginning to regret it," she added.

"Those things never work," Gig said with an air of sad experience.

"Where are we going to drink our beer?" Joan said. Her mood had changed and she felt happy—she was in the world of women again.

"I thought we could buy a couple of cans and bring them up to Barbie's place," Gig said. "You might want to meet your neighbors."

"You mean the girls who live in the apartment under me?" Joan smiled. The idea was appealing. She wanted to meet more Lesbians, even if they weren't the nicest kind. "Good idea," she said to Gig.

They stopped at the grocery where Gig bought a few cans; then they went up the steps of Joan's building and knocked on the door of the first floor front apartment.

"Who is it?" a high-pitched voice said on the other side.

"Gig and a redhead," Gig said.

Barbie opened the door. She was a small butch, with a GI

haircut. She wore an old white shirt much like the one Gig wore.

"Hi," Barbie said. "Come in. Just in time to help us paint."

"We just stopped in for a minute," Gig said, handing her the bag of beer cans. "I wanted you to meet Joan."

"Oh, yeah, you live upstairs." Barbie smiled. It was a warm, friendly smile. "Hey, Madge," she called, "we have company."

Madge, a bleached-blonde femme, came in from the kitchen, untying her apron. "Oh, hi." She stopped when she saw Joan. "You live upstairs."

"Yes," Joan smiled.

"That's Joan," Gig said, sitting on the old sofa in the small living room. The apartment was in a mess. Barbie had some cans of paint out and half the ceiling was finished.

"I'm glad to meet you, Joan," Madge said, extending her hand. She was a shy girl, nervous, but still full of warmth. Joan was glad Gig had brought her here. She had always been a little afraid of her neighbors. To strangers they looked fearfully rough, like a wild bunch, but Joan saw that was only the impression their clothes and shrill voices gave. Now Joan saw that her downstairs neighbors were no different than any young married couple in a tenement district, a little foreign-looking to outsiders, but not in the least sinister.

Meanwhile, Joan felt Gig watching her with amusement and eagerness. It obviously made her happy to introduce her friends to Joan; Gig was proud of her friends.

"I hope you'll excuse the mess," Barbie said, a trifle embarrassed, trying to kick a paint can away from the middle of the floor.

"I like it," Joan smiled. "It's not a mess—it's progress. You're making this into a lovely apartment."

"Thanks," Barbie said with a certain pride. She handed the bag of beer to Madge who went into the kitchen and opened the cans then brought them back.

"Joan's new in the life," Gig said when she had sipped her beer. "I decided she needed some friends."

"well, by all means, come visit any time you want," Barbie said. The invitation reflected her spontaneous good nature, which was echoed in Madge's face.

"Thanks," Joan said, "I will. And you must also come visit me."

She felt very happy. Gay life wasn't a long hermitage, after all. There were lots of friends to be made, close friends, because there was the feeling that each of them was in the same boat. It was like belonging to some minority group, like being a Negro, or a Jew, except even closer than that, because the whole world was against you and you had no Africa or Israel to go to—only a melodramatic memory of an island called Lesbos.

Joan sat on the other side of the sofa and waited for Gig to carry on the conversation. Gig was sitting in obvious great comfort, sipping her beer, much more at ease with Joan than she had been two days ago when they had met in the Yellow Page. So much had happened since then! Joan could scarcely believe it had only been a weekend. First Gig, then Jay, and then Kim.

Kim. Joan felt wonderfully different and scared now for a moment, scared because Kim was going to be away for two weeks, scared that too much might happen before Kim returned—with Jay, with Marc, with Gig, with school, and even with her parents; or that some speeding car might level her on the street before Kim returned; or that Kim's train might jump its track. It was the same frightened feeling that Joan had felt when her parents first left her and her sister alone in the big empty house one Saturday night, the same scared feeling she'd had when she took a bus unaccompanied for the first time, two stops and back to see how it felt to do it—the feeling of fright that comes when the cord begins to break and one feels cold and alone in the world, completely alone.

"What are you thinking?" Gig asked, sensing Joan's preoccupation.

"Oh, nothing." Joan eluded her interest and tried to pay attention to the present. Barbie and Madge were sitting in the deep easy chair, Madge on the arm of it and half in Barbie's lap. Both seemed so secure with each other and satisfied with life. Joan envied them. Their life was not exactly what she had in mind for herself and Kim—she didn't want Kim to look so butch or to feel herself so completely femme—and yet she wanted to be together with Kim in just such a home situation, on a Sunday, painting the ceiling and stopping for beer and conversation with visiting friends. Joan wondered if that would ever be possible for her; she told herself firmly that it could.

"When are your exams going to be over?" Gig asked. She had decided that was worrying Joan.

"Tuesday after next," Joan said automatically, and then it occurred to her again that it would still leave three days before Kim came back.

"What are you studying, Joan?" Barbie asked, largely to keep the conversation going.

"I may be majoring in Psychology," she said. She didn't want to talk about herself just now. She was too full of her own thoughts.

"Good—we need more of those," Barbie said. "But I hope you're not going to try curing gay kids."

"No, I'm not one of those idiots," Joan smiled. She knew what Barbie had meant: there were too many theories about what to do with inverts. Joan believed that homosexuality was as natural for some people as heterosexuality was for others. Trying to change one into the other was like sticking white carnations into a vase of green ink—absolutely artificial and in bad taste.

"Do you think you'll be able to take time off for the beach on Saturday?" Gig asked.

The invitation surprised Joan and pleased her. "Yes, perhaps," she smiled. "But not Coney Island, please. I want a clean beach."

"There's one in Far Rockaway where all the gay kids go," Gig said. "I thought the four of us could bring sandwiches and make a day of it. I don't have to be at work until nine that night."

"Thant sounds swell, Gig," Barbie said, looking at Madge to see if she were also nodding.

"It's agreed, then," Gig said. She quickly drank the rest of her beer and waited for Joan—she had promised Joan only a short visit here.

Joan finished her beer also, stood up and said all the usual things one says when a short visit is over; and then she and Gig were outside the apartment and Joan turned to go upstairs. She paused for a moment, seriously resisting an impulse to invite Gig to her place. Then she realized that she would have to tell Gig about Kim eventually—it was not fair to lead Gig on. As if knowing Joan's thoughts, Gig covered Joan's hand with hers.

"I've been thinking about the other night," Gig said.

"I met a girl at the 'Dial yesterday," Joan said quickly, before Gig could go on.

"Oh." Gig paused, and then, "A butch?"

"No. That is—not completely." Joan found it difficult to tell her. She didn't want to hurt Gig and, more than that, she wanted always to be her friend—what had happened between them the night before would, for Joan, always mark the beginning of her life.

Gig made a quick recovery. She smiled and patted Joan's head and said, "I keep getting fooled by that red hair. When are you seeing the mouse again?"

"She's no mouse." Joan smiled too. Gig was allowing herself to be a little jealous. "Her name's Kim and she's a WAC. She won't be on leave again for two weeks."

"Then what are we standing here for?" Gig said. "We should celebrate this. Why don't I get another couple of cans and meet you upstairs?"

"I don't think that will be wise," Joan said carefully. She was sorely tempted and shocked at herself at the same time. Kim had barely left, and yet she was afraid to be alone even for one hour. Something inside of her had been jarred, was now clinging to an apron string. It was the fear of this strange new world and the excitement of suddenly finding herself free in a meadow full of flowers, all wanting to be picked.

"Some other time then, Red," Gig said. "See you Saturday." She winked and turned to go and then added, "For God's sakes wear fly front or something, will you? I don't want you should go around breaking the wrong hearts out on the beach."

Joan laughed. "All right, I'll see what I can find that looks butch."

Joan turned and went happily upstairs, all tension eased. She studied uninterruptedly for about two hours and then her telephone rang. It was Marc.

"Hi. We just got out of the movie," he said. "Want us up?"

"Might as well come over," she sighed. "I'm slowly developing conversion hysteria up here."

Marc laughed and hung up. A few minutes later he and Jay were at the door. "Come in," Joan said, unlatching it, and then went back to sit on the bed with her books. She was used to having Marc and Jay over and continuing with her work at the same time.

Marc and Jay were in a particularly gay mood this evening; they swished into the apartment. "Doll, welcome to the family," Marc said. "Jay's told me and I think it's fabulously funny."

"Oh that," Joan blushed; she had nearly forgotten what had happened with Jay—it was only part of a long set of similar memories and Jay's face was indistinct, as the many faces of the others were—near strangers, and all alike; there had been the sailor whose blonde hair had struck her fancy and who had turned out to be a virgin; the actor she had met in the Positano who had a strange fancy for girls' underwear; the bookish young European who spent the evening trying to give it all some meaning; the ex-G.I. in her Chem class who read her from Henry Miller; the many others—thirty or more—and now finally Jay. She had been able to do this, had wanted to, because she was imitating David; she had forced herself to alley cat, and to like men because David did. And always she had been a man with men, like David.

"Just look at her blush," Jay said, teasing Joan. "I think it's marvelous. Why don't we all move in together?"

"I don't like *menages*," Joan said, but it was not a sharp retort. She knew she would have to get a few things clear—especially now that she had found Kim. Before Kim, Joan might have considered keeping Jay around—after all, he was good company and Marc's lover to boot. But now she wanted to separate herself from men, even from Marc. She did not want to be married to Marc anymore; she wanted to belong only to herself—and to a woman like Kim.

"But it would be so mad," Marc went on jokingly, "the three of us living happily ever after. And if you found a girl, that would make four."

Joan smiled. "I don't think you'd ever approve of any girl I might find." Se paused to see Marc's reaction. She caught his eyes as they flashed away from her; she had struck home.

"What makes you say that? Of course I'd approve of her," Marc said.

"No, doll, you wouldn't," Joan said authoritatively, "and I don't think she'd quite approve of you. Not all Lesbians are as wild as I am. I haven't been quite myself these past few months."

Marc stopped queening and it made his entire appearance suddenly masculine. Joan, noticing, though: Odd, the way they can turn it on and off like that.

"What's the problem, Joanie?" Marc said.

"The problem is that I'm regretting having married you," she said, responding to his seriousness with friendly frankness. "You see, I met a girl last night—"

"Not that character who came to our table this afternoon," Marc interjected, unable to hide his dislike of Gig.

"That 'character' is a damn nice kid," Joan snapped.

"Look, Joan," Jay dared to sit beside her on the bed and take her hand, "Marc's just concerned about you, as I am. We know you're still a babe in the woods about gay life."

"Of course, I understand," Joan said, softening a little. "I really appreciate the way you two watch over me. But in a way now I'm feeling trapped by both of you. Marc—" she turned toward him, "aren't you planning to be around Reno in the fall? It would be so simple to get an annulment—I'll pay for it." She immediately regretted having put it so bluntly. She didn't want to hurt him.

Marc sighed and paced a little more and finally turned. "All right, Joanie, if that's the way you want it." He sighed again and sat. "I guess it's all my fault. I shouldn't have gotten you into this. I should have known better."

His words freed her and immediately she could be warm to the two again. She wanted to kiss Marc for being so understanding about her change of mind. "Can I make both of you a cold drink?" She got up, full of new life, went to Marc and rubbed the top of his head fondly. "Thank you, Marc."

"Anything will be fine," he responded, looking up at her. His pure blue eyes, very young though very old, were as innocent as they were the day she had first met him in the Positano. They were eyes any girl could fall in love with, eyes like David's. But Joan felt no man's eyes could ever attract her now; now she belonged only to women. And something more marvelous had happened this weekend—she was over David. It was as if David had never existed, nor had any other man in her life.

Marc and Jay stayed only a little while longer that afternoon. For the rest of that week they left her alone. Joan wrote the paper that was due for English and did a better job on it than usual, forcing herself to stay long hours at the library digging up more material in an endless chain of research that was not really necessary to pass the course; it was a good way to keep busy.

On Saturday morning, Madge and Barbie rang her doorbell. "Hi, Madge said. "Gig said she'd pick us up here. Are you ready?"

"Almost," Joan said, finishing with the basket of lunch she was packing. She had prepared many sandwiches, wanting to treat the others as well even though they had brought their own lunch. The idea of going on a picnic at one of the gay beaches thrilled her. She had always wanted to be part of the crowd, had always wanted to be taken to a gay beach.

"Say, that's some outfit," Barbie commented good-naturedly.

Joan stood for a moment and turned with pride. She had bought Bermuda shorts with a fly front to comply with Gig's request, but they didn't make her look butch. The striped man-tailored shirt she wore made the outline of her breasts more distinct and her white knee-high socks only accented her beautifully proportioned legs. Even her red hair, tied tightly back to look like a short haircut, only made her seem more sophisticatedly feminine. Her lips were rosy without makeup, and the sun would quickly redden her cheeks. And then there was the matter of the bathing suit she was wearing underneath—it had been sent by her parents and she was too fond of it to wear something else. She had always wanted to look like Sheena the Jungle Queen, and now her bathing suit would do it. It was a leopard-skin one, and it would by no means hide her bosom.

"I wonder what's keeping Gig," Barbie said. Just as the spoke, the doorbell buzzed and Joan opened the door.

"Hi, kids," Gig said. She was dressed in white Bermudas with a white man's jacket to match, and was better groomed than Joan had ever seen her. Her shirt was a brightly patterned Cuban sport shirt and the entire combination made her very much like a man. One would have to look three or four times to decide that she was a woman, and even then, one wouldn't be sure. Her deep tan gave her a look of strength.

"I've got the car outside," Gig said, picking up Joan's basket.

"Swell," Barbie said. She took up Madge's bundles and the four went downstairs.

Gig's car was an old white convertible and the top was down, folding messily around the back seat. Barbie and Madge took the back and immediately settled comfortably in each other's arms. Joan sat next to Gig in front, feeling a little nervous, much as she had felt on her first date with a boy back in high school.

"How have you been, Red?" Gig said as they drove down the street.

"Fine," Joan said. She disliked Gig's name for her but she knew Gig was teasing her with it. In the sun, despite her masculine appearance, Gig now looked quite attractive; Joan tried to suppress a feeling of desire. It had been a week since Kim and Joan's body, not used to any form of celibacy, was beginning to take notice. She was afraid that the beach would make things worse—the sun always made her passionate. Again she tried to think of Kim and tried to put the memory of the night with Gig into its proper place, to be filed under: my colorful past.

But the thought of Gig would not stay in that category so easily. Gig's face was beautiful and her broad smile, displaying two rows of perfect white teeth, let a look of wholesomeness that Joan had missed seeing in her last week. Last week Gig had been all in shadow, part of a large, frightening environment called the Yellow Page. Now, in the sun, with the grass and trees of the parkway pleasantly on either side of them and the blue-green ripples of the bay beyond them, Gig was a human being and an attractive woman. Despite the haircut, despite the clothes, Joan could think of her only as a woman, remembering the sweet softness of her flesh and the gentle lines of her woman's body in the half-light.

Joan suddenly wanted to know more about her—where she was born, how she spent the last few years, her plans for the future. For the moment she forgot Kim, seriously considering Gig.

"You're awfully quiet, Red," Gig laughed teasingly. "What's on your mind?"

"Oh, lots of things," Joan replied cryptically. She didn't want to reveal her thoughts. "What are you thinking?" she countered, deciding to take the offensive.

Gig glanced her way for a minute then quickly returned her eyes to the road. "I'm thinking those shorts look very femme on you," she said and smiled.

Joan laughed. "I've given up trying to please you. It's ridiculous for me to think of myself in any one category." She was being impish now, deliberately teasing. She wanted Gig to know how feminine she felt.

Gig grew serious for a minute, apparently about to get something off her chest. "Joan, I guess I behaved pretty strangely last week," she said. "You see, I thought you were just another broad, strictly out for kicks."

"I was," Joan said. She was not about to deny that she ad been a broad for the last six months—that she had led a very strange life. In a way she was sorry—it had been only unpleasant, except for last week. But in a way she was not in the least bit sorry, because now she knew for certain that no man was her type and that practically any woman was. Understanding that, she wanted to slow down, wanted to be pure and innocent again, wanted to belong to someone she could love—to one woman. But now she was still shopping: there was Gig and there was

Kim, and there might be someone else next week or the week after. Her body, used to freedom, could not easily draw the line at where an evening's date should end.

"I mean, I didn't know I was your first," Gig corrected herself. "I should have gone slower."

"You did very well," Joan answered. "It wasn't what happened that disappointed me," she went on, "it was what didn't happen." She looked hard at Gig and spoke firmly. "It's the thought of the Yellow Page I can't stand, and the way you draw the line over what's masculine and feminine. Those standards strike me as a little sick. I don't understand what the difference is between 'broads' and 'virgins' and why they shouldn't both be treated as women—as something sacred. And most of all I can't see how one can be a Lesbian and still be attracted to a woman who thinks she's a man." She paused for a moment, letting her feelings cool down, then added, "I'm sorry, Gig. I just had to get that off my chest."

"That was a pretty loaded chest," Gig winced carefully.

Joan looked at the pure blue sky. Being able to talk so bluntly to Gig had made her less afraid of her desires. She was able to breathe the air and feel the sun without thinking of Gig. She was able to plan the day in her mind and to plan, just for today perhaps, on being a saint. She kept the memory of Kim's face firmly in her mind, Kim's serious, sad face; it was beautiful.

6.

THEY reached the beach and, bundles in hand, walked to the far end where all the gay kids were. They stopped several times to say hello to couples they knew. Joan waited patiently through each conversation, marveling at all the faces she already recognized. At the far side of the bay she thought she saw Jay and Marc. But she didn't walk over—in fact, she hoped to avoid them entirely.

Gig found a clean spot on the sand and opened the first blanket, and Barbie and Madge followed suit. Joan put down her basket and helped them. The air was so pure here, and the water reflected the sky. It was difficult to think of the dirty city being so near. Once settled, each girl removed her outer clothes and emerged in her bathing suit.

Gig whistled. "Hey, look at Sheena!"

Joan blushed. In defense, she decided to whistle at Gig's suit. It was a black Olympic model, very professional, and exposing to their best advantage her strong back and long legs. Gig also blushed. Barbie and Madge wore conventional suits, old fashioned and—Madge's especially—in bad taste.

The four of them sat down and Barbie began applying suntan lotion to Madge's back. Joan took out her own bottle and offered it to Gig. Gig took it and embarrassedly rubbed it on Joan's shoulders. She was uneasy about touching a girl in public. Joan smiled when she realized this, and took the bottle to put the lotion on her own arms and legs.

"Are we going in the water before we eat?" Barbie asked, not knowing whether to spread out the tablecloth.

"Let's get our feet wet first," Gig said, getting up. She extended her hand to Joan and pulled her up.

"We'll watch the stuff till you get back then go in ourselves," Madge said.

Gig saluted and took Joan by the hand. They walked to the edge of the beach where the waves came roughly up at them. But the water was warm and they went in until the waves splashed up to their middles. Gig put an arm around Joan's waist, holding her back from the pull of the water.

"You know, I can't get over you," Gig said above the roar of the waves. "No one's slapped me down like that in years."

"What's your life been like, Gig?" Joan asked.

"A mess," Gig said flatly. They met a large wave and held their ground.

"In what way?" Joan persisted. She felt almost clinical in her interest, but she also wanted to know because Gig's life might give her some clue about what she herself might expect in her own future, might give some indication of what being gay really meant.

"I've spent my life trying to get my Dad to accept me," Gig said. She sounded bitter. "You know how it is with Italian Catholics. A daughter's supposed to get married and have children and all that, or else stay home with her Mom."

"Do you have any brothers?"

"Just one, eight years younger." She gave a short laugh. "He's queer, too. Funny, isn't it?"

"Sounds genetic," Joan said.

"Naw," Gig scoffed, almost as if she were afraid to admit it. "Everyone knows it's psychological."

"I wonder," Joan said. She dropped the subject. To Gig's sense of values, homosexuals were all as degenerate as society said they were. To make it genetic on top of that would be like saying they were all freaks.

"When did you turn gay?" Joan said instead.

"At fifteen I started to wear pants," Gig said, "but I didn't turn gay till much later. I didn't really know what life was all about until one of the boys I was dating took me to the Daisy."

"Have you ever slept with a man?" Joan dared.

"Go on, are you kidding?" Gig reacted with a sudden burst of embarrassment. "What the hell do you think I am, anyway?"

"I just wondered," Joan said carefully. She turned and walked up the beach a bit, looking at the sand giving way under her feet. Her day had become suddenly bleak—Gig was as sick as Joan had judged her to be. Joan couldn't bear seeing it. She wished she could help Gig in some way, bring her out all the way into the sun, out of the dark shadows of the Yellow Page. It wasn't being gay that made Gig's world bleak. It was the part of her that wasn't gay, the illegality of her world, the heavy finger of society pressing her down to a floor splattered with beer and cigarette butts; the labels, "degenerate" and "pervert" and "sex criminal" making her always looking over her shoulder, feeling the oppressive weight of ignorant, even malicious, judgment.

It wasn't being gay—it was the life in the bars. The bars attracted the young kids who needed to come out because there wasn't any other place for those kinds to go—no coffee shops like the beatniks had, no soda fountains like those for the rock-

and-rollers. Homosexuality was illegal, and so only criminals, only syndicates would touch it, would provide the necessary meeting places.

"Hello, you old degenerate," Joan heard a man's happy voice behind her. She turned and saw Jay. "Marc sent me to get you."

Joan smiled. "I'm with friends." She turned and looked toward Gig, who had stood quietly watching her all the time, afraid to start another conversation because they all seemed to end badly. "Gig," Joan said, "let's walk over and say hello to Marc."

"Sure," Gig smiled and came over to Joan with new enthusiasm.

They walked together up the beach toward where Marc and Jay had their blankets, and again as they passed people lying on the sand they waved to the or two who knew them. Seeing so many of her species on the beach made Joan feel better. She studied Gig's face, now reddened by the sun, and saw life and health in it, saw the hue of the Yellow Page vanishing from her cheeks.

Marc waved to them as they approached. "Hello, dear." He was being mockingly domestic.

"Hello, darling," Joan echoed. It was difficult to keep from camping it up out here. She couldn't see a straight person for yards. "You remember Gig, don't you?"

"I should." Marc smiled cattily and nodded to Gig. Gig nodded back silently. But there wasn't much hostility between them this morning—it was too beautiful a day."

"Sit down and have some Gin-toe," Marc said, waving a thermos.

"Thanks, just soda or something for me," Joan said, sitting. Gig sat on the blanket too and echoed Joan. Jay reached into the picnic basket and came out with two cokes.

"They're a little warm," he apologized.

The two girls accepted them and then looked toward the waves as they drank.

"What are you two doing out here?" Joan said.

"We might ask the same of you," Marc smiled. "We come

here every weekend."

"It's a lovely beach," Joan commented. There was a long silence. The sun seemed to snatch thought away from their minds so that no one wished to talk. Finally Marc spoke.

"I called Mother long distance yesterday," he said carefully. "I told her we got married."

Joan started. "Why did you do that? I thought we had decided on Reno."

"Impulse, I guess," he shrugged. "I was hoping you had changed your mind."

"No, I haven't changed my mind," Joan said quietly. She understood that Marc had an intense fear of his mother discovering his homosexuality—that was the strongest reason for his having gotten married. "I guess you can tell her later that we're getting divorced," she said.

"Yes, I thought I could do that," Marc answered. "It'll probably make her glad that she's gotten her son back. She took the news badly yesterday."

"Then there's no harm done," Joan said.

"No, no harm done," he repeated. "As a matter of fact, Dad spoke to me on the telephone for the first time in years." He stopped for a moment. "They've invited us to spend a week up there in Vermont. Dad's sending the train fare by wire. I'd like to go, Joan, if you're game."

Joan cursed him mentally. She didn't want to spend a week out of town with Marc. And yet she knew that this had been a part of their bargain long ago—to meet each other's parents and to play this game for their sake.

"It should be fun," she said unenthusiastically out loud. "But I can't go until after next weekend. I'm expecting a guest from out of town."

"Good." We can hop a train Monday morning," Marc said. It was settled, and he sighed with relief.

Joan got up and Gig rose after her. "We'll have to be getting back to our own crowd," she said. "Come over later and say hello."

"Fine," Jay said, waving to them. And Marc nodded.

Gig had been silent all this time, as if she had little to say in the company of men. But she remained silent as she walked back with Joan.

"Barbie and Madge must be cursing us for taking so long," Joan said to break the silence.

"No, they're just out her for a tan," Gig replied. She was lost in her own thoughts, fighting the sun that beat on her head.

They reached Barbie and Madge and sat on the blanket next to them. "Red had some friends up the beach," Gig explained.

"We're going in the water for a few minutes," Madge said, getting up. Barbie got up after her. "Only up to the knees."

"Have fun," Gig waved. Then she lay down, her muscular body like a statue on the blanket. "Man, I want a dark tan."

Joan laughed, unable to help admiring Gig's body. She lay down beside her and let Gig take her hand, feeling excitement course through her. Now she wanted Gig. Gig's body had been the first to claim her and the memory of that night was in a way more wonderful than her memory of Kim—because it had been the first time, the first wonderful experience of knowing a woman. Yet Joan was afraid. She didn't want to be attracted to Gig. They had so little in common, and Gig was butch. Joan didn't want to be a part of the Daisy set; she wasn't going to let being gay interfere with her life in the world.

"Shall we get out the sandwiches?" Madge said, coming back with Barbie. They were both wet to their thigh. The surf was too rough and cold for swimming.

"Sure," Gig said, letting go of Joan's hand and sitting up. Joan sat up too and brought her picnic basket over so that she could reach inside.

"We brought beer," Barbie said, reaching in their cooler.

The sandwiches and beverages were passed around and they ate hungrily. When they lay down again, the sun began to torture Joan, making her restless and aware of Gig. Then Barbie put her head on Madge's stomach, and Gig dared to do the same with Joan.

"Having a good time, Red?" Gig smiled, turning her head so

that she could look at Joan.

"Yes," Joan lied. The overly dull conversation had only intensified her desire for Gig—there was nothing else to think about. Barbie and Madge and even Gig seemed mentally starved, knew nothing of interest except the everyday gossip of the Daisy set and the latest fashions that looked good on Madge.

"How about another walk?" Gig said.

Joan nodded. Anything to get away from the boredom of the beach. They got up and walked toward the refreshment concession where they could sit at a table under an umbrella.

"It's been a deadly four hours," Gig said when they sat.

All at once the conversation had been saved. Joan perked up. "The worst time I've had in years," she agreed, putting her arm on the iron table and leaning toward Gig.

"I hope it isn't me," Gig smiled.

"I hope not," Joan said.

"It's been such a long time since I last had to keep up a bright conversation," Gig apologized. She was looking down, for a moment feeling awkward. "Do you know what I mean? A real deadly rut."

Joan nodded. She understood that Gig was trying to describe the monotony of the Yellow Page and the Daisy—like quicksand in the way it sucked you into its pattern: the pattern of the coarse and ignorant, those who never made the grade except for the amount of beer they could drink and the money they could earn from day to day waiting on tables or hustling.

"Why don't you go to college?" Joan impulsively suggested. "It's the best way I know of getting out of any rut."

"I'd love to," Gig sighed. "But first I've got to get a high school diploma. I quit when I was sixteen."

"Yes, I suppose it's hard," Joan said. "But why don't you start anyway? Take an equivalency test. If you pass, they might let you take the extra courses you need right in college instead of in night school."

"Yeah? I didn't know you could do that," Gig said. She made a note of it in her mind and the two were silent for a moment. Joan wanted badly to help Gig, as if by pulling Gig out of her rut she might prove that there was hope for all the others.

Gig took her hand. "You know, I think I need you around to tell me things like that."

"Don't rely on me for everything," Joan smiled. She took her hand away self-consciously, wanting to reject Gig and yet not wanting to—being afraid because Gig was attractive in her bathing suit out in the sun where her skin had the coloring of health.

"Hello, Gigi!"

Joan turned toward the voice behind her. It came from a woman in a bathing suit, fortyish but attractive, who was walking toward them and waving.

"Hi, Di." Gig waved back and stood. "Come, join us."

Di pulled up a chair on the other side of Gig and straddled it—but she didn't look butch even though she was trying to seem clumsy. "How have you been?"

"I want you to meet Joan," Gig said, "Joan, this is Di."

Joan said hello and then studied Di. Her manner was housewifeishly aggressive. Joan had seen her around before—that night at the Sun Dial, and also before at the Yellow Page and the Daisy. Di was one of the regulars.

"Oh, are you two going together?" Di asked in good-natured nosiness. She seemed to be interested in Gig herself.

"Not yet," Gig said, grasping Joan's hand. "I'm still giving her a sales talk." That made Joan blush angrily. She didn't want to be thought one of Gig's conquests.

"You couldn't find a better salesman," Di said to Joan almost cattily. "When did you two meet?"

"Two weeks ago," Gig said. "Joan's going to N.Y.U."

"How nice," Di said. "That's my husband's alma mater."

"Your husband's?" Joan was puzzled for a moment.

"Di's an old married woman," Gig said. "She just had a baby last year."

"Yes," Di smiled self-consciously, as if having a baby was not what she had wanted. "Well, maybe we'll run into you two kids later on." She got up again.

Joan and Gig waved goodbye.

"Is she straight?" Joan asked out of curiosity.

"She's bi," Gig said, following Di with her eyes as she went down the boardwalk. "The baby was accidental. She's taking it beautifully, though—never saw a prouder mother."

They got up from the table and walked back toward Barbie and Madge. "I used to have a terrific crush on her," Gig laughed a little, reflectively. "I couldn't stand her husband, though. I got too possessive about her, I guess."

"I'm sorry," Joan said. For a moment she had glimpsed Gig's past. And then more of Gig's past greeted them—two butches on their way to get ice cream. One had a girl's name tattooed on her arm.

"Hi, Gig," the taller one said. "Why don't you come over later and have a beer?"

"Thanks, we're not staying much longer," Gig said. Joan saw she was embarrassed at knowing them; she didn't introduce Joan.

"I guess everyone comes to this beach," Joan said when they walked on. That was true. The faces here were the same as the ones in the bars. She might see them all again tonight if she made the rounds.

"That was part of the rough set," Gig said to explain the two. "I think they push dope—but I've never dared find out."

"Does dope go with gay bars too?" Joan asked.

"Not in all of them," Gig said. "Some rough places pose as gay spots but are really full of junkies or prostitutes. They keep the rough gay kinds around to throw the cops off their trail. They'd rather pay off for a gay bar than pay off for dope or for running a house—which is what the bar's really doing. A few of the butches push dope for a living, some even pimp."

"In other words, that's the sick set," Joan summed it up.

"Yeah." Gig was upset by her own words. "They're the ones who make it rough on the rest of us. Straight people can't seem to tell one butch from another." She stopped and looked at Joan for a moment. "You know, what riles me is that those kids weren't really gay to start with. Lots got that way serving time in reform school and now they're butches simply because they're tall and tough."

"But I don't understand," Joan said. "I've seen the wreckage of some of those beer bottle fights they're supposed to have over a femme. Why would they want to hold on to a girl that way if they're not gay?"

Gig shrugged. "The subject's getting too involved—there are too many reasons to explain it. Partly, I guess, they really like their girls, and partly it's bread and butter to them, if they're pimping for her. You know what I mean?"

They walked on and Joan thought about it, forcing herself to reflect on it despite the unpleasantness of the facts. It was enraging to think that prostitution and dope should hide under the label of gay.

They continued walking. A flock of clouds covered the sun and took the color from the beach, making the water gray and the bodies on the sand dull specks of dark and light. It was a trifle cold in the breeze.

"Darn," Gig said, "I had wanted to get wet again."

"It'll clear up in a while," Joan said. "Let's anyway."

They stopped at their blanket and Joan picked up her bathing cap.

"Meet a lot of the kids?" Barbie asked.

"Not too many," Gig said. "We're going back in the water now."

"It's awfully cold," Madge said. They were still lying together on the blanket, Barbie's head on Madge's stomach. Madge's small feminine body had begun to burn.

"We'll probably be back in a minute," Gig said. She and Joan went to the edge of the water together. The incoming tide was causing rough surf and there were few shells on the beach. Gig locked hands with Joan and they both went toward the waves. The first wave hit them like ice, but then it was warmer and they walked further, so that the waves came up to their knees. The rushing water tried to unbalance them, but Gig's strong grasp on Joan's hand was stronger than the tide. Then Gig pulled Joan closer and held on to her waist. The touch of Gig's hand on her bathing suit made Joan warm.

"Don't be afraid of it," Gig said, half meaning the tide.

"I'm not, really," Joan said meaningfully.

A large wave surprised them now, coming up to their thighs. They both jumped from the cold, and then laughed.

"How about spending the evening with me?" Gig said, grasping Joan's waist with both hands.

"I don't like the Yellow Page," Joan answered.

"It's a job like anywhere else," Gig said. "How about later, then? I might beg off early tonight—say, midnight?"

Another large wave came; its force threw Joan against Gig and made her tremble from the contact. "Don't say I'm not your type," Gig said, searching her face.

"Let's go back," Joan said, turning toward the beach. She forced Gig to let go of her waist and, walking ahead of her, went back to their blanket. But running away from Gig had solved nothing. She knew she didn't want to be faithful to Kim anymore; she knew she wanted Gig.

"Had enough?" Barbie laughed when she saw them returning so soon.

"Not quite," Gig answered. She looked up at the sky. It was still cloudy. "I think it's going to rain, after all," she said.

"We're ready to leave when you are," Madge said, putting more oil on her red shoulders.

"In that case, let's pack up," Gig said. "It's almost time to go anyway."

She helped Barbie put things back into the cooler bags and Joan dried her legs and put on her shorts over her wet bathing suit. She didn't want to stop at the locker room to change. She wanted to get away from the beach, away from temptation. Then she heard a familiar velvet voice behind her. "Hello, Joan."

She turned and saw David. He looked so different here, in a bathing suit with a fellow behind him—looked so much like Marc and like Jay.

"Dave!" Joan exclaimed. "I guess everyone really does come here."

For a moment she felt weak, but then the feeling vanished. She wasn't weak about David any longer, though warmth was still there; she hadn't yet stopped loving him. "I'd like you to meet Gig," she said, "and Barbie and Madge." She felt a certain victory at being found here, a certain recovery of pride in front of David.

David smiled at the others and then looked back at Joan. "How have you been?" he asked.

"Just fine," Joan said. "Why don't you give me a call one of these days? It'll be nice to see you again. So much has happened these past few months."

"Yes, I can imagine," he said with a little embarrassment. "Perhaps I will," he added, "in a month or so. Well, 'bye now." He turned awkwardly and went on with his friend.

Joan was shaken and Gig saw it. "An old ghost?" she asked.

"Something like that," Joan said. She continued packing but her thoughts were quick and scattered. David's appearance had jarred her—had made her realize that there was no one yet to take his place, neither Kim nor Gig. Life for Joan was still a merry-g-round of trying to forget him. If that were so, there was no point in avoiding Gig; she wasn't able to love or belong to anyone. She might as well have fun, she decided. Her shock had shaken the flicker of loyalty she felt toward Kim.

"Suppose I drive you kids to a movie," Gig was saying to Barbie and Madge. "Then I can take Joanie somewhere else." They agreed.

Joan let herself be led back to the car and sat like a robot next to Gig. She wasn't going to fight anything anymore, she was just going to let things happen as they might.

Gig sensed her preoccupation and took her hand. "You're beautiful when you're thinking," she said. Joan smiled and said thank you. But the world was far away.

Gig dropped Barbie and Madge at a movie on Eighth Street and then drove on with Joan. "Where do you want to go?" Gig asked.

"I want some coffee or something," Joan said.

They parked in front of one of the Bohemian coffee shops that featured a poetry reading that day. "I've always wanted to see one of these," Gig said. She seemed to be trying to please Joan's taste rather than her own.

They entered the dark café and ordered iced espresso.

The crowd was young and strangely dressed. The young men weren't gay although they seemed gay to the untrained eye—wearing sandals and jewelry and strange haircuts. The girls were all in jeans or leotards. This was Beat Generation style, and all the teenagers who hung around N.Y.U. were imitating it, making it more and more extreme as they added their own fancies to it.

"So that's what the new movement looks like," Gig said. She held Joan's hand across the table, feeling quite insecure in the surroundings. "Do you really understand their poetry?"

"Sometimes," Joan said. "And sometimes it's not worth understanding. There are a lot of people just riding along, pretending to be poets."

"That's true in any crowd," Gig said. "About people who ride along, I mean."

"I guess so," Joan said. She didn't really feel like talking. She wanted to go home and be alone for a while. Her life was going too fast and she didn't feel as if any of it was real anymore. She wanted to be alone and discover once again what was real.

"Why don't you spend all of tomorrow with me?" Gig was saying, still holding her hand. "You could show me the Metropolitan Museum or something."

"You're sweet," Joan said, squeezing her hand. "I don't really feel that intellectual, though. Perhaps another time."

"Joan, why can't I reach you?" Gig asked. Her eyes were very serious as they searched Joan's face.

"It's my own fault," Joan said. She took a deep breath. "I'm sorry. I'm only half here. Did you say something about midnight tonight and all day tomorrow? Why not? Come over and pick me up when you're through work."

Gig's expression brightened, but only for a moment. "You're being very strange," she said. "I'm almost afraid to be falling for you."

"No, don't fall for me, please," Joan said in an anxious rush.

"Don't, or we'll have to end it right now. I don't want love. I'm not ready for it yet."

"Then it's just sex you want," Gig said. She bit her lip. "That's too bad," she sighed. "That really is too bad." And Gig lapsed into silent thought and the two exchanged few words until it was time to go. Then Gig accompanied Joan to her door and left her on the steps.

Gig didn't come up at midnight. Joan waited up for her, but knew she wouldn't come; that was for the best; Joan did not want to hurt her and Gig could have been hurt—she had been leading with her chin all day. Something just wasn't right between them—somehow Joan knew that, knew that some important spark of interest was lacking. There was only sex, nothing more. But Joan also knew something else now: it wasn't right between her and Kim, either. There was no love between them.

Would it ever be possible to love a woman? Joan feared that it might be impossible—that too much was in the way of such a thing happening. The biggest barrier was fear, a fear to begin loving. For love was a deep involvement which could easily destroy both partners if the balance wasn't right—the balance between the world and the lovers, and the balance between the lovers themselves. Joan thought that perhaps this was the reason many gay couples broke up after a year or two—because they were afraid to love each other completely, afraid because of the uncertainty that surrounded gay life and gay relationships, the lack of social and family recognition, the lack of legal standing. It took guts to love under those circumstances, and guts to keep on loving for years afterwards.

Joan felt the slow terror coming on—the terror of seeing herself alone, changing partners as often as changing clothes, perhaps going on drinking binges like the middle-aged women in the 'Dial who became a little too loud or cried at the bar. She wondered if this was all there was to look forward to. Yet a brave spark of hope in back of her mind made her silently repeat the names of people she knew—people in public life, people of the past, and the names of couples at the bars who seemed to break that rule, seemed able to stay together. "Remember how many heterosexuals have divorces," another voice repeated. Perhaps there was hope—if there was courage.

7.

JOAN'S finals were on Thursday and Friday. She took them, felt she had passed with a high grade, and breathed easier. School was over for the summer and Kim was expected Friday night. A great sense of freedom possessed Joan and she forgot everything except the weekend.

Kim arrived at eight, put her suitcase down, and Joan kissed her. It was a long kiss, building for two weeks; Kim's mouth was delicious.

"Baby, what a long haul," Kim said. She broke away from Joan and lit a cigarette. "I thought they'd never give me the pass."

"Trouble again with the Army?" Joan asked. She sat on the bed and watched Kim's restless tapping on the rug as she smoked her cigarette.

Kim nodded. "Yes, it's starting again. I can see it coming." She sighed. "Let's forget about it for the rest of the weekend." She put down her cigarette, walked up to Joan and fondly held her hand. "And how has it been with you?"

"Hectic," Joan said. She took Kim's hand and kissed it lightly on both sides. "How much time do we have?"

"Until late Sunday night," Kim said.

Joan watched Kim's restless figure, measuring with her eyes the pleasing slimness of Kim's waist and appreciating her restless feet with their small and perfect ankles. Then she looked up at Kim's face. Remembering Kim's features had been hard these two weeks—they had been a vague blob in Joan's mind—but now they were clear and beautiful, her eyes sad and blue.

"Let's go out to dinner." Joan abruptly stood up.

"Where do we go?" Kim echoed her sudden enthusiasm.

"I've heard of a jazz club that serves shish-kebab on skewers,"

Joan said. "Their floor show's supposed to be tops."

"That's the place for us," Kim said.

They kissed again because they couldn't bear to leave the apartment just yet, and this time the kiss was more intense; Kim's hands electrified Joan's body so much that she had to break away—or postpone dinner.

When they reached the Club Vantage, across the Village from Joan's apartment, the entertainment had not yet started. It was the perfect time to order dinner. They had found a corner table for two lit by a candle where the stage could easily be seen. It was a dark, cave-like place, made to resemble a nigh club on the Paris Left Bank. Kim ordered bourbon before dinner and Joan had a vermouth.

"That's a potent drink if I ever saw one," Kim chided Joan.

"I'm already drunk," Joan laughed. She watched Kim expertly mix her drink and wondered if there were some storm raging inside her. It was the same storm that had raged beneath the surface that night in the hotel room.

"Let's eat soon," Joan said. She touched Kim's hand across the table and Kim's hand responded by grasping hers.

There was another long moment of silence as Joan studied Kim. Kim's helplessness and sadness were something new for Joan. She had never met anyone so silently stoic. She felt needed, simply because Kim had said nothing about needing her.

Joan hailed the waiter, taking the lead, and ordered dinner for them. Then she watched Kim finish her bourbon.

"I like this place." Kim finally spoke.

"I'm glad," Joan said. They moved their chairs closer together so that they could both see the stage. The floor show was beginning, the orchestra setting up their instruments. Then their shish kebab arrived on skewers. Kim ate slowly and without appetite.

"You'll be raiding the ice box later," Joan warned.

"No, I won't," Kim answered. She left the rice and potatoes, then ordered another bourbon.

"What's the matter, darling?" Joan said, holding Kim's hand

under the table.

"Let's not talk about it," Kim said.

A tall Negro singer was introduced—a beautiful, angular woman with a voice of baritone range.

The show, exciting beat and the rhythmic movements of the woman's body made Joan forget Kim for a moment, making her part of the atmosphere of the cave-like club that was so much like the Paris she wanted to visit someday. She wondered if she would go there with Kim.

Then the insecurity of the evening gripped her again—Kim's silence and her drinking. Joan felt shut out—even Gig had been better company. Gig had strained to make good conversation and Kim wasn't even trying.

Joan lost herself in the beauty of the singer, in the statuesque regality of her angular form and the voice that vibrated through it. Joan was spending this evening alone.

Hand in hand, they walked back through the park. It was past one A.M. and the music was still in their ears.

"Isn't it a lovely night?" Joan risked a cliché.

"Yes, lovely," Kim said. She stopped by the fountain and traced the lines of the stone with her foot, then emitted a long sigh. "I guess I'm not much company."

"Just your saying that makes it better," Joan said, taking heart. "What's wrong?"

"Everything. All of life," Kim said. It was as good as no reply.

"Let's go home," Joan said.

Kim kissed Joan when they had barely entered the apartment, a serious kiss that left no doubt about the rest of the evening. Joan responded hungrily, clinging to Kim's body, letting this make up for the lack of mental contact she had felt all evening. There was no restraint between them now, no need for conversation.

That was the beauty of Kim—she could be pleased so easily, could express ecstasy at a touch: Joan's lips on her palm, Joan's hand at her breast. They seemed never to grow tired; when sleep came it caught them almost by surprise.

Joan opened her eyes again in the middle of the night and found Kim smoking a cigarette in the half-light.

"What is it, Hun'?" Joan folded around her lap, resting her head on Kim for a pillow.

"It won't work," Kim sighed, "it just won't work." She began to talk. "I've been feeling guilty over you for two weeks." She stroked Joan's forehead and blew a stray hair away. "Every time someone came up behind me, I thought for sure now they were going to call me in, that they knew all about us. Do you know the feeling? Hunted. I had my cab circle around three times before I stopped in front of your door."

"Oh, poor baby!" Joan embraced Kim's waist and pressed her head against Kim's belly, trying in some way to reassure her. But she could give no reassurance. The possibility remained: Kim might be under surveillance.

"I broke down and confessed to the chaplain about you," Kim continued. "He understood and all that, but you see, in my religion it's wrong. I should be home having babies." She broke away from Joan, stood up and paced the floor. "No matter which way I turn the whole world's against me. I just don't know how to fight the world."

Joan sat, watching her, wondering what she might say. She was bursting with reassuring words —about the stupidity of religious beliefs which grew not from some god but rather from men of the past who sought to impose their own repressions and ambitions on others through the guise of religion. Joan had studied the past, had traced the growth of nationalism of the Jews that led them to condemn the homosexual civilization around them, had traced the path of Christianity and its attempt to break away from Roman rule by assailing Roman morality. Joan had studied the rise of Protestantism too, and its struggle for power under the label of reform. Sex had been included in the moral revision of the times, and degeneracy came to mean not only the act of lying or stealing or taking a life but also sexual deviation and excess. At some time in history, Nature had become a dirty word, and all natural impulses, things to be repressed. And now the world was sick, its citizens slowly killing themselves through other vices to forget the ones they dared not practice.

"I'm here to help you fight the world," Joan said at last. It was all she could think of to say.

"But you're not—" Kim turned. "You don't really love me and I haven't had time to start to love you."

It was said and it was true. They could never become close to each other on one weekend every so often. And if they did see more of each other, would that help? They had really so little in common—except sex.

"You're still in love with Bea," Joan said. "And it's true—I really haven't seen fireworks yet about you. But does that ever really happen?"

"Yes, it really happens," Kim sighed. She crushed her cigarette out, went back to the bed and took Joan in her arms. "Let's get some sleep," she said.

Joan closed her eyes, fitting snugly in the hollow of Kim's shoulder, and felt at least one consolation: the warm body beside her was soft and deliciously familiar; this at least was right—it was a woman's body.

After breakfast in the morning they played tennis and then ate a big lunch. For a while they forgot. Kim spoke of her family and how she hoped to return to Indiana after college. She wanted to open a business close to home so that she could be company for her aging father. No, it was unlikely that she would have a roommate come with her—two women living together would be too obvious in a small town. But of course she might change her mind, might find she couldn't live without a friend. Or—and this shocked Joan—she might work things out, might get married.

"Don't get married unless you really love him," Joan said.

"Love has many forms," Kim answered.

Joan disagreed. "Marriage means love in all its forms. Otherwise it becomes a starved and awful thing."

"Don't give me all that textbook psychology." Kim rubbed Joan's head fondly.

They went to a movie after dinner and came home early.

Joan's telephone was ringing as they entered. It was Joan's younger sister, calling from White Plains.

"I've been trying to get you for hours," Ginger said.

"I've been out for hours," Joan countered playfully.

"Mom wants you home for Sunday dinner," Ginger said. She was repeating an order.

Joan sighed. She had been able to put off going home with the excuse of having to study. But now school was over.

"I can't." she said. "I have a weekend guest."

"Bring her along," Ginger said.

Joan looked at Kim. Somehow that seemed like a good idea. There would be grass and trees up there. "Do you want to come to dinner at my folks'?" Joan asked her.

"Why not?" Kim shrugged.

"We'll take the twelve-thirty train," Joan told her sister.

She chatted for a while and then hung up and looked wearily at Kim. It had been a strenuous day. In a way she was glad she was going home tomorrow. Being alone with Kim was wearing on her nerves. There was too much left unsaid between them and too few places to go where liquor could be avoided.

They spent that night less tempestuously than the one before. Their bodies had become accustomed to each other and love making seemed almost dull, a mere repetition of old actions. Joan wondered why this was so. Perhaps because love or any feeling of permanence was lacking.

They woke up late and had breakfast at the Positano.

"When's your next pass?" Joan dared to ask.

"Not for a while," Kim looked down. "I'm getting two weeks' leave, which I'll have to spend with my dad. I won't be back in town until mid-August."

Joan nodded. She didn't say anything, didn't ask the precise date. Kim could look her up if she wanted to.

Joan tried to ignore the great sadness she was feeling. Kim didn't consider their relationship serious. To her, family and marriage to a man were more concrete, more important than Lesbian marriage. She could never consider Joan or any other woman equal to a man, equal to a husband or family.

After breakfast they went back to the apartment and changed clothes. They would have to wear skirts to White Plains. Kim put on a hat but Joan laughingly took it off her head; it looked absurd on Kim. They were early and sat in the empty car, waiting for the train to start.

"We don't have to stay in the house," Joan was saying. "Mom and Dad can become quite wearing—they're so desperate about making me a part of the family."

"Why aren't you?" This was strange to Kim, who needed to feel close to her parents.

"I never was." Joan lowered her head. It was difficult to pin down the reason for her separateness from her family. She had always felt like an outsider mainly because she reacted differently to everything than the rest of her family and wanted different things from life. It had always been that way. The world had never seemed completely real to her until she had met David, and even then the world had not been quite on its right side. It had not balanced itself until that night with Gig. After that, everything had suddenly come into its proper and most clear focus.

"When did you learn you were gay?" Kim asked.

"When I was very little," Joan remembered. "I looked at myself in a mirror with one of Father's hats on. It struck a familiar chord. I looked like a woman I had once seen crossing a street. Instinctively I knew what she was, even knew the name—Lesbian. I must have heard the word from some adult, but it stuck in my mind and I knew it. But most of all, I knew that I had fallen in love—with my own image in the mirror. It looked so much like that woman who had crossed the street." Joan paused. She had forgotten that incident until now, had repressed it. She had not remembered it all the while she had been in love with David. She had even forgotten for a time the crushes she had had on teachers in school, had forgotten the days and months of dreadful agony when she longed for something she could not express, the years of loneliness when she felt apart from everyone else in the world. "But I don't think it's narcissism now," Joan added. "It's not seeing my own image that makes me prefer women. It's something much more complicated, as complicated as the reasons why some people are heterosexual instead of homosexual."

Kim laughed. "You certainly take this gay bit seriously," she said. "I wish I could feel as natural about it as you do."

"How did you start?" Joan now asked.

"In the Army," Kim said. "I joined the Army for some unknown reason, liked being with women because I had never been interested in men. But I didn't realize about myself until I had been in a while and met Bea."

"It's funny how we seem to be unconscious of ourselves for so long," Joan said. "I could have been happy all through childhood if I had known just how I was different. Not knowing made me make all sorts of mistakes."

"Would you have people go around corrupting children?" Kim said. She could not understand Joan's statement.

"No, of course not," Joan said. "But there's a difference between corrupting and informing. All these terrible taboos and the guilt and fear they cause are really doing the corrupting. Perhaps if I had been told about homosexuals at an earlier age—and not in a way that was meant to frighten me —I would have understood my attraction for David."

"Who's David?" Kim didn't know about Joan's past and Joan began to fill her in now, trying to whitewash the last few months as much as possible; she was certain that Kim would pass judgment on them, would find her past shocking, even immoral. Joan realized now for the first time that she felt great shame herself about the number of men in her life; she wondered if she could ever forget that she had been little better than a whore in what had been a desperate attempt to deny her real feelings. And what a dreadful waste of time those men had all been—and how fulfilling it had been to spend one night with Gig!

Kim listened with interest, and displayed none of the shock that Joan had expected. On the contrary, Kim seemed glad to hear that Joan had made every possible attempt to try changing.

"And what about you?" Joan paused.

Kim frowned, obviously unwilling to talk about it. "Just once, with one of the guys stationed out on Long Island—after the thing with Bea. I threw up all night."

They arrived in White Plains with regret—they had finally begun to talk to each other and interruption came too soon. They walked from the station to Joan's house and Ginger met them as they came up the street.

"Hi. Mom sent me to the store," she said. She was wearing a frilly dress. Ginger always wore very feminine clothes, even in the heat of summer while trimming the roses in the yard.

"We'll come with you," Joan said. They walked with Ginger two blocks farther to the small grocery store. "This is Kim," Joan introduced her.

"Hi," Ginger blinked. Joan wondered if Ginger could see through them, could instinctively know that Kim was more than a friend. But Ginger wasn't aware of things like that.

"How did you do in school?" Joan asked.

"Fair," Ginger said. "I'll be a senior next year, you know."

"Got your college picked out?"

"I thought I'd come join you at N.Y.U.," Ginger said.

For a moment Joan dreaded what she had been prepared to hear. Ginger's coming to New York would mean that they would have to share an apartment—their parents would expect it. That would make for a difficult situation. For a moment she remembered Marc and was glad that she had married him. Perhaps he would give her an excuse. Better to pretend living with Marc than actually living with Ginger.

They walked back to the house carrying the groceries. Kim had been silent the whole time, but she was not tense about meeting Joan's family. In fact, she was relaxing, taking in the fresh air and the smell of Mom's cooking that crept into the living room.

"Hello, Mom," Joan said, dutifully seeking her out in the kitchen.

Her mother, a taller woman than Joan and very much a beauty

in her day, turned from mixing the salad, her hands covered with oil. "Hello, dear," she said. Her voice had the forced overly emotional tone that Joan was used to hearing.

Joan allowed herself to be kissed on both cheeks and then found a chore to do to keep from talking. She had nothing to say, although she knew that her silence always made her mother more desperately try to communicate with her. "How did you do in school?" she asked Joan as she continued to prepare dinner.

"Just fine," Joan said vaguely. She knew the questioning that would follow. Her parents had expected her to return home as soon as school was out and spend the summer in White Plains. But Joan had told them a month ago that she planned to go to summer school in the city.

"Does summer school start right away?" her mother continued. "Won't you have any vacation?"

"It starts in two weeks," Joan said. "But a bunch of the kids are going camping before it starts," she lied. She had to cover her visit with Marc's parents some way. "I thought I'd go with them."

"Oh," she heard her mother's disappointed voice. "Well, I suppose it's all right. Will you take Ginger?"

"Can't," Joan felt herself forced to make the lie even larger. "It's strictly within the sorority." Her mother had never gone to college, and it was easy to tell her anything about sororities and make her believe it.

"That's too bad. That's really too bad," her mother said.

When Joan came out to set the table she found Kim being entertained by Ginger, who was showing her old pictures of Joan and herself.

"Soup's almost on," Joan interrupted them.

They prepared to go to the table. Only Joan's dad was missing. He came in the nick of time, as always, leaving his car parked in the driveway. He was a real estate agent, and seemed always tired from talking and driving.

"Hi, Dad," Joan said with the same reserve she always showed her parents.

"Hello, Joan," he sighed wearily, then hurried to change his shirt and wash his hands.

At dinner, Kim had less difficulty being comfortable with Joan's family than Joan. She was able to talk and joke freely. Joan envied her ability to be at ease and to fit in so easily. For Joan, a great stone wall was constantly present, made up mostly of guilt because she had always felt herself different from the rest of her family. The wall had protected her, hidden her from the others and had confused them about her true nature. The wall had been necessary—lest they try to change her, try to impose their will upon her. Still, she was sorry for them because its being there made them unhappy. Yet the lack of a wall would have been worse—would have left her totally unprotected before them. She was sure they would never accept a daughter who was "queer," was sure that they would try to change her, and would stop at nothing to accomplish that change.

Dinner was spent in good humor despite Joan's tension; nothing of importance was said or asked, not even about her plans to come home for a week before fall. After dinner, Ginger suggested a movie and Kim and Joan went with her. Joan fought her restlessness to do something else, to go off alone with Kim somewhere where they could be free to talk. She consoled herself by heightening her awareness of Kim sitting next to her, of Kim's leg touching hers in the dark of the movie.

They took an early train back and Kim didn't plan to leave until the middle of the night. They still had a few hours more.

"I'll write you from Indiana," Kim said spontaneously. "The mail won't be censored there. Perhaps I can come back two days early and we can have that weekend."

Joan squeezed Kim's hand impulsively. It was so wonderful to be wanted and liked. Her good humor stayed with her all the way home; the two women joked and played like children.

8.

JOAN tossed in her bed, turning away from the hot sun shining in her face and for a moment forgot it was Monday. Kim's silken imprint was still on her skin and on the sheets and pillow beside her, and the air was filled with Kim—the smell of her clothes and the odor of her cologne. Then Joan awoke and remembered that it was Monday and wanted to roll over in bed again. An awful emptiness was all around her and this was a dreadful day. Kim was gone—and Monday was the day Marc was going to take her to Vermont.

She looked at her clock. It was late—Marc would be coming for her any minute. She got up quickly to go and splash herself with cold water, trying to ignore the headache, the hangover of missing Kim. Over the bathroom sink she found a note, written in Kim's careful handwriting.

"Joanie, forget what I said and let's play it cool," it read. "I'll look you up when we're both a little saner. Kim."

Joan had expected something like this but still Kim's words cut like a knife. She crumpled the note in her palm and flushed it down the toilet. A moment later, Marc rang the bell.

Marc was wide awake and in a sport shirt, happily carrying his suitcase with the air of a vacation-goer. "There's an eleven-thirty train," he said cheerily.

"I'll be ready soon," Joan said, refusing to hurry. She put on her most feminine summer print and white high-heeled sandals, trying to look as much as possible like a happy young bride. She had packed two suitcases and an overnight bag the day before and came out carrying them. "Train or no train, I've got to have coffee," she said grouchily.

"We'll grab some in the dining car," Marc said, taking the heaviest valise away from her. "Come on, dear." He said the last only partly in jest—he was playing the role of husband now.

"No kibitzing," Joan smiled, for a moment slipping into the role herself. After all, she would have to pretend for the entire week.

She locked her door and they rushed down the stairs and hailed a taxi. They didn't bother putting the suitcases in the trunk; Marc put them on the side of their seats and sat close to her. Joan tried to accustom herself to Marc's proximity. She knew he would be sitting close to her all week, putting his arm on her shoulder, perhaps kissing her cheek, or pretending to whisper something sweet in her ear. Marc could behave beautifully in public.

Marc sensed her discomfort and began to chat nervously, telling her about the estate, its hundred acres on the side of a mountain with a wide brook running through it—the swimming pool that had been dug at the widest part, and the trout fishing they might do in the river close by. The vision of greenery helped Joan a little and she smiled, trying to think of this visit as a much-needed vacation.

They reached the station with time to spare. Once aboard the waiting train, they made their way to the dining car. If they were lucky they could stretch breakfast into lunch and remain in the comfortable dining car for the whole trip.

"I expect you won't get along with Mother," Marc continued, describing his family. "But you needn't worry about her. She'll do her best to be nice on the surface. Dad's the one to worry about. He'll pass judgment on you in the first ten minutes—after that, you'll be fairly safe."

"Do they know about you at all?" The waiter had brought them coffee because they had asked for some right away and Joan started drinking nervously and trying to concentrate on Marc's briefing. She didn't want anything to go wrong for him.

"Nothing for certain," he looked down. "Rumors have gotten to them, and then there was my sudden discharge from the Navy. And Dad's always called me a sissy since I can remember."

"I'm sorry," Joan said. She studied Marc. Her question had upset him. He didn't want to remember the Navy business.

"Let's enjoy our breakfast," he said, suddenly ending the uncomfortable conversation. The train was pulling out of the station and speeding through the long black tunnel that took it out of Manhattan. And then they were out of the tunnel and crossing the long barren stretch beyond.

The silence gave Joan a chance to think about Marc. She had done remarkably little thinking about him, considering his relationship with her. Up to now she had put aside trying to understand what impulse had made her marry him, and why Marc had wanted to marry her. Now there was time to think about it. She had wanted to marry him to show David, and also to put a stop to her life as it was, to change her future and her present so that she could get out of a rut. She had wanted to marry Marc to prove she was a woman, to grasp everything she had been brought up to expect as her logical future—marriage, security, children and a man to lift heavy things and do her thinking for her. She had never wanted that sort of future, but she couldn't bear to be left behind all the other girls her age. She had married to keep up with the Joneses. And Marc's reasons had been much the same—except all of life was harder on him. It was acceptable for a woman to be masculine, but a feminine man would always be a freak, would always be persecuted socially and by the law, would always be the butt of cruel jokes. Marc had wanted to escape that kind of future. Perhaps Marc had even hoped to change, to adjust, to have children with Joan and give up men except for an occasional experience on a trip out of town, far from home and neighbors. Thousands of homosexual men had done so before him—thousands were living lives no less normal than that of the philandering traveling salesman, with a wife who closed one eye.

But Joan had not expected any of that from their marriage. She didn't want children, hated the thought of being any man's wife. She wanted someone like Kim—to belong to her wholly, without having to devote one moment of her time to anyone else, particularly a husband, a man.

"By the way, I forgot to mention it. I have a very attractive sister," Marc said sardonically, crunching on a slice of crisp bacon.

"Oh?" Joan looked up. "Is she gay?"

"Can't tell," he said. "She married one of the neighborhood playboys two years ago. Has a baby now, but I don't know how happy she is. Dad's always called her the boy of the family."

"Sounds interesting," Joan camped. Actually, the thought of being interested in a married woman repelled her. Besides, Kim was the only one in her mind at the moment.

"Let me know if you find out, will you?" Marc said. "I'm dying to make certain."

"Dear, you'll be the first to know," Joan said, finishing her eggs. But she no longer enjoyed this joking with Marc. It was too obviously an act to keep both of their anxieties down.

"Joan, do you suppose there's a chance of your forgetting Reno?" Marc ventured..

"I don't think so," she said, trying to sound as soft and kind as possible. She didn't want to spoil his dream before the end of the week. She was certain that Marc himself would realize eventually that it couldn't work between them.

Marc's sister, Ruth, met them at the station driving a cream-colored Cadillac convertible. She greeted Joan coldly, mirroring Marc's reserve and most of his blonde finely-sculptured features.

"Mom has supper waiting," she addressed Marc efficiently, her eyes quickly shifting away from Joan.

Marc put their suitcases in the back seat and they sat, three in front, Joan in the middle.

Joan felt desperately inadequate in her summer print dress. Ruth was wearing expensively tailored Bermudas and a shirt that came straight from Paris.

"You gave us quite a shock, Marc," Ruth clipped as she drove, glancing first at the road and then at them. "We decided you had gotten some girl pregnant. You're not pregnant, are you, Joan?" She looked at Joan: Ruth's eyes were penetrating and strongly observant—like a man's. Might she have been gay?

Marc laughed nervously. "You'll have to forgive Ruth, dear. She turns her New England reserve on and off as it suits her."

"No, I'm not pregnant," Joan said, countering Ruth's glance with a firm one of her own.

Ruth glanced down at Joan's body and then up at her face again. "No, you're not the type," she said.

There was a long silence now as she turned into the long gravel road that led to the estate. And then they piled out of the convertible as Marc's parents came down the roadway to greet them.

"Mother, Dad, this is Joan," Marc said, presenting her.

A tense moment followed and then Marc's mother came open armed toward her saying, warmly, "Marc has told me so much about you, dear." Only Joan felt the slight tremble in the older woman's body that showed the welcome was forced.

"Well, she's got all the right measurements," Marc's father said, sizing her. "Come on in the light and we'll look at your complexion." He offered Joan his arm and Joan took it, holding on to Marc's mother with her other hand, and they walked to the house and inside, away from the mosquitoes and fireflies. It was warm and cheerful in the house, which was conventionally furnished and compulsively neat.

"There's a light supper ready for you," Marc's mother said to the couple, and they all retired to the dining room. The air was still strained and the situation wasn't helped any by Ruth's persistent stare. It seemed to go right through Joan. She felt self-conscious to her toes.

"Joan will want to wash up, Mother," Ruth said. "Come with me, Joan." She extended her hand. Joan did not want to take it but followed after her, glad to leave the crowd.

"Where's your husband?" Joan asked, perhaps to remind her.

"Bill's working late," she said briefly.

They went upstairs to a large sweet-smelling washroom and Ruth gave her a towel. "Yell if you can't find your way down again," she said.

"I'll find my way down," Joan said. She was determined not to be intimidated. Ruth was the sort of woman who once could have easily frightened Joan.

"We'll wait for you downstairs," Ruth smiled, and turned. There was something beautifully strong about her body and the way she walked in her shorts.

Joan washed up, ridding herself reluctantly of the last traces of New York City—the soot on her neck and forehead that she had always hated but now treasured as the last remaining connection with the familiar.

Downstairs, they were all seated at the table and a place had been set for her between Marc and his mother. She sat down bravely there and put on her best smile. She wondered what had been said before she arrived. The atmosphere was very tense.

"I hope you'll like Marie's cooking. We're rather proud of her," Marc's mother said, referring to their housekeeper, who was serving them savory chicken soup.

Joan tasted it. "It's very good," she said, looking at Marie. Marie grunted and continued to serve.

There was a marked lack of conversation. Finally Marc's father spoke up. "When's Bill showing up, Ruth?"

"In time for dessert, I suppose," she answered disinterestedly. Joan wondered about Ruth. "Do you play Bridge, Joan?" Ruth now addressed her.

"No," Joan said. "But I'd like to learn."

"Never mind," Ruth said. "I'm sure you and Marc are too tired."

Again there was silence and they ate the cold roast beef and potato salad, letting the warmth of early summer become more oppressive than it should.

"Where are you two going to settle?" Marc's father now asked.

"We thought we'd stay in New York for a couple of years," Marc answered. "Joan's going to college there."

"Oh, really?" Ruth raised her head. "Which college? What major?"

"N.Y.U.," Joan answered. "Psychology. I'm not through with my Bachelor's yet."

"Oh," Ruth said with disappointment. "I have a Master's from Columbia."

Joan felt like saying, "You would," but restrained herself. "That's wonderful," she said. "In what?"

"Statistics," Ruth said coldly. The subject suited her.

"I had trouble with that this term," Joan smiled. It made her glad to be able to say it.

"It's too bad we didn't meet sooner," Ruth smiled with superiority. "I could have coached you."

"Yes, isn't it?" Joan returned her smile. "But Marc helped me quite well." It was odd and amusing, Joan's hiding behind Marc this way, pretending to love him. Joan marveled at how easily she had fallen into her part. It was the only part that was safe to play here.

"Yes, I'm sure he did," Ruth said, claiming the last word.

Marie took away their plates. Joan was still hungry but was afraid to make a pig of herself. She hoped Marc would drive her into town later, or perhaps sneak down to the refrigerator for them when everyone had gone to bed. The thought of bed did not make her uncomfortable now. Sharing a room with Marc was a lot easier than sharing supper with his family.

"How about a walk in the moonlight?" Marc said when they were nearly through with dessert.

"Sounds dreamy," Joan said, trying to seem blissful. "Would you mind, Mrs.—Mother Haines?" It was the first time Joan had addressed her that way and she waited for a reaction in the older woman's face.

"There's a perfectly lovely moon out tonight," Marc's mother answered, expressionless.

"Will you excuse us, then?" Marc got up and offered Joan his hand. Joan took it and followed him out the French doors to the back of the house, where a sweet-smelling garden completely changed the air.

"Joanie, you were wonderful," Marc whispered to her when they were outside.

Joan hushed him and looked behind her shoulder for Ruth. She didn't trust Ruth. "Darling, I'm glad I pleased them. I so much want to be a part of your family."

Marc got her cue and played his part, although they could not see anyone listening. They sat on the bench and looked at the moon and Marc whispered in her ear much too low to be heard. "Dad likes you very much, I can tell. And Mother's being her best self. I must say, though, you're certainly bringing out Ruth."

"I'm not interested in bringing out Ruth," Joan whispered in return. "You keep me away from that python."

Marc laughed, for a moment forgetting himself, and then returned to a quiet whisper.

Joan was right. Ruth was bent on following them. Now she came out into the yard and sauntered to them. "How about some ping pong?"

"I'll take you up on that," Joan said. Ping pong was a game she knew. She had been a champion in White Plains during high school days.

"We have a lighted court," Ruth said, going to a section with a cement floor, championship table and spotlights.

Joan followed her, anxious to beat the Bermudas off Ruth. A strong feeling of competition had been growing all evening. Partly it sprang from a deep attraction for the cold and rejecting blonde who looked very much like Marc—like everything Joan had found attractive in Marc despite his manhood. And partly it sprang from a desperate wish to defend herself, for she knew Ruth probably had a secret rage, a mean streak inside her.

Ruth gave her the serve and Joan took it, pretending to be awkward. She held her style back for a while, warming up and also putting Ruth off her guard. And then she hit a fast ball diagonally across the table and Ruth missed it. "Hot Damn!" she cursed.

"Just a lucky short," Joan smiled innocently.

Ruth retrieved the ball and Joan served again, this time more quickly, causing Ruth to run from one side to the other to hit the ball. Realization began to cross Ruth's face and she smiled her narrow smile again. "Sneaky. Why didn't you say you could play?" With this, she hit the ball back with great force, causing the table to resound sharply.

Joan returned the ball and Ruth missed it.

"That's three-zero," Ruth said, wiping her forehead.

Again Joan served and time Ruth returned it and Joan missed.

"Your serve," Joan smiled, tossing her the ball.

Again the furious repartee began. The strain was showing on Ruth's face. She wanted to win, needed the victory. Some fury inside her was making her play harder than she had ever played before. Joan wondered if she should let her win, if that would make a friend of Ruth. She decided to let her lead by three points, to study her reaction. They were close to the final score.

Immediately Ruth's manner changed. Self-assurance returned to her face as she saw victory was almost hers. Then Joan changed her mind. She served three times and scored on each serve. Now they were tied for the final point. She saw that Ruth was puzzled by her strategy, helplessly inferior. Joan couldn't bring herself to do it. It was her serve and she hit the ball, then when Ruth returned it she brought the paddle down with a smash.

"I'm sorry, I tripped," Joan said innocently. "I guess it's your game." Her plan had worked. She hadn't really lost, but she hadn't won either. Ruth's pride had been saved.

"We have lots of balls," Ruth said, smiling broadly and going to her side of the table. "You play very well. I bet you're a champion."

"It's been years," Joan said with feigned modesty.

They put their paddles down and walked back to the bench where Marc had been sitting, watching the battle. Joan could tell he was dying to laugh out loud.

"Your wife's made the team, Marc," Ruth said. Her arm was around Joan's shoulder, making Joan feel very uncomfortable, but she knew she shouldn't pull away from her. She had to take it for a sisterly display of affection—because Ruth would have been the first to make something of Joan's feeling of discomfort, the first to notice that Joan was physically aware of her. Ruth was out to trap her, for some obscure reason; most probably for sport. Joan decided that it might be an interesting week after all—not because she would let herself want Ruth, but because it would be such a pleasure to reject her. She wanted to teach Ruth a lesson about breaking hearts that she had never bothered to learn at Columbia. Joan was certain that Ruth knew the score, and had teased other women before herself.

The three of them went back in the house. Ruth's husband, Bill, had arrived and was seated in the dining room with Mother Haines, eating his supper. Ruth went over to him and kissed his forehead with an air of routine. She showed him less affection than she might have done kissing her pet Boxer lying in the corner of the living room. Then Joan was introduced to Bill, an office-worn, introverted fellow not much older than Ruth, with all the proper measurements of manhood—six-feet tall and broad-shouldered with curly hair of an indefinite shade and hair on the back of his hands.

"Come on. I'll show you where to unpack," Ruth stood again and faced Joan, "and then I've got to take Bill home. We don't live here, you know." She took the steps one at a time but with a bounce up toward the bedrooms and Joan and Marc followed her. "Mom's moved into your room, Marc," she talked as she went. "Her room has a double bed, so that's where you're staying."

Joan and Marc smiled sheepishly. They had been prepared for that, but still it bothered them. Perhaps I can sleep on the rug, Joan thought—it not occurring to her that Marc should be the one to offer, according to normal standards.

"Well, here you are, you two." Ruth stopped in front of a cheery room full of curtains and ruffles. "Just fill up the closets and push all the other junk to one side." Then she turned and extended her hand to Joan. This time Joan took it. It was a firm, friendly grasp. "Welcome to the family, sister-in-law. Well, goodnight, al." She skipped down the stairs again to the dining room.

Joan and Marc sighed with relief.

"With Ruth on your side you're sure to win Dad," Marc said as they began to unpack. Joan grunted, meticulously unfolding her clothes and putting them on hangers. Her hands were trembling from the tension of the evening and she hoped that she might turn in almost immediately. She needed a good night's sleep to face the morning here. But first she wanted something more to eat.

"I'll go raid the icebox," Marc said in response to her request and promptly went downstairs. By the time he had returned Joan was in her nightgown, feeling uncomfortable because she never wore a nightgown, and was sitting on the bed.

Marc closed the door and brought the tray to the bed saying, "Mom had it all ready. She said she knew you must be hungry because you ate like a bird downstairs. I hinted to her that we didn't want to be disturbed."

"You mean we can go right to sleep?" That was good news to Joan. She bit into her roast beef sandwich with new vigor.

"I also borrowed a bottle from downstairs," Marc said.

"Just like a picnic," Joan smiled, lifting her glass.

"You know, Joanie, it could always be like this," Marc said slowly.

"There's one thing missing, Marc," Joan answered seriously. "I do find you rather attractive at the moment, but only because you look like Ruth."

"Yes, I know what you mean," he smiled sadly. "And I find you attractive because you slept with Jay." He placed the end of a potato chip on his plate. "But are we so sure we can't change? Maybe it's all just a phase, like they say."

"I'm sure somehow it's not," Joan said. But within her she wasn't sure. She couldn't be sure because she had never given the other side a chance. Might it have been all right, if she had spent the rest of her life with David? At one time she had thought so. And the thought of being a Lesbian all her life —like the girls in the Yellow Page—thoroughly frightened her. In vain she tried to remind herself that all of gay life didn't necessarily have to be connected to a gay bar—that there were Lesbians spending happy lives together in homes and apartments all over the country, living no less full a life than other childless couples were living. But Marc had presented a choice to her: the wide, rosy way of straight life with all its social advantages and accepted pleasant responsibilities. She compared that to the narrow rocky road of what she felt within her to be the only right path—the path that rang true, deep in her nature. Yes, gay life was the harder road, the road with more hurdles and less glory, with precipices on either side—on one side places like the Yellow Page run by underworld vultures, and on the other side a pit full of hissing serpents of public opinion ready to strike at her weakest points, at her good name, her career, her privacy, her civil rights.

"Joan," Marc spoke up bravely, "why don't we give it a try?

Just this week. At least then we'll be able to look back at it all our lives and have an answer for people who say we didn't give it a chance."

"Is that why you married me, Marc?" Joan was very serious. She knew that this had been in back of both their minds when they said yes to the funny man in City Hall. They both had wanted to find an easier way to live life.

Marc nodded guiltily.

Joan stood and paced the floor, digging one fist into her other palm, fighting the strong revulsion she felt for any man's body. It would be a shock to sleep with Marc after Kim. And suddenly another thought occurred to Joan, a thought which had crept up from time to time these past months and which she had put aside as a necessary risk. "And what if we find I'm pregnant as a result of this experiment?" She was certain this had happened to many a Lesbian before her. Perhaps it had even happened to Ruth, if Ruth were truly as gay as she seemed.

Marc didn't answer. Joan knew he had always wanted a child, had spoken of his wish to be a father—but he was too aware of responsibility to be a father and still remain a homosexual.

Joan paced the rug some more. It was a very difficult decision to make. Her entire being rebelled at the thought of loving a man, of fitting into the role of a wife. It had rebelled in the same way about Gig, except that it had been easier to be with Gig because she was physically a woman. True, if a meeting of the minds carried any weight in a relationship, mentally she was very close to Marc. Would it be so bad to live with Marc the rest of her life? Would it be so bad to have all that Ruth had—her self-assurance, her independence, her freedom to move about and take what she wanted, the best from everyone—without a care or feeling of responsibility because there was always something permanent to fall back on at home—a convenient husband? Perhaps Joan had misjudged Ruth, but she knew other married women—had seen them pointed out in the media by Paul and Marc and others at the Positano—who hid behind respectability and still kept a harem of other women on a string, while they proudly showed baby pictures.

No, she decided, if I change it's got to be all the way, without a thought of women again. This realization shook her with such pain that she knew it showed on her face. She was not religious, but now she was seized with a religious feeling: "Forcing myself to be normal must be my cross," she thought. "I should have the courage to face ." She turned and looked at Marc.

Marc had put the tray on the floor and sat watching her, a nervous look in his eyes. Joan knew it was a difficult time for him too, knew through Jay that Marc had never slept with a woman.

With the same scientific air that had guided her actions since Paul, Joan decided to give it one last try—more for Marc's sake than her own, more as his psychologist than as his wife. She might very well help Marc adjust, either one way or the other. This alone was worth the effort—the pain and discomfort of having Marc after Kim.

She tossed him his bathrobe which was resting on a chair and said, "Are you going to bed with all your clothes on?"

"I wasn't sure what had been decided," Marc said, catching the robe with nervous hands.

"It's been decided," Joan said coldly, with the air of aloofness she was used to assuming with men. But then she stopped herself. She would have to be tender with Marc. She could easily break him.

She went over to where he sat and pressed his head to her waist, running grooves through his curly hair with her fingers. Marc responded like a child, looking up at her with innocent blue eyes that seemed to trust her implicitly. Somewhere in the back of her mind Joan felt the ridiculous reversal of this wedding night: Marc the virgin and she the teacher.

She unbuttoned his shirt for him and ran a ringer down his white chest to his belt buckle and then snapped it playfully and walked away from him. She had learned one thing from Jay—femininity, not masculinity, would attract Marc to her.

She went about the room turning off the lights, leaving on only a night light at the window. When she returned to the bed Marc had stripped to his shorts and was holding his bathrobe on his lap, self-consciously. "I won't look at you," she said. She turned away from him, lay down and pulled the sheets over herself.

Marc got into bed and began to rub her back, working out the tense hostility in her muscles and his own fear of her body. It was easier this way. He could pretend she was Jay. Joan was glad he did not want her lips. She would give him anything else, but her mouth especially belonged to Kim.

Ruth knocked at their door the next morning. "Wake up, love birds, I want to take Joan swimming."

"Have a heart," Marc answered, groaning. "What time is it, anyway?"

"Nearly noon," Ruth called back. "Marie's about to serve lunch."

"I suppose we'd better get up," Joan yawned. They both dreaded the day ahead because they couldn't be themselves in front of Marc's family.

"Just get into your bathing suits," Ruth said. "There's no point in dressing."

"All right," Marc said, "but go away, damn you!" He threw a pillow at the door and they heard Ruth's bouncing steps move down the hall.

"Hi," Marc blinked to Joan.

"Hi," Joan stretched. They were still friends this morning, although their bodies were terribly hostile, unwilling to show each other the slightest touch of affection. The evening had been a strange kind of flop—mechanically perfect but completely lacking in the sort of emotion Kim could evoke from Joan with only half Marc's effort. And for Marc it had been a dull bore in much the same way. Only friendship would make it possible for them to last the week together.

They put on their bathing suits, no longer self-conscious about being naked in the same room—because now there was no attraction between them. Then, with beach jackets over their suits, they went down to lunch.

Ruth, in a Bikini, was fixing a salad in the dining room. The patio table was set for three. "Mom's shopping in town," she explained. "Dad went down to the lake to try out a new outboard motor. He was sort of hoping you'd join him, Marc. Why don't you borrow my car after lunch and bring him a sandwich?"

Marc grunted, trying to hide the joy he felt about being welcomed back to the family fold.

"I hope you like this salad, Joan," Ruth turned to her now, "it's home grown."

Joan nodded and then gave herself a large helping of tuna fish and hardboiled egg. The country air was affecting her appetite. She hoped she wouldn't gain weight.

9.

THEY finished lunch and then Ruth tossed Marc her car keys and said to Joan, "We'd better go right in the water or we'll have to wait an hour to digest."

Joan followed as Ruth led the way to the brook. It was away from the house and past a clump of trees, after which a clearing had been made. A concrete pool was placed here so that the brook ran through it. There were flowers around its edge, water lilies and violets, enhanced by the shining blue glints of hovering dragon flies.

"We can sunbathe if you don't want to get wet yet," Ruth suggested.

"Let's dunk first," Joan decided.

Ruth got on the primitive diving board and dove in like a professional. Joan followed her. The brook was cold, a contrast to the noon heat. It woke Joan completely and she swam to the side of the pool where Ruth joined her.

"I understand you have a baby," Joan said, trying to make her conversation as feminine as possible. "It's odd to think I'm an aunt."

"It's odder suddenly to become a mother," Ruth laughed. She lifted herself out of the water and sat by the side of the pool. "Do you really love Marc?" she asked abruptly.

"Why should you ask that?" Joan was flustered and swam a little away to hide her embarrassment.

"I don't know . . . Jealousy, I guess," Ruth laughed, coming back in the water and swimming after her. "I can't bear to think you've taken him away from me. We were quite close when we were young, you know. I used to fight all his battles for him, against Dad and the kids at school."

"Marc isn't the sort who needs a champion," Joan said quietly. She crossed the pool to avoid being close to Ruth but Ruth swam with her.

"I don't mean that he was ever afraid," Ruth corrected herself. "It's just that—well, you must know him by now. He's in no way competitive. I've never seen him get fighting mad or try to win a game."

"He has more important things to do," Joan said. She lifted herself out of the pool and Ruth came up and sat next to her. "I have no respect for a man who's all brawn," Joan added.

"Neither have I—anymore," Ruth said with some weighty meaning behind the words. She returned to the water and swam across the pool. Joan decided to pursue, wanting to find out just what Ruth was trying to say to her. It was better to be on the offensive than on the defensive.

"Just what are you getting at?" Joan said, following her out of the pool and sitting on the deck chair beside hers. The sun was strong on them and they felt the heat despite their wetness.

"Put some lotion on my back, will you?" Ruth handed her a bottle and turned around, unstrapping the bra of her Bikini.

Ruth's body was firm and her breasts full and needing no support. It embarrassed Joan to se her without her bra. She had always felt partly an impostor when other women undressed in her presence, and yet there was nothing she could do. She couldn't wear a sign that said she wasn't of the same sex. With nervous hands she spread the suntan lotion evenly on Ruth's back, stopping whatever pleasure might arise from touching Ruth—stopping it because it wasn't fair. Joan was a man inside and Ruth didn't know it. To enjoy touching her would be taking an unfair advantage.

"How long have you known Marc?" Ruth asked. Her tone was still disinterested, as if none of it mattered to her. Joan decided Ruth was very interested—but for what reason she couldn't be sure.

"A few months," Joan lied. It had really only been slightly more than one month, this last crazy month.

"And you fell in love right away?"

"You ask too many questions." Joan finished rubbing on the suntan oil and closed the bottle.

"Don't close the bottle. I'll put some on your back," Ruth said, turning around, her bra still off. "You can take off your suit—we're far from the road."

"Thanks, I don't need any oil," Joan said. She lay down without removing her suit and closed her eyes. The sight of Ruth's breasts made her blush.

Ruth took off the bottom of her Bikini and then sat down in her own chair, putting on her sun glasses. "You're shy, aren't you?" she commented.

"I've had a Victorian upbringing," Joan laughed it off.

Ruth didn't answer and Joan decided to treasure the silence, giving herself up to the murmur of the breeze and rustle of birds in the bushes nearby. She fought a desire to open her eyes and watch Ruth—Ruth's perfect body completely naked. It was difficult to keep her eyes shut. The sun was burning her arms and shoulders and she decided she'd better put on some lotion after all. She reached blindly for the bottle. It was lying beneath Ruth's hand.

"So you do burn after all," Ruth smiled, grasping the bottle. She handed it to Joan impishly and then abruptly rose and ran to the diving board.

Joan could not avoid seeing her and fought with her eyes not to notice all of Ruth—Ruth's dark even tan, her perfect musculature as she dove into the brook like a minnow. "Come on back in and cool off," she laughed.

Joan stood awkwardly, fumbling with the bottle, and then unscrewed the cap and put the lotion on her shoulders. Her will power was being taxed too much. Ruth had invited her in the water and swimming naked with Ruth was a lovely thought. Ruth may have been thinking the same thing—or perhaps it was all a trap, a trap set by Marc's family to learn the truth about his marriage. Or perhaps it was all naiveté on Ruth's part. Joan decided to let the game go on. Determinedly, she removed her suit and dove in the brook.

"So you're not really hiding a scar," Ruth smiled, "and you're really all there."

"You know how it is with newlyweds. I was afraid it might show," Joan said with feigned innocence. Inwardly she congratulated herself for her ability to act like the sweet young thing she was supposed to be.

Ruth laughed wildly at her joke and swam away to the end of the pool where the water was falling slowly over a small dam. She sat on the dam, letting the water come around her waist. Her skin was whiter in the cold water. Joan swam after her, determined not to be self-conscious. She sat next to Ruth on the dam, feeling the cold water rush around and between her legs, both cooling and bracing the excitement in her thighs. Ruth's breasts were so perfectly round.

Ruth studied Joan for a moment, as if she were about to say something inward, and then she said it out loud. "How serious is your marriage to Marc?"

Joan couldn't answer. She couldn't lie. She repelled off the dam and swam out in the water. "I don't like your questions, Ruth. Are you trying to spy on me?"

"On the contrary, I've already spied on you," Ruth said with meaning.

Joan turned and looked at her, treading water. "How do you mean?"

Ruth came into the water and swam past her going to the end of the pool. "I mean Dad asked me to have you investigated after Marc told him last week."

"And, of course, you found nothing wrong with my background," Joan said, hoping to call her bluff—if bluff it was.

"No, I found nothing wrong with your family background," Ruth said meaningfully. She got up out of the pool and sat on the mat near the deck chairs, drying her face. "I gave that part of the report to Dad."

"You mean there was another part of the report?" Joan asked cautiously. She followed Ruth out of the pool and sat next to her, wrapping a towel around herself.

Ruth looked directly at her. Her eyes were straightforward and intense. "You know, I was prepared to dislike you when I met you last night. But oddly enough, you don't look like a whore to me, despite the rumors."

So that was it. The private detective had gotten on the wrong trail—Joan's alley cat past with its misleading assortment of attempts at being normal. Joan had to laugh. "Now who's being Victorian?"

"I'm not Victorian," Ruth said. "Heaven knows, my past hasn't been exactly spotless either."

This admission made Joan stop and look at her. It was a strange thing for Ruth to say.

"I mean I was worried about Marc," Ruth said. "I was afraid he had married you to prove something to Dad."

"How do you mean?" Joan was still cautious.

"I know why he was discharged from the Navy," Ruth said. There was a long silence and then she spoke again. "You know, Marc and I are more alike than I wanted to realize for a long time. I married Bill to escape from that realization."

"I don't know what you're talking about," Joan said firmly. Ruth frightened her. She had never met anyone so strangely frank. Surely this must be a trap.

"Are you sure you don't know?" Ruth fixed on her face. "Well, if you don't know, then it's best I don't tell you." She lay down on the mat and looked up at the sky.

Joan dared look at her—she was very beautiful as she lay in the sun, a white towel carelessly spread across her waist—then she took hold of herself and determined not to desire her; Ruth was married and she had a baby. Joan lay down on the mat, far away from her.

They sunned themselves without conversation for another twenty minutes, then they heard the car pull up the driveway and Ruth sat up. "That's Marc and Dad," she said and quickly put up her Bikini again and Joan followed her example.

Ruth stood and extended her hand. This time Joan took it—a firm, warm, honest hand. They ran together past the wooded area back toward the house.

Spontaneously, Joan felt they were friends, felt it in the way they ran together—felt a harmony in their movements and coursing through their clasped hands. It was difficult to keep from liking Ruth, from wanting her. For a minute she remembered Kim and felt a wave of guild about it. She still felt that she ought to be thinking only of Kim. Again she wondered if she would ever be faithful to someone after having been promiscuous for so long.

Marc came toward them holding two fishing poles. "Hi. We came back for the two of you."

"I don't really feel like fishing today, Marc," Ruth said. She let go of Joan's hand and then went on ahead to the porch.

"What happened between you two?" Marc asked in a low voice.

"Nothing," Joan chimed casually. She took one of the poles and sauntered back with him to the house. She wanted badly to follow Ruth, but she forced herself to stand around and take part of the family conversation. And Ruth was busying herself with packing more sandwiches for them.

Joan allowed herself to be taken away by Marc and his dad, sitting between them in the front seat of Ruth's convertible. Standing in her bathing suit in the coolness of the rushing river learning to fly-fish helped her spend the afternoon. She caught a minnow, which she had to throw back, and Marc caught a catfish that made them all laugh. Marc's father got most of the luck—he came home with a string of bass— or were they trout?—Marc couldn't tell. They returned to find dinner waiting for them—Ruth and Mom never trusting to their luck, and Dad handed the fish to Marie for tomorrow's lunch.

"You look a hundred percent healthier than yesterday," Ruth said to Joan, smiling sphinxishly. "You were so pale when you came from the city. Love that tan you're getting." She ran a ginger boldly down Joan's arm, and Joan flushed, remembering immediately their hour at the pool. Ruth was teasing her deliberately now, being tempting and alluring. Joan followed her upstairs to change for dinner.

"Wear shorts if you have them," Ruth suggested, "I always do." Then she brought Joan a new towel from the linen closet.

Joan stood, not wishing to change in from of her. But Ruth lingered, regarding her. There something on her mind. Slowly, Ruth closed the door that led to the hall and leaned back against it until the latch clicked.

Joan didn't move. Ruth was planning a kiss. Joan wanted it to happen, and yet she also wanted to run—because Ruth was so alluring. As Ruth came toward her, however, she found herself frozen to the floor. Only Ruth's firm grasp on her shoulders made her stop trembling, and Ruth's mouth on hers—a sweet, perfect mouth—claimed her completely. The length of their bodies touched and their arms nearly crushed each other in their hast to embrace. Then Joan caught herself and forced Ruth to let go and, in a desperate effort to make her stop, slapped her.

Ruth let go instantly and looked at Joan, surprised. But then she saw Joan's rapid breathing and saw it was not a rejection. A tense smile formed on her mouth.

"I don't think you'd better do that again," Joan said.

The words were had to say. She took a change of clothes and walked past Ruth, unlatching the door, and went into the bathroom to change. It was the most difficult distance she had ever walked.

When she came out again, dressed in Bermudas, Ruth was gone—probably downstairs with everyone else. Joan walked uneasily down and joined the others, prepared to see her again, to dare look squarely into Ruth's steady blue eyes—but Ruth was gone.

"Shall we all retire to the dining room?" Mother Haines said when she saw Joan. The group did so and Joan noticed that no place had been set for Ruth. All at once the evening seemed dull. Joan's entire being grew restless. Ruth must have gone home to Bill.

Joan didn't know what to think. The thought of being a toy for a married woman's amusement filled her with rage. The memory of Ruth's beauty and aggressiveness disquieted her. How could it be possible that Ruth could belong to a man, could really prefer a man!

She ate silently and Mother Haines asked if she were ill. She said she had a headache. After supper, Marc took her out for a walk in the fresh air. It was good to be away from the house.

"It's Ruth, isn't it?" Marc said as they kicked the pebbles on the side of the road.

"I can't discuss it," Joan said. But Marc knew.

"Joanie," he took a long breath, "I haven't had a chance to discuss last night with you and I know you don't want to because for you it was dreadful—"

"Please, Marc." There was a pained look on her face.

The two walked together slowly, and then Marc took her hand and squeezed it firmly. It was the action of a friend and Joan responded. She was very fond of Marc; as a comrade, she loved him.

The crickets were subdued there by the road and a large moon lit their way, making the landscape lonely and unreal. The smell of the leaves filled their lungs. For any other couple, it would have been an ideal lovers' walk. But a great loneliness filled Joan, a longing for some other world, some distant motherland that was actually her home. Then, as if transportation had come to take her there, they heard Ruth's convertible pulling up behind them.

"Hello, you two," Ruth waved. Her outward manner was nonchalant, but Joan saw the conflict in her eyes. "Marc, you don't mind if I take Joan for a drive, do you?"

Marc turned, slightly taken aback. "I don't know whether I do or not." He turned to Joan, waiting for her to decide.

Joan looked at Marc and then at Ruth. Ruth's nerve was atrocious, but Joan wanted to see it through between them—needed to be sure about her. But she didn't want to leave Marc alone on the road.

"We can drive Marc back to the house," Ruth said, reading her mind.

Joan looked at Marc again. She didn't want to make the decision. Marc understood. "You go on," Marc said, opening the car door for her. "It's a nice night. I'll walk back."

Joan allowed herself to be led into the car and said nothing. Marc closed the door and the two drove off.

Ruth's driving was steady and fast. She didn't speak. Finally Joan broke the silence. "Where are you taking me?" she asked.

"Where we can be alone," Ruth said.

Again there was silence. Joan fought the excitement she felt, the mounting desire. She had never felt like this about anyone. With Kim and with Gig it had always been a question of symbols—of the fact that they were Lesbians and that at last Joan had found peace, an end to her search for what was right and natural for her. But with Ruth it was more than that—it was a deep feeling of animal attraction that had caught hold of her, had made it impossible for Joan to want anyone else. Joan knew now, as they drove quickly past the landscape, that no matter what happened between them, whether small or large, for the first time she was really in love; for the first time Joan could be completely belong.

Ruth stopped at a driveway that had Bill's name on the mailbox. The house was set back from the road—a two-family house with a two-story garage a little distance from it—a pleasant, quiet place.

Ruth left the car in the driveway and then opened the door for Joan. "Bill isn't living with me anymore," she stated simply. Joan followed her inside, wondering about her statement. "We put up a pretense in front of Mom and Dad," Ruth said, turning on all the lights on her way to the parlor.

Joan said nothing, taking in the surroundings and the entire situation. The house was immaculately neat. It seemed unlived-in.

"We'll have to be quiet or we'll wake up Billy," she said. "May I get you a drink?"

Joan shook her head. Ruth poured one for herself and then put the drink down without tasting it. She was nervous. Her self-assurance was no longer so complete. Joan leaned on an arm of an easy chair and watched her.

"I'm sorry about this afternoon," Ruth said. With visible effort, she stopped pacing. "I should have explained all sorts of things to you first."

"There's no need for explanations," Joan said. And there was no need any longer—Bill's absence from the house spoke for itself. Ruth didn't want Bill and that cast a new light on everything.

"I think I'm in love with you," Joan said. Despite what she had said to Kim, she had not really meant those words since David; she waited now to see how they would be received.

Ruth's was a delayed reaction. She turned away from Joan and looked at the wall and her whole body shook almost imperceptibly.

Joan walked over to her and took hold of her shoulders from behind. She rubbed the muscles of her back, breaking the tension there. Ruth reluctantly turned and buried her head deep in Joan's breast, suddenly letting herself go. Pressing against her now she cried. They were strong, controlled tears, but they were washing away the world.

Joan covered Ruth's forehead and neck with kisses, protecting Ruth within the circle of her arms until finally Ruth wiped the tears on her cheeks away with the back of her hand and looked up at Joan.

Joan kissed her and they blended again as they had done before, the kiss becoming more and more passionate with every movement of hands and bodies. But it was a different kiss than the one of before—a lover's kiss lacking all the bravado of the first.

"We hardly know each other," Ruth said, pleating Joan's collar nervously with her fingers.

Joan broke slightly away from her and looked at Ruth's angelic face, now full of conflict between passion and propriety. "Let's go slowly," Joan said. She forced herself to let go of Ruth and walked a few steps away. "Show me your house. I'd love to see your baby."

Just as she had said this, they heard foot steps coming down the stairs. "Did you want anything, Mrs. Baker?" An older woman who looked much like Marie entered the room.

Ruth started and embarrassedly said no. The woman went back upstairs to the nursery and for a moment the two were nervous. Might she have heard anything? "I'm sorry," Ruth said to Joan. "I completely forgot about Mrs. Reed. I'm always so used to doing what I please in my own parlor."

"I don't think she heard us," Joan assured her. But they were both upset by the incident.

"Let's go outside," Ruth said.

Joan followed her out of the house and they went toward the garage. "There's guest apartment there," Ruth said. "We can be alone."

"Let's not just yet," Joan said and took her hand.

Ruth's hand was still wonderful to hold, real, as concrete as the world. They walked to the back of the house and a little away to chairs that were scattered on the lawn. There they sat.

"You're still very much afraid of me, aren't you?" Joan stated.

Ruth nodded. "All through school I ran from women. Do you know that feeling of terror?"

"Yes." Joan knew. Before David there had been moments like that, moments when she had realized she was different and wanted something that everyone else called wrong. Panic would grip her, make her run away from the person she wanted most to hold.

"What are we going to do about tonight?" Ruth asked.

"What do you want to do about it?" Joan countered. She knew that Ruth must make her own decision, instinctively knew that this would be the first time for her.

"I want you to stay," Ruth said. "I want you to stay with me." Her hand grasped Joan's more tightly than before.

"Then I'll call Marc and tell him I'm spending the night here," Joan said. "I'm sure he'll find some logical explanation to give his parents. He could tell them we quarreled. Newlyweds always quarrel." Joan's words sounded feeble. She knew this would put Marc on a spot.

"No," Ruth said. "I'd better take you home in a while."

They both knew that this was best and sat in silence together, still holding hands. Finally Ruth said, "I can pick you up in the morning. We can go for a drive together."

The thought of waiting was almost too much to bear and they looked at each other with anguish.

Mrs. Reed appeared then. "Telephone for you, Mrs. Baker," she said.

Ruth excused herself and Joan followed slowly after her into the house. It was Marc on the phone. "But are you sure it's all right?" Ruth was saying. Her face was a mixture of concern and relief. "Very well. And thank you." She hung up. Joan knew why Marc had called. Ruth didn't have to say it. "Marc's told Mom you're spending the night here," Ruth said. "He told her I felt ill."

"Marc's a mind reader," Joan smiled.

They walked outside again and Joan felt the conflict raging in Ruth. Ruth was still afraid, terrified of her, almost sorry Marc had called.

"Don't be afraid of me," Joan said. The calm assurance of her tone steadied Ruth and the two walked more quickly toward the garage.

The apartment above the garage was pleasant and airy, more airy than the house, and had les of the tradition of man and wife about it. Joan didn't kiss Ruth when they were inside; she avoided her deliberately, stopping the desire that was burning inside her. She would wait. Perhaps nothing would happen tonight, but she would have to wait patiently. This would have to be Ruth's decision; all of it was up to Ruth; Joan did not ever want to feel that she had swayed Ruth one way or the other.

"You take a shower," Joan said. "I'll turn on the radio. We can sit and talk all night if you want." She threw Ruth a towel she had found folded on the chair.

Ruth caught the towel with one hand and looked hesitantly at Joan. "You take a shower with me," she said.

"No." Joan sank deep in an easy chair and picked up a

magazine. "I'll take one later."

Joan felt very strong. She did not desire Ruth in the same intensely physical way she had desired Kim and Gig. It would have been enough to just lie in bed beside Ruth all night. She was enjoying a stronger emotion, the pleasure of a bond that seemed to be between them, making her want to know all of Ruth's mind as well as her body. It would have been enough simply to talk all night with her.

When Ruth came out of the shower she was hiding her figure behind her towel—a change from the time at the pool.

Joan didn't look at her and went to use the shower herself. She kept the water as cold as she could bear it, trying to chill her body and the fire inside it, for there was a fire, in spite of her resolution to be non-sexual. But the cold water was no help. She came out, wrapped in her own towel, and saw that Ruth had turned off most of the lights. Staring at the ceiling, she lay in bed, her breasts exposed above the covers. Joan tried not to look at her. She dried herself more thoroughly and then sat on the bed, not wishing yet to lie down.

Ruth looked at her then, eyes scanning the skin of Joan's throat and upper chest, following the edge of the towel that covered her body. Terror wasn't in her eyes anymore, only a nervousness that said—I want you.

Joan let the towel drop and sat, studying her. Ruth's lips were beautifully full. She bent over and kissed them sweetly, feeling her own breasts brush lightly over Ruth's.

The reaction was quick and sudden. Ruth's arms went around her and pulled Joan close; there was no question of waiting any longer. Now Joan knew a completeness she had never known before and a strange sort of joy—the world was right-side-up again.

10.

Ruth was crying softly on Joan's shoulder. The first mists of dawn were outside the window and the birds had not yet begun to sing. Joan pressed Ruth close, fighting a sleepiness that weighted her eyes. Ruth had cried softly all night, ever since Joan had fulfilled her. She was crying away her marriage and her baby, crying away the awful two years with Bill.

"When did you leave him?" Joan whispered. It was the first time that she had questioned Ruth about her separation.

"I always wanted to leave," she said. She buried her face deep in Joan, trying to escape remembering. "I finally asked for a divorce. That was the night I got pregnant." A small shiver went through her. "Do you understand? He forced me. That's why I can't feel anything for the baby. I didn't want it."

"But he's half yours," Joan said, holding Ruth even more closely. She had never seen Ruth's child, but the thought of his being part of Ruth made Joan ready to love him. And, in loving Ruth's baby, Joan felt the weight of responsibility—Ruth must not leave Bill; Ruth must keep the family together, for the baby's sake.

What a terrible thing to ask of her, and what a terrible thing to expect of herself. Joan could no longer imagine life without Ruth.

"It's no good," Ruth said. "We've been through this a dozen times. I've already started divorce proceedings—it's better now, while Billy's still too young to care."

"Then you're willing to just give him up?" The thought made Joan wince—that Ruth should deprive herself of her child.

"Bill wants him. He want to marry again. Besides," she clung to Joan tightly, bursting into violent tears, "what sort of mother would I make? Don't you see? Women like me shouldn't have children!"

"Don't say that," Joan said. She sat up and shook Ruth, then pressed her close again. "Don't you dare let the world beat you down like that! There's absolutely nothing wrong with what you are." But Ruth was in no condition to listen to her. She was letting loose after two years of strict restraint. "Listen to me," Joan insisted, pressing her cheek close to Ruth's again, "let's not think about it now. Sometimes attitudes change." The words hurt coming out. "Look, I know this much about women—a gay experience sometimes clears the air, actually makes it easier to enjoy a man." Joan was referring to her own experience with Jay after knowing Gig, and to what was general knowledge among Lesbians—that many women had been able to go back to men after knowing women, had been able to be pleased by men. In Joan's case, being satisfied by Jay had made no difference; she was still a Lesbian. But as for Ruth—perhaps Ruth was just confused, or had simply married the wrong man. She was much more inhibited than Joan, had less experience with men. Possibly her difficulties with Bill stemmed more from inhibition than from sexual direction.

"I don't want to go back to him," Ruth said.

"We'll talk about it tomorrow," Joan answered. She began to lull Ruth to sleep, soothing her taut nerves with gentle caresses, and as the sun streamed through the blinds, she finally let herself drop off, weary and full of mixed emotions.

Marc came to pick them up at noon, knocking on their door in the same gung-ho way that Ruth had knocked the day before. "Wake up, I want to take Joan swimming," he joked.

This time it was Ruth who threw the pillow at the door. She felt better this morning, almost like her old self. She embraced Joan passionately one more time and then both reluctantly got up.

Ruth was strong this morning, stoic and silent, but something about her had changed. Her eyes were softer, had a new depth. Joan blessed and cursed Marc all in the same breath—blessed him for waiting until noon and cursed him for coming at all. She had so little time to be with Ruth, so little time before she would have to give her back to Bill.

Both Ruth and Joan dressed quickly, avoiding each other because an embrace might keep them back an hour trying to pull free. With only a touch of hands, they opened the door and forced their feet to walk downstairs.

Marc was waiting on the lawn, his hands in his pockets, sporting a lovely pair of hairy legs beneath his Bermudas. "I thought we might have breakfast on the road," he said. And then, apologetically, "I had to get out of the house and come get you or it might have seemed odd."

"Thanks, Marc," Joan said gratefully.

Marc drove Ruth's car a few miles to a dairy bar where they could get decent scrambled eggs. The conversation between him and Ruth was tense and perfunctory. Despite themselves, there was rivalry between them over Joan. The situation was beginning to evoke a deep claustrophobia in Joan. She wanted to be alone with Ruth, wanted to be free to spend the rest of her life with Ruth without a care or a foreign responsibility. Impulsively, she reached over and squeezed Ruth's had. Ruth immediately responded, and they were together again, as close as they had been when they were alone.

All three were famished and ate enough for six.

Marc was the first to take the conversational bull by the horns, "Are congratulations in order for you two?" he asked. He said it carefully and with a smile meant to indicate that he approved.

"Yes," Ruth said awkwardly. She could not look at Marc directly and there was conflict on her face. "I've been getting a divorce from Bill, you know."

"I've been trying to make her give up that idea, Marc," Joan said. "It's too soon for her to take a step like that."

"I never did like Bill," Marc said. He had taken to smoking a pipe this week and now filled it with tobacco, looking at both of them, especially at Ruth. "What are you going to do about the baby?"

"I don't know," Ruth looked down. "I really don't know."

"I had an idea this morning," Marc ventured carefully. "How about the three of us going to Provincetown for the rest of the week? I can call Jay long distance and have him meet us, then the two of you can be alone—and so can the two of us."

Joan and Ruth were silent. It was too much to consider at the moment. "Neither of us feels like a holiday, Marc," Joan said finally.

"Nonsense," Marc said. "It'll be good for all of us. When the week's over, we can all decide what we want to do."

"I think Marc has a point," Ruth said. "Bill won't miss my and Mom and Mrs. Reed will be more than willing to look after the baby. Maybe we can all think more clearly away from here."

"I'll go anywhere you want to go," Joan agreed, inwardly glad at what Ruth had said. At least they would have a week—one week before it ended, had to end.

"Good," Marc said. "I'll phone Jay from here and then we can go back home and pack our things and tell Mom and Dad."

When Marc came back from the telephone booth he was full of sparkle. "Jay's meeting us at the train station in Boston—that's on our way," he said. "Now I feel more like my old self."

They paid the check and left the restaurant, already feeling the spirit of vacation. Joan was grateful that they wouldn't have to spend the rest of the week here, where everything and everyone was awkward and uncomfortable.

They dropped Ruth off and Marc and Joan returned to his parents' house. Ruth was to pack, phone Bill, and then pick them up. They would drive in her convertible.

"You know, Joanie, I'm glad it's Ruth," Marc said. "You deserve someone like her."

"It can't last, Marc," Joan said. She didn't want to talk about it. She knew what was ahead of them—a dreadful parting. And yet the experience was too wonderful to drop prematurely, in the same way that loving David had been worth all the suffering. That had taught her how to live.

"Perhaps there's some hope," Marc said. "After all, these are modern times. All gay love doesn't end unhappily anymore."

"Yes, perhaps there's hope," Joan sighed.

It was surprisingly easy to break the news to Marc's parents. They felt just as awkward having the newlyweds around and thought it was lovely that Ruth was also going and that they could have time with their grandchild. Mother Haines spoke up: "It will be a good rest for Ruth." Joan felt that unconsciously she understood her daughter's secret.

In an hour, they were ready to leave. Until the last minute Joan suppressed a great panic that Ruth might fail to arrive, might change her mind or have her mind changed by Bill. Then her car pulled up the driveway and the world was all right again. They loaded their baggage in the trunk, Marc took the wheel and all goodbyes were said. Then the three were free of everything, doing forty-five in the direction of Boston and Cape Cod.

This time Ruth took Joan's hand. It was the first overt sign of affection on her part since that morning. Joan responded by letting her head fall on Ruth's shoulder.

"I'd better put the top up," Marc laughed. He pressed the button that did so, and none too soon, for Ruth kissed Joan on the lips. It was a familiar kiss, full of the affection of last night. It left a peculiar thirst in Joan's mouth and she longed to be alone with Ruth, all the more as Ruth stroked her forehead and lulled her to sleep.

The trip to Boston took more than four hours. Toward evening, when they stopped for supper, a happy mood seized the three completely. Ruth joked and chatted with Marc like old times and the family resemblance became more marked between them. Joan largely watched and listened in her usual withdrawn way. She could not bring herself to feel part of the group because, after Kim, she felt there was such an impermanence about Ruth. And yet she was sick with love, already pining for that which she had not yet lost.

"Wait till you meet Jay." Marc sounded excited and happy. "Can you imagine that we never knew the other was gay all the time we were on the same ship? We were terrified of each other."

"When did you start?" Ruth asked.

"Some older guy on the ship—he wasn't even gay, just trade. He had me picked." Marc laughed. "It's funny, they never really caught the mad ones, just the young and naïve who were stupid enough to fall for their traps. I was crazy enough to get picked up in a bar when I was on shore leave." Bitterness set over Marc's nonchalant smile. "First they draft you, then they tempt you, then they kick you out. And it's on your record for the rest of your life."

The words struck at Ruth. She took a deep breath, unable to stop the flush of red to her cheeks. She looked angry enough to fight the whole Navy. Joan reached for her hand under the table and gave it a reassuring squeeze, stopping the rage within herself at hearing Marc's story once more. Stories like this were what gave the bars their atmosphere—places full of people full of rage.

"There's a rumor about George Washington and Lafayette," Joan joked to bring back some good humor, "and everyone knows about Marie Antoinette and the Duchess of Polignac."

They finished their coffee and left the luncheonette. Boston was ten miles away and Jay wasn't expected to arrive until late that night. They planned to take two motel rooms and Marc would go and pick him up later. They stopped at an AAA court and got a cabin with adjoining rooms. Ruth and Joan turned in early.

"Do you still want me as much as last night?" Ruth asked after she had closed the door. Her tone was uncertain, lost.

"Yes," Joan said. She looked at Ruth, quietly, studying her angelic face. She had changed so much in two days. She seemed older now, more serious. The hostility and the restlessness had left her eyes. Joan had not dared ask Ruth how she felt about her. It was too much to ask of her so soon. And yet she had hoped that Ruth would return her love a little, even if she did go back to Bill. "How do you feel?" Joan asked instead.

Ruth smiled a tired smile. "Come here," she said.

Joan walked toward her, trying to stop the trembling that always came when she was near Ruth. And then their bodies blended into each other and Joan knew that everything was just the same between them; they had not been separated at all.

"What are you thinking?" Joan asked.

"I'm thinking how strange and different this all is," Ruth said. She kissed Joan's forehead. "It's more real than anything else I've ever experienced. The reality frightens me in a way."

"It's hard to change your life at twenty-nine," Joan said. She held Ruth's hand and tried to shut her eyes for a minute, tried to forget the world outside.

"I feel nineteen again," Ruth smiled. She held Joan closely and they kissed.

"What were you doing at nineteen?" Joan asked.

"I was going to Barnard," Ruth remembered. "Those were horrible years. Did you know I lived in the Village?"

"No," Joan laughed, pleasantly surprised. "Did you have a roommate?"

"Yes. She was very pretty." A sadness came into Ruth's eyes as she remembered. "We were both heavy-dating frat boys."

"What happened?" Joan asked. Ruth now still looked nineteen. Her past might only have happened yesterday.

"I tried to kiss her one day and she slapped me," Ruth said.

Joan held her closely. "Just like I did yesterday."

"It wasn't the same," Ruth said. She let go of Joan and got up, beginning to unbutton her clothes. "I guess we'd better get a good night's sleep."

Joan watched her undress, watched Ruth's tall, Spartan body come free of the clothes that had encumbered it since morning. "Ruth," Joan said slowly, "you mustn't feel responsible for me in any way. I don't want you to feel that you have to stay with me just because I'm in love with you."

"On the contrary," Ruth turned and looked at her, came close to her, a great calm in her eyes. "I do feel responsible for you. I want to feel responsible."

There was a moment of silence and Joan was made helpless by Ruth's gaze. Then Ruth turned and went to the shower.

Joan tried to read the book she had brought with her, but it was futile. She began to undress and waited outside the bathroom until Ruth was through. Then Ruth brushed past her wetly and Joan used the shower. When she came out, Ruth had put a quarter into the motel radio and was sitting naked on the bed, listening to a cool sax.

"Come and sit next to me," she said. "I want to brush your hair." Joan did so and let down the long red braid she had twisted behind her head to keep her hair dry. "How did you manage to have such long hair?" Ruth marveled. Her firm careful brush strokes gave Joan goose pimples; when she kissed Joan's collar bone, her cool soft lips made Joan tremble.

"Don't do that," Joan said, trying to resist her.

Ruth laughed, both nervously and determinedly self-assured.

"Don't run away so much."

She put the brush down and took both of Joan's shoulders and pulled her back against her body. Their flesh touched and they could not bear to separate again.

Joan pressed against the warmth of Ruth and threw back her head for Ruth to kiss her lips.

They were nestled together in the dark, watching the lights of passing cars streak across the wall.

"I just shut my eyes and gritted my teeth and forced myself to lie there," Ruth said. "I spent my college days that way. Then I thought marriage might change things. It didn't." She stopped and pressed Joan's head to hers. "Don't you see? You weren't an experiment—you were a decision. I can't bear to live one more day with any man."

"I *do* love you," Joan confirmed and pressed her head into Ruth's breast. Ruth's story had touched her deepest emotions and she felt she knew and understood Ruth's past as clearly as her own.

"I hoped the baby would make a difference," Ruth continued, "but when I saw it, it was just like all other babies. I couldn't feel like a mother no matter how I tried. That's why I think it's for the best that Bill maries again—he's already found someone else, you know—and he wants to take Billy and have more children too."

Joan listened but could not quite believe Ruth. Ruth was protesting too much, almost as if she were trying to convince herself that she really did not love her child. But Joan saw that Ruth was tearing her heart out over her baby and wondered what would really happen later if Ruth gave Billy up. Joan wished with all her heart that she might give Ruth a child to replace him. She thought of Marc and hoped for a brief moment that he had made her pregnant. But of course that was sheer fantasy. Another baby would only aggravate and complicate the difficult situation. Joan's gift to Ruth would have to be some sort of child of the mind—a growing usefulness shared by both of them which they could leave to the world together.

Joan contemplated Sappho and Shakespeare and rolled over to sleep. Ruth's knees, fitting comfortably behind her own, and Ruth's entire form, molded in the same direction, cradled and warmed her.

Mark woke them cruelly at ten. "Check out time's in a half hour," he shouted through their door. Joan groaned. She nudged Ruth, who sprang up out of a dream, and the two walked, half asleep, to the bathroom and brushed their teen. In twenty minutes they were dressed.

Joan looked at Ruth. She seemed different. "You look strange," she said.

"I'm wearing lipstick," Ruth smiled. It was the first time she had worn makeup since Joan had met her.

"I don't really like it," Joan said, but followed Ruth's example herself. It was beginning—the adjustment. Ruth was beginning to worry that they looked too obvious. From now on they would wear makeup.

Now they opened the door for Marc and he introduced Jay standing with him; then the two men took the girls' suitcases and carried them to the car. The two girls sat in back—that might or might not seem an odd seating arrangement to others—and they drove off to find a place for breakfast.

Marc was about to avoid driving through Boston and they decided to eat on the road to Cape Cod. They stopped at a place called Polly's Tea Shoppe because Jay thought it looked so prim. "It looks like they have good waffles," he added. Marc had apparently told him to take it easy, Joan noticed, because Jay wasn't queening as usual. He could be very masculine when he tried.

"You know," Ruth mused, "being an old maid isn't going to be as bad as I thought. There's something pure about it."

"You'll never be an old maid," Joan countered. But she was glad Ruth had said that. It was a good sign.

"Have you decided what you're going to do after your divorce?" Marc asked Ruth at breakfast.

"I had planned to teach in college," Ruth said.

March seemed to have no trouble asking Ruth important questions. "Why don't you and Joan live together?" he continued. "She's got to finish up at N.Y.U. Maybe there's an opening there for you."

"Let's not discuss that now, Marc," Joan interrupted. Joan found it difficult to think of the future. She was afraid to let Ruth answer.

"I think it would be a good idea," Ruth said, looking at Joan.

"Let's not discuss it," Joan said again weakly. She dared not let herself hope. It was harder and harder to think of ultimately losing Ruth.

They reached Provincetown in the late afternoon and Jay directed them to housekeeping cabins on the edge of town that discreetly welcomed gays. Unpacked and settled in a half hour, they decided to eat out.

"There's a gay-owned place on the edge of the dunes," Jay suggested. He was the most familiar of all of them with Provincetown, strongly colonized by artists and gays, having taken a few weekend trips to it during Marc's absences. "Afterward we can visit the bards," he added cautiously.

"Let's not," Joan was quick to say. But Ruth displayed disappointment.

"I want to go," she said. "I've always wanted to see a gay bar."

The restaurant run by a bisexual couple on the edge of the dunes was a quiet out-of-the-way place with an elderly Negro pianist who played show tunes.

Ruth listened to the music seeming lost in thought. She would often ask that something be repeated because she had not heard it. This was disturbing to the three for they all understood the sign. Ruth was undergoing a struggle to decide between two worlds—and it was taking her away from both. Impulsively, Jay took Ruth's hand reassuringly. "don't try so hard," he said. "It'll be decided by itself."

Ruth responded and smiled. "It's nice to be among friends."

After dinner, the boys left them in front of the Jockey Bar and went their own way. A completely Lesbian bar wasn't of particular interest to Marc and Jay. Joan and Ruth entered bravely and then Joan sighed with relief because it was even more orderly than the Sun Dial and not at all like the Daisy.

They found a table and enjoyed the sea air that blew in through the bay windows on one side. The place was well lit, unlike the 'Dial, and its customers had the sunburned glow of health.

"Hi," a woman whom Joan did not at once recognize waved. And then Joan remembered her. It was Di, Gig's married friend. They headed toward her table, glad for a familiar face, and a joined her at Di's invitation.

"I'm so glad to see someone I know," Di said. "Is Gigi along too?"

"No," Joan said awkwardly, remembering that Gig had implied that they were going together. "Di, I'd like you to meet Ruth."

"Hello, Ruth," Di said lazily. "Do sit down, both of you."

Ruth and Joan sat, Ruth still quiet and observant. For her, this was all new and strange, perhaps thrilling. Joan was certain that Ruth had not fully realized until now how many other women were Lesbians. This particular crowd looked as normal as a bunch of college students and housewives, although in many instances more attractive. It was reassuring to Ruth.

"What brings you to Provincetown?" Joan asked Di.

"I drove up with my schmuck of a husband for the week," Di said. She winked at Joan as if she expected Joan to know all about her unsuccessful marriage. "What are you two kids doing here?"

"Sightseeing," Ruth answered before Joan could. Hearing that Di was married had made her pay attention to the conversation.

It became a tense moment for Joan—she remembered Di's accidentally becoming a mother. She wondered what meeting Di might mean to Ruth, and whether it would be upsetting.

"Where are you staying?" Di asked. "Perhaps we're neighbors."

"At the Cape Cabins," Joan said.

"Too bad," Di said. "We're at the other end of town."

The Jockey Bar was filling with couples and the lights were dimmed to prepare for the small all-girl band that was taking its place on the platform by the dance floor.

Di hailed the waitress and ordered Four Roses, straight; Joan and Ruth ordered mint juleps because neither had tasted them before.

"Does one dance here?" Ruth asked, quite surprised. She had not expected to find that this was like any other nightclub.

"One tries," Joan said snidely. Although she wanted to dance with Ruth she wanted to discourage her from doing so. She was very nervous about properly introducing Ruth to gay life. But Ruth turned on her comment.

"Joan, why have you been so damned patronizing all evening?" Part of her exasperation seemed to come from somewhere else, from a detached part of her personality.

"You know why," Joan answered blankly. She met Ruth's eyes and saw the conflict in them. "Would you like to dance?" she defied her.

"Why not?" Ruth stood and, with the same manner in which she had gone to play ping pong three nights before, she followed Joan to the dance floor.

Ruth was taller and forced Joan to follow her lead; she looked very butch on the dance floor with her athletic bearing. "What's so awful about two girls dancing?" she said as she led. "We do this every Saturday night in Vermont."

"It's different here," Joan said.

"Yes, I suppose so," Ruth sighed.

They did not dance very long, neither one of them finding relief in being so near and et so far from each other's flesh—in fact, bored because they could be doing better in private. When they returned to Di's table, they found another couple had joined her.

"This is Alice and Chris," Di introduced them, "Joan and—Ruth, isn't it?"

Ruth nodded and the two sat down again.

Alice and Chris were a refined couple with sensitive although not very attractive features, not at all in bearing like Barbie and Madge. Their diction betrayed a better education. They seemed out of place with Di, whose ultra sophistication showed edges of coarse breeding and social insecurity.

"Darlings, I hope you'll excuse me," Di said almost immediately, "I see someone I know." She left the table to rush after a very masculine older woman who had just sat down at another table with friends.

"I guess she's left us together," Chris smiled awkwardly. She was the thinner and taller of the two, although Alice, despite her more feminine features, had more assurance and vitality. Neither of them was distinctly butch or femme.

"Are you here for the summer?" Joan asked. She instinctively liked the two and hoped that they might become friends. There were no traces of the Yellow Page or the Daisy in their faces; they would be good for Ruth.

Joan paused in her thoughts and wondered why she was so desperate about protecting Ruth from gay life. Ruth had been right to lose her temper. Joan had been patronizing for two days, treating Ruth like some innocent minor. She wondered if guilt played a part in her behavior—for she felt responsible for Ruth's turning gay. But was she responsible? Hadn't Ruth sought her out, consistently taking the lead? Yet Joan felt responsible nonetheless.

"Yes, we have a bungalow near the dunes," Alice was answering Joan's question. "Why don't you visit us while you're here?"

The invitation was spontaneously hospitable and Alice paused at her own words. Then she said, "Chris is an architect and I'm usually left with little to do while she's at the drafting table. I'm a teacher."

"I'm a college student," Joan volunteered, then added, "Ruth hopes to teach." This started them off on an animated conversation to which Ruth contributed very little. But she was listening and observing, and a great deal of tension gradually disappeared from her face.

Chris and Alice had been roommates for six years and were

both certain it would last for life. They seemed still very much in love by the way that they held hands and in the way they spoke of one another. It was not a tense thing between them, not an *it's got to work or else* attitude. And they weren't demonstrative as Barbie and Madge who had seemed to be convincing themselves that theirs was a marriage on the same terms as man and wife. Chris and Alice were relaxed in their approach to love, life and the fact that each of them was a woman, no more and no less than the other.

The loudness of the music had begun to cut into their conversation and Chris looked up for a minute to see how Di had fared at the other table. She was desperately keeping up a conversation with the other woman and the waitress had just brought her another double Four Roses.

Chris frowned and bent over to speak to Alice. "Do you think we'd better get Di now?"

"Oh, let her have fun," Alice said, not paying attention. But then she turned and saw the situation and said, "Well, maybe we'd better."

Chris got up and went over to Di's table somewhat reluctantly.

"I'm terribly sorry," Alice said to Joan and Ruth. "We promised Di we'd be sure to get her home in good condition. Her husband doesn't really know about her, you see—that is, he doesn't want to know about it. So we're going to have to drive her home."

"That's a pity," Ruth said. "Will we see you two again?"

"Oh yes, that will be nice," Alice said. She paused and thought for a minute. "I have an idea. Why don't you two come with us? We'll see Di gets home and then you can come back to our house with us—unless you planned to stay here all evening."

"I think that's a fine idea," Ruth said, and Joan echoed her.

On their way back from Di's house everyone breathed with relief. Alice turned to face Joan and Ruth who were sitting in back. "I'll make us all some coffee and then we can go on with our conversation. We haven't given you two a chance to talk at all yet."

"You know, I'm glad we met," Ruth said, "very glad."

"It's practically impossible to meet gay people except at bars," Chris said as she drove. "I was saying that to Alice just before we met you two. We've been sitting home alone since the beginning of the season waiting for someone we know to drive up from New York."

"Finally Di came and dragged us out of our rut," Alice added. "I hope she doesn't have a hangover tomorrow. She's supposed to be entertaining her husband's boss and his wife."

"Di sounds as if she leads a hard life," Ruth said. "Why doesn't she get a divorce?"

"It's difficult at her age," Alice said. "She has no profession to support her, and then there's her baby."

"She has a child?" Ruth looked up. She was not really surprised; she seemed to have expected it.

"But that's not the basic problem," Chris interrupted. "Di's never trusted gay life. She's always kept her husband for security and some butch around for sex."

"Honey, don't be coarse," Alice said. "It's not Di's fault, really." She looked at Ruth and Joan again. "There's the old myth that women can't get along without men. Di's been brought up on that all her life."

"Men do make better salaries than women," Ruth commented.

"You're not telling me," Chris agreed. "I had to strike out on my own because no firm would hire women architects. The best jobs are always saved for men with the excuse that they have families to support.

"Chris and I are old-fashioned feminists," Alice said, half jokingly.

They reached their bungalow which was surprisingly near Ruth's and Joan's. This prompted Ruth to say, "Why don't you two walk over for breakfast tomorrow?"

There was a flurry of mixed conversation as they entered and then Chris went to help Alice in the kitchen and Ruth and Joan were left alone in the living room. They walked to the windows that faced the beach.

"Are you happy, darling?" Joan asked.

Ruth turned to look at her, her face still serious. She had not really smiled for hours. "I'm a jumble of emotions," she said.

Joan moved to stand near her and dropped her head on Ruth's shoulder, enjoying the feeling of closeness. Intense feeling was growing inside her despite all the uncertainty about Ruth. It had become almost impossible to think of life without Ruth now—or to remember a past which had been lived without her. Joan had not realized that real love could come so spontaneously and so completely. That she had been too quick to say she loved Kim made her feel ashamed—she had no way of knowing then that real love was a thing this encompassing. Kim. Joan thought of her for a moment and knew that even if Ruth left her and Kim returned, no similar relationship was possible. What Joan had felt with Kim wasn't true love. True love was Ruth, would always be Ruth.

"You know, Jay gave me some good advice," Ruth said, holding Joan fondly. "Everything will all be decided for me. I can see that now. I really have nothing to do with it. I can't change what's natural in me. The best I can do is try to repress it. And then someday I might grow to be what Di is, completely dependent on a husband I despise, with a child I don't want, sneaking off to attract some woman who wants no part of my mixed-up life."

"You'll never be like that," Joan said. "I can see you at forty going into politics or something just to get away from home. You'll sublimate it all and probably be the first woman President."

"Why bother," Ruth said, "when I can have the whole world just by being with you?"

She bent over and kissed Joan lightly on the lips.

"Does that mean you're in love with me?" Joan dared to ask.

"I have no right yet to say that," Ruth said. "I have nothing to offer you except confusion and a great feeling of guilt."

Ruth and Joan walked on the beach to their bungalow. They could see lights and knew that Marc and Jay were already home. "I suppose they're wondering where we are," Ruth smiled. With that smile, she became like her old self. The evening with Chris and Alice had somehow helped build the image of a new world for her. It was possible to live like normal human beings—just like everyone else; and Chris and Alice had proved it. Theirs had not been the strange twilight world that the blurbs of paperback novels described; Chris and Alice were living in the sun.

"How's the apartment situation in New York?" Ruth spontaneously asked.

"Fair," Joan said. "A lot of walking can find one."

They stopped and listened to the roar of the incoming tide. "What made you want to kiss me that first time?" now Joan asked. She had been reluctant before to question Ruth's feelings, knowing that searching her own motives was difficult for her.

"I think I was repeating what happened ten years ago," Ruth said. "I must confess, Joan, that then you meant nothing more—were nothing more to me than a symbol. You were Marc's wife and therefore you had to be a Lesbian, or at least know about homosexuals. It was my desperate attempt to communicate with you."

"How deeply I can understand that," Joan said meaningfully.

They reached their front porch and quietly went inside. "Thank God, you're back," Marc said. "We were just going to go look for you."

"We met some nice people," Ruth said. "They're coming over for breakfast."

It wasn't long before everyone decided to go to bed. Joan and Ruth took the bedroom that faced the ocean. Marc had insisted; he was being romantic about what he now called their honeymoon.

"I feel we don't really know each other," Ruth said when they were alone. "Could we talk all night?"

"You talk; I'm tired," Joan said, sleepily lying down.

Ruth sat next to her and began to rub her back. "Do you know about fairy tales?" she said. "I used to devour them as a child, but I was always the prince. I especially liked Sleeping Beauty."

"Then kiss me," Joan chided, turning to face her.

Ruth meant to kiss her lightly but Joan held her lips with her own and made the kiss a passionate, arousing thing.

"Stop," Ruth laughed. "Here I am, trying to mate our minds for once."

"All right, talk to me," Joan said. She rested her head on Ruth's lap. "But if you lean over me with those lovely breasts, it'll be at your own risk!"

Chris and Alice arrived for breakfast at noon. Ruth cooked, and when Joan tried to help, she was shooed out of the kitchen. There wasn't enough room for all of them around the table so they spread out buffet fashion in the living room.

"What grade do you teach," Jay asked Alice.

"Third and fourth," Chris answered for her. "She's in one of those tough schools you've heard about."

"Do you mean you work with juvenile delinquents?" Jay said, quite interested.

"Some," Alice said. "My classes seem to behave for the most part."

"Do you have any problem about being gay and being a teacher?" Ruth asked as she served the scrambled eggs.

"Do you mean about being found out? Some," Alice said.

"Not exactly," Ruth said. "I mean, do you worry that your being gay might in some way corrupt your students? So much talk is always going on about the corruption of minors . . . "

"And just what would I want with a minor?" Alice laughed, taking hold of Chris' hands.

"What I mean is—by just their being exposed to you. Some people think homosexuality is contagious that way—subliminal influence, and all that."

There was a silence for a while and then Chris spoke. "Alice's classes develop less behavior problems and learn more than any other teacher's in her school. Her principal commended her at the end of last term."

"Ruth is concerned about becoming a teacher herself," Joan defended her.

"I think Ruth should indeed be concerned," Jay said. "I think we all should be concerned. Maybe it's particularly up to us to see that children develop into happy and useful adults, not bar hops or drug addicts or unmarried mothers. We know consciously and more than most what it's like to have what seems an unanswerable problem and how easy it is to feel desperate. And if some kids seem unavoidably inclined toward homosexuality, then it's also up to us to make things easier if we can."

"How would you go about doing that?" Ruth asked.

"Alice can tell you the part she plays," Chris said before Jay could answer. They turned to let Alice speak.

"It's funny, but I swear you can pick them out even at that tender age," Alice smiled. "I have a sweet little kid in Four-A right now. She won't wear anything but boys' clothes. She's the youngest of a Puerto Rican family and she gets hand-me-downs from her brothers. She goes around saying she's a boy. I'm sure she's not really gay, but she's mad at the world for having made her a girl. Her mother's a prostitute, I suspect."

"What are you doing about it?" Ruth asked.

"I gave her a project," Alice answered. "She's directing the class play, and has also been made poet laureate for the assembly period. It's done wonders for her socially."

"Would that prevent her from turning gay?" Marc asked.

"I don't know whether it will or not," Alice wrinkled her forehead in concern, "but it certainly might prevent her from turning into one of those bull-dikes who hang around the Daisy."

"Wouldn't a heterosexual teacher have done the same thing?" Ruth asked.

"Perhaps," Alice answered, "and perhaps not. She might have ridiculed the child instead to make her wear dresses. That happened to me when I was ten."

"Well, we can see that it didn't work," Jay laughed. "You know," he went on, again serious, "it's amazing how many things people try doing to prevent homosexuality—but there is no rule that seems to work. Sometimes I think homosexuality is like Topsy—it just growed." He laughed at his own line and the others joined in.

"How about going to the beach?" Marc stretched and changed the subject. Everyone but Ruth assented.

"Why don't you people go on ahead?" Ruth said. "I should really drive to the supermarket to get the rest of the shopping done." She had a dull, pensive look on her face that discouraged them from trying to change her mind.

"Do you mind if I go with you?" Joan said, hoping that Ruth would not mind.

"I guess you can help carry groceries," Ruth smiled. She was still being cold but it was more toward the whole company than to Joan. The others took their cue and left.

"What's the matter?" Joan asked when they were alone.

"I couldn't hear myself think," Ruth dismissed the question. She gathered the breakfast dishes and piled them in the sink, still with the same withdrawn look on her face. Efficiently she washed and stacked them to dry then, finally, broke the silence. "I'm sorry if I'm so damned moody," she said.

"It does seem like a horrible world, doesn't it?" Joan answered.

"All of life is hideous," Ruth said. "I'm fighting a dreadful premonition about today."

Joan laughed. "Do you think they're going to drop the hydrogen bomb?" Then she became serious. "Are you trying to tell me you want to go back to Bill?"

Ruth looked at her a moment, studying Joan's face and her eyes. Her own face softened. "Come here," she said.

Joan went to her and let Ruth take her in her arms, holding on tightly, afraid to lose her.

"Do you think I feel any better with the country club back home?" Ruth said. Her voice was tender and her embrace reassuring. "When Bill goes out in the sun he gets a red, leathery complexion and every hair on his arms shows. He sweats and he smells of sweat and his beard is rough and scratchy." She lifted Joan's chin now and kissed her lightly. "When you play in the sun your skin turns ripe like a peach and soft as silk. You don't sweat—you perspire, and it's the odor of the woods and flowers. How could I possibly prefer Bill to you?"

Joan instinctively knew what Ruth meant and a great feeling of relief shot through her. Ruth was as much a Lesbian as Joan. It wasn't just the fact that men were of another sex but that they were completely different, beings somehow totally alien from themselves. This was the true test—the contrast and comparison between men and women was so drastically clear that not even the handsomest of the male could compare with the homeliest of the female. Men's flesh was firm, not soft; their odor sour, not sensual; and the taste of their lips was acid, not achingly, familiarly sweet. For all women this might not be the case. To Lesbians it was so and irrevocably so, despite psychoanalysis, despite social disapproval, often despite themselves—as Ruth had shown when she tried to live with a man.

"There's something else," Ruth said. "I feel as though I've only been half alive until the last few days. It's as though I've finally found the spectrum in which reality and the world appear in more than one dull shade. I'm finally seeing the color of life. Now that I know what living is really like, I can't go back to that other halfway world. I could never go back to a man, not any man. I think if it were a choice between doing that and dying, I'd choose death." She stopped and her face was deeply serious. "For the first time in my life I think I'm feeling love."

It was said, and it had been said so quickly. An infinity of barriers had crumbled. The momentum of the crash flung them together in a kiss that was passionate and free. They were one being and all fear of the other's mind and soul was gone from each.

Finally the broke apart. "I should call Bill," Ruth said. "I should tell him that I'm going to New York instead of back to Vermont."

For a moment both of them were giddy with joy. Ruth's call would make them free, would allow them to live only for each other. They started toward the main house and the pay phone, then Joan halted. "What about Billy?" she asked. That stopped the dream and Ruth's face grew serious once again.

"I guess things are never that easy," she said. "I'll have to go back and see things through. I've got to be sure Bill's new wife will want Billy; otherwise—"

"Otherwise we'll have to keep him," Joan finished. "I understand other Lesbian couples have brought up perfectly normal children," she added, trying to be light. Then she sighed. "I suppose two mothers are better than none at all—or half of one. Your trying to bring Billy up alone might make you too unhappy to love him properly." Joan was saying that because she wished it to be so, and in its way it held some logic. But there was always the conventional opinion—that it was wrong for homosexuals to bring up children. "Have you met Bill's mistress?" she asked, changing the subject.

"Only in passing," Ruth answered. "She's a sweet young thing. I don't think there's anything to worry about, except perhaps her brain. She didn't seem too bright." She sighed wearily. "I suppose I'd better call home anyway and see if everything's all right."

They walked to the main house hand in hand, their feelings a mixture of happiness and tension. Then Ruth nervously made her call. Mrs. Reed answered her ring. "Hello? This is Ruth Baker. I just wanted to be sure there were no problems with Billy."

"He's fine, Mrs. Baker," Joan heard Mrs. Reed answer. She pressed close to Ruth to hear both ends of the conversation. "He ran a little temperature last night, but the doctor said it wasn't serious."

"Then it's all right now," Ruth tensed then relaxed. "I shouldn't drive back, should I?"

"No, I'm sure there's no worry," Mrs. Reed's assuring voice said.

Bill cut in suddenly. "Ruth, is that you?" His voice was very upset. "Damn your leaving now. What kind of a mother are you, anyway? Billy ran a high fever all night."

"high fever! But I didn't know." Ruth was upset again. "I'd better come home."

"No, don't bother," Bill said sarcastically. "Doris and I sat up with him. He's over the crisis."

"Then you don't want me back, is that ?" There was hurt in her voice, but not because of Bill's rejection. Joan saw how much it meant to Ruth to feel herself a responsible mother.

"It's obvious you don't care enough to come back," Bill said, "or you wouldn't have left Billy like that."

"Now, wait a minute," Ruth had taken enough. "I told you where I was going and you agreed that Mrs. Reed could take care of him. You're forgetting that I saw Billy through the measles and whatnot all year without your help."

"Well, you won't have to be burdened anymore," Bill said. There was mean bitterness in his voice. Then it became matter-of-fact. "We don't want you back, Ruth. Doris can take care of Billy. I wouldn't want my son exposed to a woman like you." He clicked the receiver down.

Ruth's hands were shaking as she finally hung up.

"What did he mean by that?" Joan asked.

"He meant about us," Ruth said. "I told him about us before I left. I felt it was the only fair thing to do."

11.

THEY left the main house in a state of shock. Ruth said, "I need a drink." Joan suggested that they stop at a bar on their way to buy groceries. "But only one drink," she added, "because I have to drive."

They took the car and drove into the town proper. They walked to the Jockey Bar because it was a place they both knew.

In the daytime, the Jockey Bar did not seem to be the same place it had been at night. Only those inevitable strange few who preferred the darkness of an air-conditioned club to the bright heat and sunlight of the beach were sitting on stools, hunched over their drinks. Joan recognized with discomfort one of the two butches Gig had spoken to at the beach—the taller butch with the tattoo, who was now very drunk. Joan looked with concern toward Ruth. The Jockey Bar was not the sort of place to cheer her up. But Ruth had already sat down at the bar and Joan had to sit next to her. Ruth ordered a scotch and water and Joan asked for a ginger ale.

"What kind of a drink is that?" the tattooed butch commented from the other end of the bar. She had recognized Joan and was trying to start a conversation. Joan ignored her. "How's Gigi?" the butch spoke up again. "I don't know," Joan answered reluctantly, hoping to discourage more talk. She turned again toward Ruth who was downing her scotch with a look of disgust. "How do you feel now, darling?"

"Remind me never to order scotch here," Ruth said, taking one more swallow and then putting her drink down. "Let's go."

She put money on the bar and they walked out into the sunlight again, heading in no particular direction, still trying to lose the tension aroused by the phone call.

"That was a hell of a place to go to," Ruth said after a while. Joan realized it would be best to drop the matter.

In a few minutes they turned toward the supermarket and there efficiently bought what they needed. The task helped them forget for a moment.

"My God," Ruth said when they were back in the car, "that means I might never see Billy again. He's going to grow up to hate his real mother." The thought filled her not with grief but with anger, anger at Bill for his betrayal. For betrayal it was: Ruth had been honest about herself and Joan; she had never condemned Bill for Doris, yet now he condemned her for Joan. She had been willing to let Billy go without a fight until now, but now she was sorely tempted to fight for her baby. Bill had made her angry; what he said had been untrue and unfair.

Ruth started the car with determination and drove at a rigid speed back toward their cabin. "I'm going to fight," she said.

"No, you can't fight," Joan stated blankly. "You'll lose and so will everyone close to you."

"No judge in the world would give Billy to Bill and Doris," Ruth said.

"No—but he wouldn't give Billy to you, either," Joan said. "Can't you see? It would be a bloody court battle and Billy would only lose both parents."

"They reached the cabin and Ruth came to an abrupt halt. "I guess you're right," she sighed. She was beaten and they sat in the convertible for a moment recovering. "Damn the world,"

Ruth finally said. "Damn this awful stupid world!"

Joan touched Ruth's arm and Ruth recoiled. "No, please don't touch me. Just leave me alone for a while." She got out of the car and brought the groceries to the cabin; she said nothing more.

Automatically they dressed to join the others at the beach, simply because there was nothing else to do. Joan watched Ruth silently putting on her bathing suit and felt that they were again far apart. She wondered if Ruth could ever forgive her for the loss of Billy—for it had been on her account, in a crazy mixed-up way. Long after Ruth had forgotten Bill's insult she would remember that if not for Joan she would have kept her baby. She would not remember that she had planned to give up Billy before Joan had even appeared. But through Joan she had been taken from an acceptable life and brought into a strange, new and frightening world; only this would Ruth remember. Joan wondered what she could do, what sacrifice she could make to clean the slate between them, to make Ruth forget Billy.

Dressed in their bathing suits, they got into the car again, drove down to the public beach and walked to the gay section on the end where the crowd had gone. They found them all happily lying on blankets and eating frankfurters bought at the refreshment stand.

"Hi, join the mob," Jay hailed them. Ruth and Joan walked over silently and as silently sat on the corner of the blanket.

"What's the matter with you two?" Marc asked.

"Ruth had an argument with Bill," Joan explained briefly.

Chris and Alice came back from the water's edge to greet them. "There's a grounded devilfish down there," Chris said, "four feet long."

"It's only a skate," Jay corrected her. "Let's go look at it." He got up; Joan and Ruth followed him, like sheep, to the edge of the breakers. "Ugly, isn't he?" Jay commented. He cautioned them to watch out for its tail.

The ragged breakers were menacingly close, and the presence of the devilfish made the whole scene more frightening. The power of the ocean made itself felt very strongly to all of them. Only Ruth turned away and walked along by the water's edge.

Joan watched her with concern.

Jay stuck a stick at the edge of the skate's open stomach that contracted and retracted like a large Cyclops' eye. "It's first cousin to a shark," he said. But Joan wasn't watching the skate. Ruth had gone into the water.

"What's the matter?" Jay asked.

"Ruth's gone swimming," Joan said. "It looks awfully rough. I'm going in after her." She left Jay without another word, her eyes on Ruth who was expertly cutting through the breakers on her way to deep water.

"Ruth, wait!" Joan shouted from the shore. "I'll swim with you." But Ruth did not turn around.

For a moment Joan was afraid to go into the turbulent water. She had never swum in open ocean and knew nothing about fighting currents or giant waves. But she had to reach Ruth. An unreasoning conviction overwhelmed her—Ruth intended more than a mere swim.

Joan took a deep breath and rushed against the waves, only to find herself submerged and then flung back on the beach. Jay reached her but she got up determinedly and rushed forward again, this time riding a wave and reaching the second line of breakers. Swimming was easier and she shouted above the water for Ruth to wait. But Ruth was already quite a distance out in deep water.

Joan followed her, straining muscles against the icy current that fought to pull her in another direction. Fatigue caught her almost immediately but she kept on after Ruth. Whenever she could she shouted Ruth's name, and the water splashed in her face and mouth. She seemed to gain ground and they were only a hundred feet apart, but Ruth did not hear her. From the beach came the shrill sound of a lifeguard's whistle—they were dangerously far from shore.

"Ruth, turn back!" Joan shouted again and then wrackingly coughed out more water. Her arms were exhausted and she tried to kick more with her feet—then the water suddenly became unbearably cold and she doubled over with a cramp. She fought to keep her head above water, panic stricken, and gurgled a call for help. She was sinking, fighting the cramp that twisted her persistently in two. Her arms waved helplessly above her head and her good leg tried to kick her up to the surface but it was hopeless, and her air was going. Dizziness began to cloud her brain and she stopped struggling, holding on to the last bit of precious air.

"So this is how it ends," she thought. She felt a dreadful anger at the sheer waste of it. She wanted to live, and she wanted Ruth to live. She thought a moment of the crowd on shore, and of Marc and Jay, felt sorry for them and for her parents. Her air was gone and she ached to exhale, but still she held her lungs full, knowing how awful water in her lungs would be. "This is a terrible way to die," she thought.

Her cramp was gone, but it was too late. She had no strength to surface, and she was blacking out. With a final burst of life she though of Ruth and wished Ruth were at least here with her, not drowning in some other part of the ocean. Then, as if she were dreaming it, she felt Ruth's body pull her close and Ruth's hand under her chin. Ruth had come, and she was pulling them both up, back into the air. Joan relaxed and exhaled.

There was such a little distance between life and death. Only the matter of a few feet to the surface. Ruth held Joan afloat, both of them coughing too violently to speak. Lifeguards were coming toward them with a boat. They allowed themselves to be pulled up and rowed into shore, still coughing and breathing the air that now seemed very precious. No explanations were asked of them. One lifeguard said sternly, "You're lucking you're both alive." Then the men went back up the beach to their posts.

"What happened?" Marc asked as he came to them.

"Joan got a cramp," Ruth replied. They were holding hands and Ruth, exhausted, pulled Joan's head to her shoulder. "You little idiot," she said softly. "You thought I was going to kill myself."

"Weren't you?" Joan asked guiltily.

"Why should I do a stupid thing like that? I was just working off steam over Bill," Ruth said.

"All's well that ends well," Jay said. He and Marc handed

each girl a frankfurter and a cup of coffee and wrapped them both in blankets while Joan looked sheepishly at Ruth who was obviously much amused. But something had happened to both of them out in the water. They were changed. They were in love again.

Chris and Alice noticed it first. "Say, the two of you should be alone," Alice said. "Marc let the cat out of the bag. Why didn't you say you were honeymooning?"

"I thoroughly agree," Jay said. "I think we should send them off on a drive somewhere. There's a whole lot of the Cape they haven't seen."

Ruth smiled at Joan. "Want to go on a long drive?"

"It might be fun," Joan shivered, "if I can ever warm up again."

Ruth laughed and got up, pulling Joan up with her. "Come on, we'll go back and change. There's a lighthouse a few miles back we can look at."

They said goodbye to the company and went to the car. Two minutes later they were back at the cabin and Ruth helped Joan out of her wet suit.

"I should really be angry at you for pulling that dramatic bit," Ruth said, watching Joan's pitiful shivering. "But I can't seem to think of anything except how glad I am that I finally heard you and saw you go down. When I went after you I was determined either to save you or drown trying to save you. That's how much you mean to me." Ruth held her close and made Joan stop shivering.

"I'm glad the lifeguards came in time," Joan said. She put her arms around Ruth's neck. "It was foolish of me to have thought you might try suicide. I should have known you were too sane for that. What's wrong with me? I could have killed both of us!"

"I think we'd both better trust each other," Ruth said, pressing her close with both hands.

They dried themselves and changed clothes, taking jackets along in case they would be gone past sundown. They kissed again and left the cabin for the car. They were going to the little lighthouse Ruth had spotted, going there because it was as good a place as any to be alone, away from people they knew.

"Why don't we eat dinner out?" Ruth suggested. "I'm dying for some lobster." Joan agreed. It was so wonderful to be free of the crowd for a while.

They reached the lighthouse and stared at it blankly, taking in the white cleanliness of its walls against the pure blue sky. The air was cool and clear here and the ocean not so frightening because of its distance from the cliffs where they stood.

"You know, I think this could go on forever," Ruth said. She took Joan's hand and they walked back to the car.

They ate at a roadside inn that looked out on the ocean. "I'm dying to go back to New York with you," Ruth said. "I want us to find an apartment right away. This vacation's too much like being a gypsy." There was a desperate eagerness in her voice. Ruth hadn't stopped talking since they left the lighthouse. "Joan, I've got to feel I belong somewhere that's real."

Joan took Ruth's hand across the table and squeezed it hard. "You belong with me," she said in her firmest tone. "There's nothing more real in the whole world."

She suddenly discarded her seriousness. "What kind of furniture shall we buy?" She folded her paper napkin and made a square on it with her pen. "Let's plan our living room."

They couldn't afford rent over a hundred, they agreed, and they had to have two rooms. What about Joan's parents? Wouldn't they object to Joan's living with Ruth? What excuse could they give? Joan thought of using Marc, and then decided that would only complicate matters. She would tell her parents that living with Ruth would save on rent. If worst came to worst she would get a part-time job and pay her own way through college. She wouldn't mention the marriage to Marc unless her parents tried to force her to leave Ruth—that was one advantage to her marriage; her parents no longer had a legal say in her life. That could prove a valuable asset. "I don't suppose there'll be much trouble," she added. "I'll be twenty-one in fourteen months."

They talked for a while about Ruth's finding work. She was certain there would be no problem. She could teach, and if there wasn't a teaching job immediately available, her background in statistics could get her an executive position just about anywhere.

That took care of practically every immediately important topic. There was still the matter of Joan's telling Kim, however. Joan didn't look forward to that job, but it would have to be done as soon as possible. Her one consolation—a comfort despite the heartbreak of Kim's note—was that Kim had never fully cared for her.

"Why don't we take the train back tomorrow morning?" Ruth said. "We can leave the car with Marc and Jay until they're ready to drive back."

It was settled. They were going back. An air of serious responsibility seized both of them as they left the restaurant. This was their life, they had chosen it, and it was going to go on through their private small eternities, for better or worse. Those vows had meant nothing when Ruth had married Bill and when Joan had married Marc, but now, unspoken, they mattered as much as life itself to each of them, to these two women in love.

When they drove back it was already dark. The crowd was toasting marshmallows in front of the cabin.

"Had dinner yet?" Marc hailed them. "We saved a steak for you."

"Yes, we have," Joan said, but the steak was too tempting and they decided to have a second dinner.

When they had nearly finished their second meal, Marc took Joan aside and asked her to walk a while with him. "Hey, Joanie, how about a walk?" he had said, and the look on his face was serious. Joan put down her plate and left Ruth for a minute.

"How's everything?" he asked as they walked along.

"Fine," Joan said. She had little to report. There was still confusion in her mind, confusion and fear. She was very seriously in love with Ruth and, having won her, she was afraid to lose her—Ruth, who was so strange and beautiful and who was ten years older. Joan knew she couldn't possibly give Ruth all the things she had been accustomed to having since her childhood. In New York there was no rambling estate or well-furnished mansion, no cool brook to leap into. Joan's furnished room hardly resembled what Ruth had left behind. And yet there was the strong hope still clinging—the hope that flared in Joan when she saw Ruth's eyes look at her fondly—that perhaps their love could make up for the lack of expensive setting.

But was Ruth really in love with Joan? Or was she just in love with Lesbians? Ruth had no other experience with women. Joan could compare Ruth to Kim and Gig and find her deliciously superior. But Ruth had no criteria for Joan. If Ruth went to the Sun Dial, would she find herself attracted to ten others? Everything had happened so quickly between Ruth and Joan. Joan feared it would end with the same speed once Ruth met someone else.

"What do you two plan to do?" Marc broke her silence. He seemed to want to discuss something important.

"We ere going to tell you that we planned to go back to New York tomorrow," Joan said, "if it's all right with the two of you. We'll leave the car and you can follow us later."

"I guess that'll be fine," Mark said. "We thought you might want to be alone. But I meant after that—are you thinking of finding an apartment? Jay and I have been talking and I think we've come up with a pretty good idea. Why don't we all live together and have a real crazy family?" His eyes were blinking with eagerness now. "we'll be able to pool rent on a really extravagant layout that way. What do you say? Would you like to live with your husband?"

Joan thought for a moment. On the surface Marc's idea was quite practical. But then she remembered how irritable she became in large groups, especially where there were men present, and how even now Ruth and she were going back to New York early to be alone, to grow closer to each other. "I'll take it up with Ruth," Joan said, "but I don't think either one of us wants to. I'm sorry, Marc." She noticed his disappointment and put her hand on his. "You know, it's refreshing to have a husband who's also a good friend."

Marc brightened immediately and smiled. "Thanks. Actually, I guess it wouldn't be such a good idea. It might have been for Jay and me because we love to camp it up, but you girls are always more serious than we are. Joan—" He stopped and found the rest difficult to say. "I've been meaning to thank you about the other night. You don't know what it's meant to me to find out—about women, I mean. All my life I've worried that I've been a coward—that I've just been afraid to sleep with a girl. Now I know it was more than that. It all goes much deeper. I realize that I can never be anything but gay—that if I had tried living a normal life with you, or any woman, I'd have grown to hate her. I guess that's the way you've always felt about men, isn't it?"

"Yes," Joan said blankly. She felt impatient. She didn't want to remember that night. It had filled her with great disgust—not because Marc had been worse than any other man—in fact, next to Jay he had been best—but because she had realized that if their love-making had succeeded, it would have meant spending the rest of her life with Marc—and the thought of spending the rest of her life with any man sent a wave of rebellion through her entire being.

They walked back to the others then, pointing at constellations as they went, happily taking in the beauty of the night.

Joan stopped and looked at Ruth who had finished her steak and was trying her luck with a hot marshmallow that insisted on dropping off the wrong side of her fork.

"Hey, how about going to bed?" Joan asked softly.

Ruth looked up and smiled. Her mouth was sensuously narrow, her eyes full of the stars. "Sure," she said.

They stood, sensing that they didn't have to excuse themselves, and said goodnight to the others. Then they were alone in the cabin and the whole scene changed again. Ruth, lovely Ruth, standing there, lazily, running a finger across the table, half looking at Joan, her graceful body laughing at a silent joke. Joan was laughing quietly too. She closed the door and leaned on it. "Ruth, do you love me? You've never really volunteered the information."

"No, I haven't," Ruth said. "Do you mind if I'm so slow about these things?"

"No, as long as you're sure," Joan smiled. She went to Ruth

who put her arms around Joan's waist and kissed her. It was still so right, so exquisite to be kissing each other.

"I want you to tell me all about yourself," Ruth said, sitting on the bed and taking off her clothes to prepare to shower. "I've told you about me and now I want to know more about you. You know, I'm really very insecure. Being an ancient twenty-nine I worry about you, Joan—I worry that someone as young as you are might lose patience with an old woman like me."

"I like your being older than I am," Joan said. "It makes you more a person than any other woman I've known."

"That's because I'm not tottering yet," Ruth laughed. "But what about when you're twenty-nine and I'm nearing forty?"

"We'll both be twice the people we are now," Joan said. "I think I'll love you twice as much."

Ruth yawned and stretched, "Well, at least we'll have ten years to adjust to growing older." She had taken off her clothes and now went into the shower. Joan decided to follow her in. They stood together under the cool water and their bodies felt accustomed to being close.

"It seems the only things we've done since we've met is go swimming and take showers," Joan laughed.

Ruth laughed too. "Have I told you what I thought of you that time in the brook?"

"No, what did you think?" Joan asked, slightly embarrassed by the memory of that important day.

"I thought you were the most beautiful naked woman I had ever seen. I wished that I could sketch and had brought a pad and pencil. What did you think of me?" Ruth reached over Joan for the soap and Joan caught her lips for a moment.

"I wondered if your breasts still had milk in them," she chuckled. "Now I know."

Ruth laughed self-consciously. "How I tortured you that afternoon. I was doing it on purpose, you know. I was determined to seduce you. But you refused to make the first move, so I had to."

"I'm glad you did." Joan came very close to Ruth and the water trickling down their bodies filled them both with desire.

They could wait no longer. They embraced and kissed and Ruth felt for the faucet and turned it off. Then she gently lifted Joan and clumsily carried her out of the shower. Joan grabbed a couple of towels on the way out of the bathroom and wrapped one impishly around Ruth's head.

"What sort of hat is that?" Ruth laughed. She put Joan down in the middle of the floor and took the towel, half drying herself.

"Your skin is so white," Joan said. She grabbed Ruth's towel and finished drying her, all of her, and Ruth, in turn, took it back and dabbed Joan's breasts, her thighs, her back, as their arms and legs wound around each other again in an interminable, indefatigable full-bodied embrace.

The next morning Marc drove them to the ferry for Boston. This was the most direct route. From Boston they would take the train back to New York, ". . . and we'll join you in a few days," he said. "Who knows, maybe we'll find out more about each other, motel after motel, in that romantic convertible of yours."

Ruth laughed. "Don't try to do too much in one vacation."

Marc left them and again they were alone, on the ferry to Boston. Ruth and Joan dared to hold hands out in the open, looking out on the water, the water that only yesterday had been grim and nearly fatal. Now, as the ferry cut through it, leaving a clean white line of foam, it seemed beautiful and calm, incapable of treachery.

"I'm so glad we're alive," Ruth said. "Sometimes when I get angry I damn the world. But that has nothing to do with life. Life is something so special. I don't believe that it should be taken away, not from anyone or anything." She turned to face the headwind and the sun's rays fell on her golden hair. Joan thought her a beautiful vision against the blue sky.

"Have you always felt this way?" Joan asked, forcing herself to talk and not stare at Ruth like a love struck idiot.

"Not always," Ruth said. "There was a time when I wanted to die. There was a time when I was so unhappy, so confused and alone—Marc can tell you what a strange being I've always been." She stopped and looked seriously at Joan. "Didn't you think I was strange when you first met me? Don't you think I've changed considerably in the last few days?"

"It's hard to say. I didn't know you well enough before," Joan said.

"well, I have changed," Ruth smiled fondly. "I'm suddenly relaxed and happy. It's all because of you, Joan. I'm deeply grateful to have found you."

They noticed that they were being observed by several couples near them and so they walked up the boat toward the helm where there were fewer passengers. There they clasped hands again and absorbed the beautiful day.

The rest of the time on the boat and on the train to New York they talked about themselves in an effort to communicate all that they had ever thought and felt about their lives. Ruth told Joan of the time she built a tree house of her own, away from the one her father had built, and how she had stubbornly sat in it for hours because he had laughed at her attempt at carpentry. She showed Joan the scar on her leg from the gash she had gotten when the house finally had given way under her weight.

"I built a car out of a crate and an old baby carriage," Joan countered. "I rolled it down a hill and nearly crashed into a truck because I forgot the steering wheel and brakes."

They laughed. Their childhood had been so alike—both had been strong-willed and tomboyish children fighting a world, and parents, that tried to make them into girls.

When the ferry came close to the city Joan remembered Kim and lapsed into silence, again concerned with the problem of just how to tell her. Ruth saw Joan frown and asked her what was wrong.

Joan hesitated for a moment. Then she decided she should keep nothing back from Ruth, no fond memories of someone else, no silent problems. Slowly she told Ruth about Kim, about the way Kim had left things up in the air before Joan went to Vermont with Marc, and that now there could be no question of her choice. Kim was in the past. "And yet I feel she needs a friend," Joan concluded. "I'm afraid she's facing an awful lot alone. I wish we could help her."

Ruth smiled. "I feel I owe her something for having stolen you from her."

They decided to call Kim at camp as soon as they reached New York. Perhaps they could go up and see her on Sunday and somehow explain the situation. Joan was certain that Kim would understand and would wish them luck.

The train ducked into the long tunnel that led to Pennsylvania Station in New York. Each fought a sudden feeling of excitement and fear. At the end of the tunnel their life was beginning.

12.

WHEN they left the station, Ruth stopped to take in a deep breath of good old smog-filled New York air. "I haven't been here in two years," she said. "Smells great!"

Joan laughed and hailed a taxi to take them to her house.

"This is the same part of the Village I lived in!" Ruth exclaimed when they stopped on MacDougal Street.

"My room doesn't have a skylight," Joan warned her.

"Mine didn't either," Ruth said.

They got out and took their own baggage, too full of excitement to share their entrance with the cab driver. "I should carry you over the threshold," Joan volunteered but Ruth laughed. "Let's wait 'til we get upstairs."

One flight later, as Joan nervously unlocked her door, she remembered with horror that she hadn't cleaned before she had left with Marc. The bed was unmade and the ashtrays were full of Kim's cigarettes.

"Well, I'm waiting," Ruth said. She had put down her suitcases and stood with an impish smile on her face, waiting for Joan to carry her across the threshold.

Joan laughed and put her arms around Ruth's waist, raising her just far enough from the floor to carry her the few inches onto the rug. They kissed, sweetly, despite the open door.

After they had washed and rested for a while they decided to eat dinner in one of the coffee shops downstairs. They dressed in shorts for the occasion and chose the Gas House Café because it had a sign outside that said "Poetry Reading Tonight."

"I've always wanted to see the beatniks in action," Ruth said..

"They're just teenagers," Joan said. "The real beatniks have fled."

They entered the dark basement and sat at a small table and ordered hamburger plates, ignoring the coffee stains on their menus. Joan looked around to find familiar faces. Somehow she hoped to see someone she knew so that she might introduce Ruth. She wanted to absorb Ruth into her life, make Ruth a part of her past as well as her present. But there was no one she knew, just a lot of strangely dressed children. Then she saw Gig pop in at the door and wave. Joan waved back and motioned for Gig to join them.

"Hi, Red," Gig said, coming to their table. "Where have you been? I wanted to take you to the beach the other day."

"Please don't mention beaches," Joan laughed. "I almost drowned at one yesterday. I want you to meet Ruth. Ruth this is Gig."

Ruth and Gig nodded to each other and Gig inspected her carefully.

"Ruth and I are roommates," Joan said slowly, wanting to leave no doubt about what she meant.

Gig did a double take then a broad smile spread on her face. "Well, this calls for a celebration," she said. "As a matter of fact, when I saw you two duck in here I came after you. Barbie and Madge are having a party tonight and I thought you'd like to come."

Joan hesitated. But for no purpose—Ruth's acceptance was prompt; "I think that would be fun."

"But I thought you wanted to rest," Joan tried to cue her, afraid that even the best of the Daisy set might prove to much for Ruth to meet right now.

"But I want to meet your friends," Ruth said.

Joan could say nothing more so she turned to Gig. "All right, we'll drop in after dinner."

"Okay, see you then." Gig saluted and left the coffee shop.

Joan turned to Ruth with concern. "I think I ought to prepare you for Gig's crowd," she said. "They won't be like Alice and Chris."

"I didn't think they would be," Ruth said. "She's from the Daisy Bar, isn't she?"

"How did you know?" Ruth's knowledge of gay life surprised Joan.

"Every Villager knows the Daisy crowd," Ruth smiled. "At one time, seeing obvious Lesbians frightened me. But now it doesn't somehow—no woman frightens me anymore. I'm rather curious about the party tonight."

"I still wish we weren't going," Joan said. The thought of being with the Daisy set filled her with impatience. They were no longer quaint to her, only unbearably adolescent, like the crowd in the café.

"We'll only stay a little while," Ruth consoled her.

Gig's short visit had started a flurry of conversation behind them. An unshaven man who seemed to be of the of the owners of the coffee shop was making obscene remarks about her to two fifteen-year-olds with pony tails.

Ruth looked up angrily from her hamburger; Joan took her hand. "You'll have to get used to that," she said.

"I don't see why I should," Ruth said. "I don't see why I should at all." There was a flush on her face as she finished her dinner and she snapped a little at Joan.

"You'll get ulcers that way," Joan said.

"This whole nation will get ulcers if they let that go on," Ruth flared. "Hitler and Stalin both started on the homosexuals before they got around to persecuting other groups. I'll bet that man's a Communist." She turned around and said the last loudly, and it stopped the conversation in the coffee shop for a moment.

The unshaven man turned red and ignored her remark.

"Let's go," Joan said, throwing money on the table.

Outside, they tried to calm down but they were both shaking

with rage.

"Are you sure you can take this sort of life?" Joan asked her, trying to make Ruth laugh a little again.

"You're asking a D.A.R.," Ruth smiled. "What sort of a person would I be if I didn't have the guts to fight for the right to exist? It's a family tradition." She took Joan's arm and led her down the street. "Let's go meet your friends."

Madge opened the door when they knocked. The party was already in full swing, the apartment completely redecorated with red, white and blue banners. Only then did Joan remember that this already was the Fourth of July weekend.

"Come on in," Madge said.

There was a large crowd and the phonograph was playing. It looked like the Daisy without men—but the absence of men made it more pleasant and festive, unlike the professional atmosphere of the Daisy. Barbie came over and Joan introduced Ruth. Drinks were placed in their hands and they found a quiet corner of the floor and sat down, watching the two couples who were dancing expertly in the middle of the room.

"Hi," Gig said, coming out of the kitchen, a white apron over her slacks. She sat down next to them for a moment. "You don't mind if I announce your engagement, do you? We'll have a toast."

"It's not an engagement," Ruth corrected her, "it's a marriage."

"It's not a marriage yet," Gig countered. "Wait a few years before you say that."

Ruth looked at Joan and smiled, clasping her hand fondly. "I guess that's a good piece of advice. How about it, Joan? Do you think it'll last long enough to be called a marriage?"

"That depends on you," Joan smiled. "I'm helplessly in love."

"That depends on you, too," Ruth said. "I'm in the same

condition about you."

"Stop it—you two lovebirds are killing me!" Gig put her hands over her ears. She called for the music to be stopped and shouted for quiet. "I want to propose a toast to a couple of maniacs," she said. She raised her glass.

"To Ruth and Joan, who are no longer alone."

ArtemisSmith 1959

APPENDIX 2013

**COLLECTED PAPERS
IN THE
PHILOSOPHY OF SEX AND LOVE
UNDER THE
INFORMATION SCIENCES**

FUTURE SEX
HUMAN SEXUAL EVOLUTION BEYOND THE SPECIES LEVEL

by artemis smith

© 1969-1974 by ArtemisSmith. All rights reserved.

ABSTRACT

An alternate proposal to the present concept of human sexuality stressing human sexual evolution beyond the species level, subsumable under the modern trend toward the unification of science. It is argued that the modern shift in the concept of mind toward theories of information exchange leads to a reinterpretation of all conscious experience as the result of communications-exchange processes, and that this is continuous with the reinterpretation of all physiological phenomena as information-exchange phenomena, under the unification of science. Accordingly, human sexual behavior, as a subspecies of psychobiological behavior, is reinterpreted as a communications activity.

The sociological implications of this view are that sexual freedom may be held subsumable under present Constitutional guarantees covering higher forms of human communication. The evolutionary implications of this view are that human sexual activities, and the quality of the pleasure resulting there from, may extend well beyond the involvement of the natural sexual organs with which we are genetically endowed.[10]

---

[10] ArtemisSmith (Annselm L.N.V. Morpurgo, M.A., APPA-CPC) has an M.A. in philosophy from The City College of the City University of New York and a CPC from American Philosophical Practitioners Association. She is a poet and multimedia artist working in epistemology toward the formulation of a new concept of mind utilizing information-science theory. As a science and medical writer, she has covered work done on the split brain at Cal-Tech, and work on conscious processes done at Foundation for Mind Research by Masters and Houston. She has just presented a preliminary model of conscious behavior, including an information-science definition of consciousness, for the British Computer Arts Society at University of Edinburgh, Scotland, and an educational psychology paper for the 1973 ACM Urban Symposium in New York. She is artistic director of The Savant Garde Workshop and has been produced off-Broadway, has made films, has published novels and poetry. She has been an adjunct lecturer at Sarah Lawrence and CUNY:Queensborough Community College.

Introduction.

The object of this investigation is to arrive at a reformulation of the concept of human sexual identity adequate to meet the requirements of today's trend toward the unification of science. The moral revolution has also awakened the need for a new philosophy of sex which takes into account the human rights of women and the sexual minorities. In the revolt against the old morality, there has been too heavy a reliance on the scientific and medical professions to dictate what the new morality should be; while a conscientious job of doing so has been often performed by physicians and psychologists, questions about what is truly moral are best answered not by science alone but by science and the value theorist. In the past, mistakes have been made by scientists for lack of some central viewpoint - thus Freud, for example, evolved psychoanalytical approaches to both women and homosexuals which, though advanced and liberal for his time, were ruinous in psychotherapy. This paper is one of a series written from a central viewpoint on the nature of conscious processes, based upon an information-science concept of mind, designed to aid both the scientist and the legal theorist by providing them with some philosophical considerations relevant to theory of value in their own, 21st Century idiom. It is also a proposal, from a multimedia artist working in philosophy, for a new concept of human sexual identity.

I. The present concept of human sexuality.

The etymology of the word "sex" is from the Latin "sex(us)", akin to *secus, secare,* meaning to cut or divide. Its preferred lexical definitions are:

1. Either the male or female division of a species, *esp.*, as differentiated with reference to the reproductive functions. 2. The sum of the structural and functional differences by which the male and female are distinguished, or the phenomena or behavior dependent on these differences. 3. The instinct or attraction drawing one sex toward another or its manifestation in life or in conduct. 4. Coitus, *v.t.*

This common lexical definition is technically inaccurate from the standpoint of the life scientist who discerns in some lover, primarily bacterial, life forms more than two sexes (as much as ten!) involved in the reproduction cycle. It is also inadequate for the psychobiologist when considering behavior deviant from the normal behavior associated with structural and functional differences. If the objective of the categories "male," "female," etc., is to divide the species into subspecies solely according to reproductive functions, then terms such as "homosexual," "bisexual," have no meaning when applied to humans; but these terms do not have meaning for the biologist (it is incorrect to refer to amoeba as "homosexual," to flatworms as "bisexual," since amoeba engage in "fission" and flatworms are "hermaphrodites"). Despite the fact that an analogy of sexual deviance exists in lower animals, terms such as "homosexuality" are restricted to variance in human behavior involving sophisticated psychosociological functions above the reproductive functions (such as "love"), not clearly discernible in lower life forms.

Increasing psychobiological evidence that all mammalian sexual behavior is as much dependent upon chemical differences in the brain as it is upon the structural and functional differences in the reproductive organs has further rendered the primitive division along strictly external physiological lines highly arbitrary and, realistically, useless. The difficulty in drawing a clinical division raises the question whether any division according to "proper sex" in psychology and sociology is at all useful, and whether it would not be better to do away with sexual categories altogether in ordinary language.

Whereas in medicine the problem of who can and who cannot engage in a particular act of intercourse or reproduction is still an important though increasingly complex question (especially as sexual prosthesis in the form of surgery, test-tube incubation, or mechanical alternatives becomes perfected), the problem of isolating sex differences which are essentially relevant to sexual activity in humans would seem too technical a differentiation for everyday needs (I.e., to remind someone daily that they are male or female, "heterosexual." "homosexual," "bisexual," "asexual," "polysexual," etc., may soon be regarded as punctilious as reminding them daily that their blood type is Rh-negative or positive!).

A strong argument for retaining sexual distinctions in ordinary language is, however, that a consciousness of such distinctive characteristics is functionally related to the successful engagement in a sexual act. It is argued:

If sexual activity, now admitted to be a normal and beneficial physiological function, is to be engaged in regularly and with mutual satisfaction, an awareness of the sexual characteristics of both partners must be psychologically maintained on a frequent enough basis to permit sexual attraction and stimulation to occur.

It is further argued that thoroughly obliterating the difference between the sexes may lead to early sexual confusion resulting in a less-than-optimal sexual adjustment, thereby educating heterosexuals to become bisexuals or homosexuals.

But the question of what constitutes an optimal sexual adjustment is precisely the issue under investigation. It can seriously be counter-argued that the optimal sexual adjustment for one segment of the human population is detrimental to other segments, thus the educational problem is one not of teaching everyone to do one thing, but of enabling each to do "his own thing."

For the purpose of our investigation, however, we will assume that an awareness of the sexual characteristics of both partners is a necessary condition for the proper performance of a sexual act. What we wish to inquire is precisely which characteristics are to be isolated as distinctly "sexual."

a. The problem of sexual objectification.

The problem of isolating objects, events, syndromes, qualities, from the environment is an epistemological one. It has two stages:

i. the classification of "raw data" from the periphery of perceptual reception into alternate, hypothetical and cursory categories, each of which represents an equipossible interpretation of given data; and
ii. experimentation with alternate hypotheses and selection of successful categories.

The activity of (i.) is perceptual, the finished products of (ii.) are concepts. Objects are differentiated and recognized by this process, and regulate the formation of concepts.

Sexual differentiation in lower animals is a perceptual, not a conceptual, activity (i.e., dogs do not ask each other whether they are male or female, they "sniff each other out" and then react according to their chemical determinations). An analogy of sexually deviant behavior in lower animals does not occur because some dogs or pigeons have "homophile" feelings - that is, not because they happen to fall in love - but because of some gap in their perceptual activity, either innate or acquired through frequent proximity to members of the same sex. Thus, two male dogs who would normally quarrel may acquire tolerance and even "friendship" for each other. Such perceptual gaps may even occur interspecially: cats may become attached to mice, dogs may make sexual advances to people, etc. It seems ridiculous to regard such perceptual confusion as sexually deviant behavior. While there is certainly some conceptual behavior occuring in lower mammals, sexual neuroses involving moral conflicts are difficult (though not impossible, in the case of "shame" in dogs, and more notably in chimpanzees) to instill.

In the human case, our recognition of sexual difference seems to proceed almost totally through the application of concepts learned by rote and imported without the use of perceptual examples. (Thus, we get our fingers slapped when, as infants, we attempt to explore ourselves or our siblings; anatomical differences are hidden from us by clothing and sexual differences are reintroduced as differences in attire, social roles, grammatical inflections.) If sexual deviance is a learned rather than a natural form of behavior, improper concept-formation is its cause and notoriously improper concept-formation more frequently occurs when perceptual reinforcement, in the form of actual clinical experience with the objects talked about, is not provided. (Thus doctors, lawyers, carpenters do not become competent practitioners until some internship is undergone.) Only in the case of naturalists (i.e., some nudists) does sexual differentiation occur in the order of perception-conception, and there seems to be little problem among such naturalists about sexual confusion.

If the above are plausible assumptions, it would seem to follow that as the sociological picture becomes more "unisexual" due to the need to insure sexual equality for everyone in the society, the obliteration of artificial means for sexual differentiation must be accompanied by greater opportunity for direct perceptual differentiation to take place - if we want children to develop their natural sexual preferences. This may not insure a completely heterosexual society, however.

b. What is undesirable sexual objectification?

It can be argued that

> leaving children to their own perceptions without some conceptual guidance particularly of a moral kind is dangerously haphazard. Children left to their own devices are far more likely to grow into savages than into responsible citizens. A completely naturalistic rearing of children in naturalist families is due not to the degree of freedom such children are permitted, but rather that naturalists are highly-opinionated, rigid moralists to begin with! Therefore, to avoid undesirable sexual development, perceptual exploration ought to be guided by correct concepts. The problem of determining which concepts are correct is one left to the value theorist, once the limits of pathological development are established by the clinician (i.e., it is up to the clinician to determine how much homosexual activity leads to a loss of potential for heterosexual activity, etc.).

It is difficult to see why there should be any restrictions placed upon sexual activity above and beyond the usual moral restrictions placed upon *any* pleasurable activity. We ought always to be aware of the consequences of our actions, and ought never to act in ways that degrade or dehumanize either ourselves or other human beings (and we might also add a concern for other species as well). Accordingly, learning the manners of sexual interrelation would seem to be an extension of learning the manners of all social conduct.

This view is particularly appealing to the proponents of sexual equality. They argue that the adoption of optimum criteria for sexual objectification and sexual behavior, since it affects the life-style of every individual in a community, must take into account the civil liberties, rights, and universal human needs of each person in the community; thus, while some psychologist may argue that it is more sexually satisfying for the male to treat the female as a sexual object rather than as a sexual person, this kind of behavior is immoral and ought not to be condoned. (This has the effect of limiting satisfactory sexual intercourse exclusively to love relationships, where the partners spontaneously come to prefer treating each other as persons rather than as objects for sexual gratification.)

It would seem fair to argue that

> any criteria governing the social pursuit of human preferences would have to sub serve considerations in both legal and moral theory. Thus, while most human beings would prefer to be economically well off, this does not automatically give them license to acquire either by conquest or by stealth their fair share of the world's goods. Accordingly, it would seem proper to maintain that it is legitimate for legal and moral theory to prescribe was is *not* permissible in sexual behavior; what is immoral is whatever degrades or abuses one's own person or other persons; what is illegal is any act that infringes upon the civil rights and liberties of others, as prescribed by law. The imparting of sexual mores, as a part of the moral education of the child, must conform to these requirements.

While we ultimately have no quarrel with this view, it presents some very fundamental problems, the first of which being the problem of how to reconcile moral reality with everyday existential exigencies. This is a problem that arises not only in sexual contexts but in all social contexts. More often than not, although we know what it is morally proper to do in a given situation, from an ideal standpoint, this is not what we choose to do - either because it is imprudent (and going against prudent choice is, in another sense, immoral), or because we follow much stronger emotional inclinations.

From the clinician's standpoint, healthy sexual behavior bears no resemblance to what is considered polite social behavior; persons who have this attitude in bed are very dull lovers. It is precisely because our western culture has adopted such a wholesome, moral attitude toward sexual conduct that sexual neuroses tend so frequently to arise in our society.

The moral view propounded above is not really different from that already endorsed by the three major religions, or by current legislation. The problems relating to sexual equality are not problems about how persons should morally relate to other persons, but rather problems about the definition of "female person," and "deviant person." A double standard about what is "good" for men and "good for women is held to, and arguments presented against a unisexual standard are that the physical and emotional differences between the sexes would render such a standard oppressive to both. Against sexual deviants, the argument is that this deviant behavior is not "good" either for the deviant or for others to whom he might spread his affliction and ought, consequently, to be either cured or at least prevented from attaining overt expression.

The movement toward sexual equality concerns itself not with the elimination of puritanical attitudes toward sexual conduct but with acquiring both for women and sexual deviants equal protection under the law as is presently enjoyed by heterosexual males, by redefining the concept of sexually "good" practices.

It would seem therefore that the mere shift toward a unisexual standard in our society, while it would certainly improve relations between all the sexes, will not solve the basic problem of what really constitutes an optimal attitude toward sexual conduct, one that is not "against nature" in the more enlightened, modern clinical sense of the phrase. Lovers do not perspire together, they sweat; sexual conduct is not gentile - although it may be gentle, it is just as often rugged, nasty, a release of aggression - it has the character of a sport rather than a parlor game, and what is permissible is what is sporting (and that does depend a great deal on the strength and skill of the players); even among persons who share a high degree of action, there is the tendency - the need, the lust, the temptation - to treat one's partner as object rather than as person. Sexual conflicts arise when we become aware of the contradiction that exists between what our moral sense tells us is a proper way to relate toward other persons, and our momentary desires which - when our partners consent to gratify them - makes them partners-in-crime. Thus we adopt the attitude: this is what we do in private, and the rest of the world need not know. The result is less than optimal, for it is accompanied by guilt, shame, remorse - and this is a result "against nature" if sexual behavior is a natural form of behavior.

II. An alternate proposal.

What is sought for is some kind of criterion for proper sexual objectification which will not lead to the classification of obscene behavior, when engaged in by consenting adults, in private, and with no deleterious consequences there from, as immoral behavior. Therefore it will not do for us to argue in the conventional manner that though obscene behavior is immoral, it sometimes fulfills a moral function (i.e., the release we obtain from "harmless" shameful acts, such as watching a boxing match or hiring a prostitute, leads to a reaffirmation of our moral nature when we confess our sins and determine to act morally in the future; likewise, better to hire a prostitute for our escapades than subject our loved one to such degradation). Such arguments are specious. In the first place, willfully committing immoral acts does not insure our greater morality in the future - rather, the contrary; we run the risk of establishing dangerous precedents, habits we will be unable to break. Secondly, the selection of one class of human beings, willfully and premeditatedly, rather than in the heat of the passionate moment, as objects rather than persons, is a far greater moral transgression than the original sin we are trying to avoid.

There can be no moral excuse in a truly moral society for the existence of prostitutes or boxing matches or any other institution that maintains social emotional equilibrium at the expense of some of its citizens. Such a state of affairs leads neither to sexual equality nor sexual freedom, only to the perpetuation of a slave class. One need not be a Marxist to perceive this clearly. But the alternative to such a hard-line moralistic view need not be a puritanical one. If some obscene behavior is not immoral, one may perfectly well be either a prostitute or a boxer, providing one freely consents to such behavior and is not economically driven to it, for then one is not being abused or degraded. (In some societies, such as the Babylonian, prostitution was part of religious worship, the function fulfilled by priestesses who enjoyed a very high status in the community; under such working conditions, few women would find cause to complain!)

What is to constitute "amoral obscene behavior" if the word "obscene" essentially presupposes an immoral situation? We shall obviously have to redefine the word "obscene" at some point, but not until we have explored the category. The existence of societies, both past and present, in which erotic behavior is regarded either as morally neutral or as an out-and-out good thing gives us some justification for maintaining that the concept of obscenity is a conventional one, even if most societies - if not all societies - hold some things to be obscene; the question is not whether the category has a right to be in our vocabulary, but exactly what kind of behavior should be included in it and whether some of this behavior must necessarily include erotic behavior.

Let us allow that any act which degrades a human being is

an obscene act; what is it about erotic behavior that is essentially degrading? The answer, according to our present reasoning, is any behavior which results in treating a human being as object rather than as person. But what if we are only *pretending* to treat someone else as an object - what if we are only playing? The woman who dresses herself up as an ostrich, the man who permits his penis to be adorned with pecans and chocolate sauce, is not seriously saying: this is who I really am. We err when we think that we unmask our real selves in bed; we do just the opposite - we engage in fantasy and masquerade. It is important to distinguish between the acts that we perform in different contexts and *who* we are; we are not simply the sum total of our acts, though some acts - those willful, premeditated, truly immoral acts we perform not in play but in earnest with disastrous consequences either for ourselves or for others - are acts by which our own conscience and public opinion judge us to be human or something less-than-human.

Social and sexual free-play, sport, games, ritual, dance, theater, art, may all be seen as alternate forms of human recreation; they are expressions of our creative nature; it is not only natural for us, but absolutely essential for us to diversify our lives, explore new avenues, think of new games to play. To do otherwise is to grow old and rigid, to lose our awareness of the present.

But the fact that we sometimes indulge in fantasy need not intrude upon the rest of our lives. Why should a man who likes to pretend he is "masculine" and a woman who likes to pretend she is "feminine" act the part around-the-clock? To do so is to engage in infantile behavior; there is a proper time to play, and a proper time to be serious. We ought to unmask ourselves when we hop *out* of bed. As civilized beings, we are more truly our real selves when we are fully clothed in the vestments of our own choosing than when we parade in our birthday suits. Evolution beyond the species level begins with the assumption of such a viewpoint.

III. Postscript on the unification of science.

Thus far the view propounded here has been confined to a nontechnical analysis of the present concept of human sexuality, in ordinary language. However, a much more fruitful approach to the creation of an adequate theory of human sexual behavior, for the future development of the species, may be given by its inclusion under the concepts of information theory. This alternate description may also have important consequences for present legal theory, for it may be possible, once a central view of the universe which gives an account of moral phenomena as well as physical phenomena within the scientific idiom has been formulated, to justify many of the current civil liberties claims of the sexual freedom movements under already-existing legislation.

In governments whose political structure incorporates a separation between church and state, and particularly in nations which hold to this separation due to the presence of powerful rival religions, each of which might transgress upon the rights of the others, it is fitting that the question of *what is moral* be relegated to a nonsectarian body of professionals qualified to determine axiological issues; this does not mean a body of theologians delegated to the task of sitting at some form of religious congress, for such a body would no more be qualified to determine policy on moral issues by majority vote than the U.S. Senate would be qualified to determine, ultimately and without further recourse for appeal, the legality of its own legislation. What would suffice to constitute fair representation for the views of each of the religions in such a nonsectarian body of professional axiologists is that, discrimination not being present in the hiring or appointing of such professionals, the personnel would be representative of the nation's conflicting ideologies. However the formation of such a body, consisting of genuine professionals in axiology (rather than some legion of decency composed of prominent and pious community leaders who are mere amateurs at the task), depends upon the existence of a genuine science of morals, continuous and synoptic with the physical sciences; such a profession would, just like the legal profession, lean for its determinations upon precedents and paradigms, but also upon the empirical determinations of the lower sciences and, where these conflict with older views, the task of such a body would be to formulate new compromises.

The concept of what is moral, in a nonsectarian state, is a negative concept. Whatever is moral is that which is not expressly indicated as being immoral. (In our society, the concept of what is legal is analogously a negative concept: whatever is legal is that which the law does not explicitly forbid; this means (a) that a statement of the law, in formal language, exists on record, (b) that its application acquires a list of precedents which determine its future application in particular cases, (c) and that the law remains consistent with the entire body of law, as that whole body of law comes to be interpreted, in the future as well as in the present.)

From the standpoint of our present, highly inadequate moral legislation, the explicitness of the phrase "acts against nature" which precedes the enumeration of forbidden sexual practices, is questionable in that the sciences have long since rejected the concept of nature to which it pertains (moreover, it was not a nonsectarian concept to begin with). Accordingly, it may be argued that while it is perfectly proper for a science of morals to forbid "acts against nature," what constitutes the class of such acts must be determined by scientists.

It is doubtful, however, that a body of moral theorists drawing their conclusions in a manner continuous with the physical and sociological sciences would consider "acts against nature" of primary moral significance; scientists regularly act against nature, and boast about it; the entire concept of man's evolution beyond the species level is a defiance of nature.

Accordingly, a body of modern moral theorists would be much more likely to concern themselves with the determination of "acts against humanity." This is not a departure from the real sense of the prior, religiously-oriented view, since it was formulated to serve the needs of an anthropocentric universe. The old sense of "acts against nature" includes the suppressed phrase, "of man." No scientist will argue with this reading; the question, however, of what is the real nature of the human species is an open one since, because of our highly adaptable nature, we are to a large degree in control of our own future.

a. The adaptational character of human nature.

Since the central characteristic of our scientific concept of human nature is its adaptational quality (intelligence being a subordinate concept in present theory, since intelligent behavior is an analogue of adaptational behavior), and the scientific concept of what is "good" for a species being point-for-point identical with what is "healthy" for the species, as empirically determined - the line of argument for justifying a judgment of what constitutes an "act against humanity" is whatever act either limits or impairs an individual's optimal physiological, psychological, or sociological function, thereby threatening his powers for adaptation (i.e., his freedom, as a being with self-governing powers of intelligence, to remain master of his own fate).

Questions about which are the particular "acts against humanity" to be forbidden become much less arbitrary and easier to handle from this viewpoint, since a large body of science exists to test and research our hypotheses in a reliable manner, even if conflicts between moral theories are still prevalent. As the unification of science becomes more and more complete, the future of negative concepts such as "what is moral" and "what is legal" is even more easily determined than that of positive concepts - since the main problem that science cannot solve is "what is true" in an absolute, intertheoretical sense, whereas the problem of "what is contingent," also a negative concept, is much easier (since whatever is not explicitly contradicted by the unified body of theory is, theoretically, still possible).

b. Sexual behavior as a communications activity.

The descriptive level which holds the most promise for the unification of the languages of science is that provided by the information sciences. Therein, adaptational activity of all kinds, including the biological, is regarded as a communications process whereby information is assimilated from the environment by the adaptational unit, which then accommodates its further experimental acts upon the environment; through such probing, also known as perception, the adaptational unit is able to acquire those patterns of action which prolong its survival, by arranging its perceptual input into alternate strategies of action and selecting from among these, through a process of optimization, the appropriate response. A truly detailed description of this view cannot be given here, but an interesting feature - for legal theory - may be found in the reinterpretation of sexual behavior as a form of communications behavior, and this may be used to illustrate the ways in which the unification of science may be able to resolve questions about morals in the near future; how soon this will happen depends entirely upon the liberal inclination of the courts, since there arguments are, from the standpoint of the scientist, valid under the present body of knowledge.

It may be argued that all acts of sexual reproduction are acts of human communication, and therefore Constitutionally guaranteed. (They are also guaranteed by custom, but our objective goes further.) The legal argument for legitimizing sexual deviance in any of its nondestructive forms follows from the above in this manner: all attempted acts of human communication which fail are nevertheless covered by the same Constitutional guarantees, just as an attempted act of free speech or free association, which failed, would still be covered.[11] The participants could argue that their attempted act failed because of an error in perception; they were unable to perceive that all the requisite conditions for reproduction were not present in the sense that the more important perceptual cues, those which enabled them to engage in a sexual act, were forcefully present so that the volitional aspects of the act were depressed, and were not present on other occasions when they were exposed to stimuli having other requisite conditions for reproduction but lacked the more important perceptual cues. A mistake in perception, unlike a mistake in judgment, is involitional.

To illustrate the force of the above argument, we may take an analogous example. Suppose a physician were asked to testify in the defense of a man arrested for urinating against a wall in a back alleys, after a policeman had followed him there and waited to catch him in the act. Suppose the physician were to offer the following explanation: this man is a patient; as a child he was improperly trained and as a consequence cannot urinate in lavatories - it is a phychobiological impossibility for him, due to his early trauma; he therefore urinates only in back alleys, after taking proper precautions at not being been; he must urinate sometime, even if he can hold himself for long periods, therefore he must sometimes break the law; the policeman went out of his way to catch him; his actions hurt no one and, in fact, were less offensive than the public defecation of pets on city sidewalks in full view of everyone; the only way to correct his problem medically is to fit him with some ambulatory catheter which would almost immediately irritate him and lead to serious infections, thereby providing a remedy far worse than the original problem; his recognition of lavatories and walls is perceptual, and he is perfectly aware of the difference between

---

[11] The only attempted acts at reproduction not covered by the above would be those in which contraception occurred, since the intention to reproduce would be explicitly denied by the act of contraception.

the two types of places, and what people are supposed to do in either place, but his personal associations with each place have been irreversibly transposed, so that his involitional response is always inappropriate; the fact that urinating is a controllable reflex act is immaterial, since it is nevertheless an act which must be performed at some time and can only be performed, by this particular man, outside a lavatory; the fact that he always takes great care to find a lonely spot where no one will see him should indicate his willingness to obey the spirit of the law, even though he cannot obey it to the letter.

We would probably find the man not guilty, and the trend in current legal theory is to be more lenient in the case of sexual deviance as well. But the urination case seems more acceptable than the deviant's case in that we are already accustomed to the behaviorist's notion of stimulus-response arcs, and the problem of simple, straight-forward psychological inhibitions. Sexual acts, because of their socially more complex structure, are problems in perception on a much higher level; not only the sexual deviant, but just about everyone, has a problem in their sexual perceptions (e.g., we all have our distinct "types" to which we are attracted, and those which we wouldn't go near under any circumstances). The fact that these are actually problems in perception rather than intellectual quirks is simply illustrated by the fact that there are many people (e.g. those our parents would like us to prefer) that we intellectually know we *ought* to be attracted to, but simply aren't.

Now that we have argued for the above view, however, we wish to point out that it is only an interim argument, less than an optimal one, that can be offered to secure civil liberties for the sexual freedom movements. It is not optimal because it appeals to the force of involitional acts, whereas the objective of any sexual freedom movement should be the finding of suitable arguments for holding that any sexual act performed in private, between one or more consenting adults, which does not have deleterious consequences either physically, psychologically, or socially for any of the parties, or their progeny, or the community, is perfectly moral and should be legal. Furthermore, for acts of this kind to be moral, they should be volitional - the result of human optimal choice for all individuals concerned. Arguments of this kind, under the unification of science, would have to proceed from demonstrations that whatever act was being considered would not in any way impair the health of the parties involved, or the community, and would therefore not be judged immoral.

c. A humanistic analogue.

Any reference to the involitional quality of a sexual act is most unsatisfactory for the programme of achieving human evolution beyond the species level. If we wish to be masters of our own fate, we ought to also be captains of our own body; thus it would seem that relying upon the notion of mistaken perception, and erroneous attempts at reproduction, are degrading ways to justify the commitment of acts which are pleasurable, subjectively chosen, and in many cases are accompanied by the highest moral feeling of love for one's partner. To regard the sexual expression of love as an illness, due to perceptual malfunction, seems quite grotesque in view of the fact that the sexual expression of love is good for everybody, and its repression deleterious for most people in both a psychological and sociological sense. And even in those cases where the sexual expression of love has no concrete object (i.e., in those cases where one's partner is merely a stand-in fulfilling an organic need), it seems perverse and primitive to regard the satisfaction of a basic physiological function as, in itself, either moral or immoral - although its irresponsible release might be thus regarded (i.e., such as in cases where both parties do not consent to it, or when one of the parties is fraudulently misled into thinking that a real expression of love is taking place).

The objective of such a humanist programme for sexual freedom is not to provide a carte-blanche rationale for all forms of what is presently categorized as obscene behavior, whether deviant or merely lewd, but rather to draw an enlightened philosophical line between what are to be considered acts of sexual "fair play" and sexual "acts against humanity." The latter are to be deemed obscene and legislated against, both with respect to their actual performance and to their promotion or advertisement in the communications media. The result of such a humanist programme will be to limit, in the interest of public health, far more of what is already permissible under the present inadequacy of the law, than what it will permit. Thus the objective of such a moral revolution will be the enlightened reorganization of social values with regard to sexual behavior, rather than the blind elimination of restrictions.

Looking now to the future, we may one day come to reject the argument propounded in (b) above as inadequate on the following grounds:

i. Though human sexual behavior is a form of communications behavior, its primary purpose is not reproduction, and if reproduction follows from such an act, it is either by accident (which can be corrected by way of abortion), or by erotic choice (i.e., reproduction through sexual intercourse is just another sexual game we play.)

ii. The class of sexually deviant acts which count as errors in perception are all those involitional acts which violate the rules of sexual "fair play," and these are to be distinguished from a second class of sexually deviant acts which are volitional and performed as "acts against humanity," being errors in moral perception. The former are subject to medical treatment, the latter, subject to punishment.

It seems plausible to argue that human evolution beyond the species level will render reproduction through sexual intercourse an entirely optional act; accordingly, the whole notion of sexual division of the species along reproductive lines will be antiquated; there will therefore be no real reason for maintaining that reproduction is the purpose, overt or covert, of sexual behavior; and its subsumption under the notion of communication will render the concept of sexual intercourse as merely another medium for social intercourse. The rules for "sexual fair play" will thus conform to the principles for what constitutes social propriety in general - mutual consent between social peers being the primary consideration (i.e., gaining the consent of a halfwit is not the same as gaining the consent of a social peer; thus it may be wholly immoral behavior for one or more sophisticates to entice a simple soul into an orgy, just as it is considered nonsporting for four card-sharps to entice an unsuspecting greenhorn into a serious poker game).

What will constitute involitional acts resulting from errors in perception are those compulsive acts such as exhibitionism (unless the parties watching are consenting adults) now generally recognized as belonging to that class, except for deviant acts between consenting adults which, under the new formulation, would no longer be considered deviant acts; there would, however, be a public health clause covering some acts even when performed between consenting adults (e.g., the willful spreading of venereal disease as a sexual "kick" as has become prevalent among some highly promiscuous groups), and to guard against the exploitation of persons of low intelligence or the economically disadvantaged or the brain-damages (e.g., those persons who at present are exploited as prostitutes or in the pornographic trades). However, the whole notion of what constitutes exhibitionism or sexual exploitation will be so liberalized as to present very little problem except in those areas where sexual conduct will be a definite threat to public health.

A greater emphasis in the new obscenity laws will be put against volitional acts resulting from errors in moral perception; this is because moral perception is not a reflex act but rather involves the higher-order integrative functions: it is a form of "seeing as," rather than a form of "seeing." To see someone *as* a sexual object is different from reacting sexually to someone; we cannot control our reactions but we can, in the case of controlled reflexes, hold ourselves in until another consenting adult who evokes a similar reaction in us happens to come along; moral perception is the perception of objects as related to a particular "attention set" - that context of human interrelationships that marks us as social beings having a large degree of mutual respect. The notion of punishment for failure to conduct oneself morally makes sense only if such punishment works to promote the retention of such an "attention set" as a primary context for social intercourse; since moral perception seems to be a natural phenomenon in most people, emerging during the course of natural psychological development, most of the emphasis on future moral education will focus not on the artificial imposition of such an "attention set" but on preventive educational measures to insure that the natural formation of such an "attention set" is not impaired by behavioral practices which would tend to depress it (e.g., to encourage children to mistreat animals would tend to generally dull their perception of others' pain, whether animal or human; to expose the unsophisticated to mass-media simulations of sexual orgies - especially those of a sadistic type - would be to teach forms of behavioral adjustment to analogous situations in real life, rather than merely to entertain).

In general, the guiding principle governing what is to be deemed morally neutral in situations involving social intercourse of a sexual type are those acts, and mass-media reenactments, which do not unduly stimulate sexual behavior in a community to the exclusion of other forms of social intercourse. There are certain kinds of sexual practices which encourage promiscuity of a type not recommended for reasons of public health; there are mass media simulations which are decidedly pruritic and ought to be reserved for situations in which sexual intercourse is intended during or afterwards, rather than indiscriminately displayed. Moreover, if the question of consent is of primary importance, as it should be, such practices and media programming should be made available only to the sexually mature. (This could be handled by giving out licenses, to persons who have undergone the requisite training in sexual behavior to understand and fully control the extent of their participation.)

d. Aesthetic, pruritic, or obscene?

It is hoped that by the adoption of a humanistic code of sexual behavior that the class of stimuli labeled pruritic or obscene will be so substantially revised as to present no problem for a professional association passing on moral issues. The symbols of sexual play that we find today obscene will simply be relegated to the class of the comical in the arts, a form of buffoonery which no one takes seriously and carries no special onus of immorality for those who take part as performers. The more serious forms of sexual interplay, such as is found in genuine art films, will remain relegated to the realm of the aesthetic in that they point not to the act itself but to what is communicated by it.

The real locus of obscenity in any given situation is not an act that is performed *with* another human being, but rather that an act is being performed *against* another human being or group of persons. We are justified in reacting with horror at a display of pornography today simply because we are aware that the participants are being degraded and dehumanized; this is not due to the acts they are performing, but society's attitudes toward those acts and the persons who perform them. We are all well aware that there can be no moral excuse for treating any portion of humanity as sexual objects in earnest rather than in play - and encouraging these to be used, abused, and shut out of the moral community for "permitting" themselves to be thus exploited, when such "permission" is not free consent but a socially-imposed pattern of sexual behavior and sexual identity which the ignorant victims of social degradation mistake for a real reflection of their "inferior" moral nature. And even as we point to the prostitute, the deviant, the nonconforming female, as engaging in moral impropriety, we condone wars, prejudice, ghettos, and hard-core poverty, without going into equal reactions of visceral revulsion.

The conditions of present morals legislation work to create conditions which are not only obscene but genuinely atrocious. Any approach to finding ways of justifying human sexual free-play which does not result in the dehumanization of a large portion of the players should be most welcome; its overall effect on the morals of the community should be cathartic. The advantage of the communications-theory approach to this problem is that it enables us to give an account of sexual intercourse which transcends the primitive biological stratus of purely physiological activity and brings sexual behavior, in humans, in line with the rest of human symbolic behavior.

All human sensori-motor activity is perceptual and leads to intellectually integrated concept-formation. There is no fundamental difference in the intellectual content of information gained through the use of one set of senses rather than another. Sexual concept formation, and the perceptual activity which gives rise to it, is primarily one of tactile orientation. (The fact that we come to learn the differences between objects first through the use of our tactile sense, even as we learn to distinguish them with our eyes, tends to give us the subjective impression that this sense has a more basic ontological significance for us - objects learned by touch are more "real," more "concrete" than those learned primarily by sight or hearing, and are consequently "less symbolical" on a subjective level.)

Tactile perception, which requires greater proximity to the object, and has a completely different temporal spread than our faster senses (i.e., it is much faster to see or hear a phenomenon, as a gestalt of a certain kind, than it is to touch it), is nevertheless a form of perception requiring as much intellectual integration as any other kind, and is subject to intellectual sublimation just like all our other senses. We come to "see" a touched object *as* an object of a certain kind or another kind. The communications aspect of sexual behavior is precisely our coming to "see" ourselves and our partners primarily by touch. The fact that sexual satiety depends not only on the performance of such sensori-motor accommodatory activity, but on the degree to which we are able to integrate it intellectually into some kind of image or fantasy, corroborates this view.

The question of human evolution *to* the species level, in the sexual case, may have been one of coming to "see" the objects of a sexual act as objects of a sexual kind, belonging to living bodies capable of an awareness of their potential for sexual pleasure. The question of human sexual evolution *beyond* the species level may turn on whether the objects of a sexual act come to be "seen as" objects of higher-level communication, belonging not only to a living body but also to a social and moral being - with whom we are actively engaged in an act of preverbal communication, a denotation activity in which the objects pointed to are not the objects "seen" by touch but objects of a much more complex kind. The fundamental type under this kind of symbolization activity falls is no longer the merely "sensual," but the "aesthetic," and, in the case where the moral relation that subsists is highly prevalent in awareness, the "beautiful."

Annselm LNVM **1969**

ArtemisSmith's
TOWARD A SCIENTIFIC EXPLICATION OF SYNESTHETIC PHENOMENA THROUGH KINESTHETIC STIMULATION
(its relevance to sexology)

By Annselm L.N.V. Morpurgo (ArtemisSmith)
© 1974 and 2011 by ArtemisSmith. All rights reserved.

INTRODUCTION

What follows is part of a general trend to form and articulate a central theory of aesthetics from an information-science viewpoint.

Application of information-science concepts to neurophysiology, especially in the area of sensorimotor learning, has placed the study of kinesthetic behavior such as occurs in improvisational dance, as well as other movement phenomena including the enjoyment of sexual interplay, as basic to the study of aesthetics when viewed as an extension of human epistemological activity engaged in by the psychobiological system.

In particular, some recent successes in prosthesis for the blind through the use of a multimedia tactile-visual substitution system, in which kinesthetic response plays a key factor, would lead psychophysical researchers to new hypotheses about the status of 'phantom limb phenomena' of all kinds and, here specifically, the nature of mutual sexual gratification therefrom.

The central hypothesis of this view of mind and aesthetic experience (under which category higher-level human 'lovemaking' may be included) is entirely dependent upon tactile perception for its continued presence, and this perception cannot proceed without constant sensorimotor experimentation at-a-short-distance in real space and time.

Such existential experimentation, falling under the larger category of epistemological behavior, is an on-going information exchange process in which the quality of consciousness produced in the observer (i.e., including a state of orgasm) is directly determined by the kinds of sensorimotor experimental strategies available to the perceiver/communicator. Such strategies proceed through kinesthetic feedback from the periphery, wherefore the phenomenon of spontaneous orgasm may be the outcome of an extension of such primary perceptual activity at the point where the agent or agents take joy in the sheer act of interplay.

The presence of "completion" in perception may occur when perceiving becomes more than a pragmatic activity—when the entire organism engages in spontaneous creative interplay with the environment and acquires options for new percepts as a result of such increased sensorimotor activity that greatly extends the adaptational abilities of the perceiver resulting in a feeling of general 'freedom' and 'well-being'.

Some years ago,[12] the author first proposed the hypothesis that human consciousness was an extension of perceptual behavior at the point where such behavior becomes creative rather than merely pragmatic. It was seen as emerging from lower-level epistemological activity which, in the process of linguistic translation within all the chemico-neural languages of the psychobiological system, acquires the kind of aesthetic ambiguity present in metaphor, i.e., of a "metasporic" synaptic state.

This hypothesis rested heavily on earlier work in learning theory (Piaget, 1947, 1963) and cybernetics (Wiener, 1948, 1961), and the philosophical investigations of Wittgenstein and

---

[12] cf. *ArtemisSmith's A Cybernetic Model of Conscious Behavior from a Multimedia Artist. 1972 Masters' Thesis, CUNY:The City College.*

Quine; the latter specifically addressed the question of translation and objectification in behavioral semantic systems.

From a neurophysiological standpoint, the author's investigations into the nature of human consciousness came specifically as a reply to certain questions posed by later-Nobel-laureate R.W. Sperry, head of the split-brain research team at California Institute of Technology (Sperry, 1966, 1967, 1969, 1970), regarding mental causality and mind-body interaction.

In 1969, the author had occasion to inspect the experimental facilities at Cal-Tech and to interview split-brain researchers and patients. At that time, I discussed with Professor Sperry the possibility of providing a logical explication of the phenomenon of consciousness, in information science terms, that would meet the rigorous requirements of the non-dualist philosopher.

In 1972 I subsequently proposed and published such an explication. This rested heavily on the findings of the split-brain team that the quality of human consciousness depends upon which cortical aptitude centers play the most active roles in the experimentation-objectification process of perceiving.

In psychological terms, this is equivalent to the claim that our 'attention sets' or predispositions to perceive are the key factors in determining which objects in the perceptual field are actually noticed; further, that the parameters of observation, as fixed by our sensory apparatus, determine the physical limits of the perceptual field. Thus, any phantom limb, whether it be a prosthetic retina or a mechanical hand or an artificial penis, determine the quality of the input and the physical limits of the perceptual field.

But the question of creativity in perception requires that we explain precisely how it is that 'attention sets' arise from which the spontaneous declarations of "I am conscious of *such and such …!*" arise.

Such ejaculatory utterances do not emanate solely from problem-solving behavior but reflect nonspecific responses to stimuli that Piaget termed the "play instinct"—*i.e.*, the tendency of the open system to engage in experimental activity for the sheer need to keep itself in a state of constant activity or else risk deteriorating into a rigid system. "Joy - immediacy" in perception is somehow related to this basic, open-system characteristic. The presence of this creative free-play, for the sake of maintaining maximum options for organismic adaptational function, is what distinguishes the open system from the closed system—the biosystem from the machine.

How the neurophysiological system leads to human consciousness may be parodied in the old game called "Russian Scandal." The game involves a group of persons sitting in a circle; the first player whispers some gossip in the adjacent person's ear, and the story is passed on to each person around the circle; when it reaches the last player, the story with all the distortions is told out loud; it is likely to be barely recognizable from the original.

So it is with the various centers of the brain—each in its own neurophysical language gives a message to some other center. At some point, the transformation of this message comes to be expressed either in spoken language or body behavior—that transformation, with all its distortions, is what appears in the ejaculatory immediacy called *Consciousness* and its overt declaration is what determines which parts of the perceptual field are most confirmatory of future expectations of perception—i.e., the next 'attention set'.

Movement is vital to human perception; without it, consciousness comes to be depressed and even eliminated. As was discovered very early in Pavlovian experiments involving the orienting reflex, the eye that is fixed upon an object and not permitted to utilize its oculomotor reflexes soon becomes unable to see; the ear that is exposed to the same tone for a length of time develops a deafness to that tone. The more perceptual experiences are associated with an object, the more vivid that object becomes. In the aesthetic experience, which includes the human sexual experience, we come to be acquainted with objects, situations, persons, in ways that our ordinary perceptual apparatus would not normally perceive; this too is movement, of a higher-order kind.

Confirmation of such a view of the entirely linguistic nature of *Consciousness*, only barely outlined here, will come from areas of science concerned with simulating higher-level conscious experience either in machines or in humans utilizing bionic replacements for lost or nonfunctioning sensorimotor apparatus—*i.e.,* as in varying kinds of prostheses.

The term prosthesis is most often associated with the crude replacement of limbs, but eyeglasses and hearing aids are also prosthetic equipment, as are artificial kidneys and pacemakers. That eyeglasses may enhance the quality of sight is of course a truism, but the true aim of visual prosthesis is to mimic the retina or other site of visual processing in such a manner as to make it possible for a blind person to "see" precisely as a normal person. To do this, it is not enough simply to supply an alternate source of information assimilation at-a-distance, such as might be accomplished through a cane or auditory scanning device; rather, the aim of such prosthesis is to create an "eye" that actually produces images directly to the brain as the natural organ does - where the image received is hooked up to the central nervous system in such a way as it can appear as an actual mental image; proof that this kind of prosthesis is possible provides a vastly significant advance in the theory of mind-brain interaction.

Below follows an account of a remarkable success in achieving such a visual-substitution system that points inescapably to the validity of the information science concept of mind, and its grounding upon kinesthetic behavior, as a prerequisite for the emergence of human consciousness of all kinds.

The prosthesis referred to is called The Tactile Visual Substitution System (TVSS) and it was developed in the late 1960's at Pacific Medical Center, San Francisco, where this research is still continuing. Principal researchers are P. Bach-y-Rita and C.C. Collins of the Center's Institute of Medical Sciences.

In the initial experiment, six blind persons, five of whom had been blind since birth, and six normal-sighted persons functioning as controls, were provided with a tactile analogy of a retina. The skin of the patient's back was chosen as the tactile surface and a grid was constructed on which 400 vibrating points capable of electromechanical activation were laid at ½-inch intervals; this grid was connected to an analog computer which digitized geometrical information received through a television camera, so as to permit the subject to receive television pictures in the form of vibratory information on their skin; the apparatus was set into a dental chair in which the subject sat, stripped to the waist.

But the simulation of sight goes far beyond the provision of a substitute retina. The oculomotor reflexes, which move and focus the eyeball, play a vital role in sight, through kinesthetic feedback to the brain; in fact, sight is not possible without such constant oculomotor activity. Consequently, the researchers equipped the television camera with a zoom lens for alternate focusing and set the camera on a flexible tripod which the patient was permitted to manipulate himself, thereby permitting his entire body to function kinesthetically in a manner approximating oculomotor activity.

After being introduced to the mechanics of the system, subjects were taught to discriminate first between various geometrical lines and shapes, and then their combinations including three-dimensional forms. After approximately one hour of such training, they were introduced to a "vocabulary" of 25 ordinary objects, such as chairs, cups, telephones. After less than ten hours of training, recognition time for these objects fell to 20 sec., and recognition time for new objects which the subjects had not been trained to *see* also fell markedly; this speed in recognition was directly dependent, in most cases, on the subject's ability to manipulate the television apparatus himself rather than through an intermediary, thus firmly establishing the hypothesis that kinesthetic feedback plays an important part in visual perception.

What was even more startling, however, was that subjects reported the locus of visual perception to be in front of them, where their eyes are, rather than on the skin of their back where the stimuli were being received. Not only this, but blind subjects were able to discover distinctly visual concepts, such as perspective, shadows, shape distortion as a function of viewpoint, and apparent change in size as a function of distance; moreover, they could recognize objects, letters, persons, and moving stimuli even from the barest cues—such as the cord of a telephone or the handle of a cup And all of these stimuli were subjectively interpreted as visual, by both blind and the nonblind control subjects!

One of the key questions raised by the experiment was why an area of the skin on the back of a person—not a very sensitive area at that—should work as well as a more sensitive one, such as a hand. The answer, still then speculative, was that most of what goes on in perception is the work of central structures of the brain which can modify and amplify even the most sparse peripheral input by linking it to a multitude of already-learned responses. Thus the important part of perceiving was not the input from the periphery, but the body's own record of motor adjustments to outward cues—the richness of the perceptual experience being directly correlated to the amount of freedom for sensorimotor experimentation available to the perceiver—how flexible was the television viewing apparatus, how finely could it be adjusted or shifted in space—that is, how closely could it mimic the motor operations regularly performed by the muscles of the eye in sighted subjects.

Questions about the quality of perception were then reduced precisely to questions about the quantity and pattern of information exchange, such patterns being determined by the kinds of motor operations permitted the perceiver.

Motor operations functioned as hypotheses in a bioepistemological experimental process, providing the spatio-temporal parameters for pre-scientific observation. *Seeing* was thus regarded as continuous with *learning* and *concept formation.*

LANGUAGE AND EPISTEMOLOGY

An epistemological activity is perforce a behavioral/linguistic process, for it proceeds by way of a syntax and rules for transformation and produces, for each signal input, a set of alternate analytical informational parameters for the next round of synthetic experimentation. Natural language, as a pattern of sound notations, is only an analogue of this more primitive neuronal information-exchange process and the very expression of natural language is in the topological *graphic language* of peripheral sensory input. A mathematical model for storage and retrieval of information in the neural network has been offered by a number of researchers, notably Sebestyen (1962), and Zeeman (1964), which has direct application to Aristotelian word hierarchies and Boolean set theory, which in turn lend themselves to natural language semantic structures as modeled by Katz and Fodor (1964). Space does not permit in-depth analysis of these issues here, however they rely on earlier work by Godel on the openness of certain axiomatic systems in geometry which permit changes in the outcome of hard-wired topological computations depending upon the adoption of new postulates.

Godel's *Theorem* has precise application in neural networks, as well as all the a posteriori theoretical constructs of the unified sciences including the multi-universe hypothesis.. Why not then also apply it to the psychobiology of Gender?

EPISTEMOLOGY AND MOVEMENT

There is a genuine conflict between schools of philosophy on the question: *If my anatomy is totally different from yours, are the objects I "see" the same as the objects you "see"*? But it is not necessary for us to resolve this controversy in order to comprehend the importance of perceptual a priori mechanisms in the temporal reconstruction of possible objects; the latter, being only a tentative and hypothetical pursuit in the organism, easily discarded upon the advent and conflicting percept, does not affect the philosophical issue of whether external reality exists independently of the perceiver, or not.

Does a person's *Gender* present a genuine dichotomy in the quality of perception that cannot be overcome by alterations in the parameters for observation such as occurs with prosthesis?

This is a shaded area.

In perception we have a hard-wired a priori set of physical restrictions upon the kinds of sensorimotor experimentation in which an organism can engage but this can change with a revision of its architecture. The natural set of movements permissible to the perceiving organism is analogous to the set of instruments accessible to the scientist for testing hypotheses. If any part of the natural set of operations is either diminished or embellished, there is a drastic variation from the norm in the kinds of objectification achieved. Despite the quantitative character of the neural input, here we have the key to the qualitative difference between *seeing, touching* and *hearing*: the spatio-temporal pattern of perceptual input differs—i.e., *what can be seen* versus *what can be touched* or *what can be heard* varies with the environment and the specific placement of the perceiver.

Congenitally blind-deaf persons limited to entirely tactile stimuli live in a two-dimensional *Flatland* of subjective space wholly limited by the length of their arms and legs with only memory contributing a third dimension; projective hypotheses about possible new tactile sensations for such *Flatland* inhabitants would be few and highly inaccurate, not occurring with enough frequency to keep up with the changing events and objects surrounding them. Yet there is nothing anatomically preventing such persons from *hearing* and *seeing* by technological extensions such as the TVSS where the pattern of input to the skin of the subject's back is quantitatively and qualitatively approximate to that normally received by the eye and ear. In all cases, the added multidimensional factor of memory, in its most basic form of semantic notation as neural *graphic language* expands and equalizes the perceptual field. *All the appearances point to the same reality.*

SYNESTHESIA AND CONSCIOUSNESS

It was John Dewey who proposed that "having an experience" is the intellectual establishment of a link between "what is done" and "what is undergone." The richer the associations connected to a particular stimulus, the richer the experience and the richer the *consciousness* of the perceiver.

As has been pointed out above, researchers on the TVSS and the split-brain have very clearly reduced questions about the quality of consciousness to questions about the kinds of information exchange taking place in the two cerebral hemispheres (Sperry, 1973, 1970). The strategy of stimulating vision through the TVSS was to create an effect of synesthesia by treating the area of the skin on the patient's back in much the same way as it would function if it were a retina; similarly, the strategy for uniting a 'split-brain' patient's distinctly separate perceptual inputs into a single consciousness has been shown to rest on the subject's ability to integrate both sets of input in a manner that converses and 'makes peace' with both sides of his surgically-divided brain and thereby permitting *informed choice*. Man *is* a social animal, as Aristotle observed, and the logic that divides and organizes language is what unites and focuses all psychobiological human interaction both internal and external.

Analogously, it is no accident that the term *copulation* is interchangeable with the phrase *sexual intercourse*. It too is a synesthetic process, depending upon a plethora of alternate experimental strategies possible between/among/within the entire field of communicators. And when the *synesthetic* experience becomes the *aesthetic* experience, the added moral factor of distinctly *Human* interaction is present. That last component requires an attitude of heightened attention coupled with profound mutual respect among the participants, whomever and how many there may be.

Annselm LNVM **1974**

ArtemisSmith : The Third Sex

the Ladder

MARCH 1961
VOLUME 5, NUMBER 6

Published monthly by the Daughters of Bilitis, Inc., a non-profit corporation, 1232 Market Street, Suite 108, San Francisco 2, California. Telephone: UNderhill 3 - 8196.

NATIONAL OFFICERS, DAUGHTERS OF BILITIS, INC.

President — Jaye Bell
Vice President — Helen Sanders
Recording Secretary — Dottie Dee
Corresponding Secretary — Chris Hayden
Public Relations Director — Jo Carson
Treasurer — Ev Howe

THE LADDER STAFF

Editor — Del Martin
Editorial Assistants — Agatha Mathys, Elaine Kingston, Millie Jensen, Jean Nathan
Los Angeles Reporter — Sten Russell
Production Manager — Patty Patterson
Circulation Manager — Cleo Glenn

THE LADDER is regarded as a sounding board for various points of view on the homophile and related subjects and does not necessarily reflect the opinion of the organization.

contents

WE'VE MOVED...4
DOG ANNIHILATES BLANCHE E. BAKER SCHOLARSHIP................5
FEAR OR LACK OF TRUST? - EDITORIAL..........................5
HOMOSEXUAL BILL OF RIGHTS SIZZLES & FIZZLES.................5
SPECIAL NOTICES FROM DOB BOOK SERVICE......................26

COVER BY BILLIE THIS MONTH IS A SKETCH OF ARTEMIS SMITH, AUTHOR OF THE THIRD SEX AND ODD GIRL, WHOSE BOOKS ARE AVAILABLE FROM THE DOB BOOK SERVICE (SEE BACK COVER).

purpose of the Daughters of BILITIS

A WOMEN'S ORGANIZATION FOR THE PURPOSE OF PROMOTING THE INTEGRATION OF THE HOMOSEXUAL INTO SOCIETY BY:

1. Education of the variant, with particular emphasis on the psychological, physiological and sociological aspects, to enable her to understand herself and make her adjustment to society in all its social, civic and economic implications—this to be accomplished by establishing and maintaining as complete a library as possible of both fiction and non-fiction literature on the sex deviant theme; by sponsoring public discussions on pertinent subjects to be conducted by leading members of the legal, psychiatric, religious and other professions; by advocating a mode of behavior and dress acceptable to society.

2. Education of the public, at large through acceptance first of the individual, leading to an eventual breakdown of erroneous taboos and prejudices; through public discussion meetings aforementioned; through dissemination of educational literature on the homosexual theme.

3. Participation in research projects by duly authorized and responsible psychologists, sociologists and other such experts directed towards further knowledge of the homosexual.

4. Investigation of the penal code as it pertains to the homosexual, proposal of changes to provide an equitable handling of cases involving this minority group, and promotion of these changes through due process of law in the state legislatures.

ArtemisSmith : The Third Sex

Diana Carleton Rhodes and Carle were early pen names for Annselm L.N.V. Morpurgo:

incorporated

post office box 5716

los angeles 55, california

May 25, 1954

Diana Rhodes
4004 Warren Street
Elmhurst, Queens
New York, N.Y.

Dear Miss Rhodes:

Thank you for your offer to write for us on assignment. We will be very happy to have you do this. The girls and I take great pride in your confidence in the magazine.

Is the peice called "Tenderness" the first of this series? We think it is indeed well written, but would like to see all of the articles before deciding. Or at least the majority of them.

But don't send them yet. I will be in New York -- perhaps you have already heard about it -- from June 6 to 12, and would very much like to meet with you and discuss our editorial plans.

Perhaps Bill Lambert or the girls have written you about the meeting at the Amato Opera Theatre, 159 Bleecker St., N.Y.C., June 7. We're counting on you're being there. I hope you can make it.

But for sure, I want to meet with you sometime while I am in NY. I want to arrange it at a time most convenient to you, but because my schedule will be very tight, I would like to know as soon as possible what time that would be.

Please write whenever you can. We enjoy hearing from you.

Very truly yours,

Ben

Ben Tabor, Secretary
Editorial Board

cc - Ann Carll Reid

Can Atheism Become a Genuine Religion?
by ArtemisSmith (Annselm L.N.V. Morpurgo)*
© 1972, 2011 by ArtemisSmith. All rights reserved.

PERMISSION TO QUOTE OR REPRINT
THIS ESSAY IS FREELY GIVEN
PROVIDED YOU PROPERLY CREDIT ITS SOURCE

*Annselm L.N.V. Morpurgo is a professional philosopher of science and Executive Director of THE SAVANT GARDE INSTITUTE. She is also known and published in the arts as poet-futurist ArtemisSmith, a cult figure and strategist of the 1950's and '60's Rainbow rights coalitions. Her works are archived at www.ArtemisSmith.com

Is the term *God* as ontologically trivial as the term *Phlogiston*?

I remember that the first time this question came up in a really serious way was when my artistic life-partner and mentor, Billie Ann Taulman, first shaved the remnants of my adolescent stubble with Occam's Razor. Fortunately, neither of us had yet been corrupted by the language analyst's need for logical precision - a sophistication that would have thoroughly apoplexied our budding artistic thought. Our naive approach was purely intuitive, commonsensical. Taulman was describing the fundamental tenets of her native Methodism; I, as an offspring of Freemason Scientific Unitarians.

Our initial question, posed as artists and poets, was: How are we to picture |God|?

> do we use the Methodist equation, |God=Love|, or the Einsteinian one, |God=Absolute Truth|?

Taulman cut through the confusion with one of her sweeping *Gestaldt* shifts:

> why contemplate |God| at all?
> why not simply contemplate |Love=Absolute Truth|?

Suddenly both of us stopped and held our breath - yes, such an equation embodied genuine pictorial simplicity, one rooted in Human genetico-moral intuition - an aesthetic equation that allowed a higher level language icon to replace all heretofore godhead idolatries:

> |Love=AbsoluteTruth=TheBeautiful|=|The Sacred|

Our artistic purpose spontaneously blended into one voice - now we knew the direction in which each of us would proceed. Together we would masterbuild a whole new metaphysic, a scientifically-based "small-c" catholicism, one better suited to the universally |True| concept of Human Identity - one that would finally succeed in sweeping all the merchants of falsehood and idolatry from the one and only universally accepted mystical intuition, wherein the notion of |Scientific Truth| might be held synonymous with |The Sacred|!

This artistic vision marked the beginning of our mutual, 'Mystical-Atheism.'

We paused to examine our new protocol:

> [Mystical-Atheism], an oxymoron?
> No!
> But isn't the Atheist's position that nothing need be held |Sacred| ultimately logically self-contradictory? Yes!
> But then, is it logically possible for an Atheist to hold anything |Sacred| and still be an Atheist? Again, Yes! despite Grand Inquisitors' best efforts to suppress this logico-political possibility.

To understand how this is possible, one must begin by dismissing all religious zealots who set up verbal pseudoconstructs regarding the psychological nature of skepticism.

There are at least two kinds of atheist positions, only one of which is logically untenable:

> 1. Atheist=nontheist/nonidolatrist, someone who may at least minimally believe in |Truth| (i.e., whether it be aesthetic or scientific or merely logicotheoretical truth) but not in any deity.

> 2. Atheist=nihilist, someone who believes in nothing, not even logic, or any belief whatsoever including their own atheism.

The latter definition, reflecting the straw-man position most often opportunistically attacked by the ardent theist, most certainly belongs to a schizophrenic fool trapped in paradox.

But not so the former, which can point to any number of perfectly sane and intelligent persons (including but not restricted to Buddhists and Ethical Culturists) who are capable of leading a value-laden life filled with Humanist ideals and commitments, normal relationships, ambitions, things believed to be at least existentially |True| and aesthetically |Beloved, Valued, Preserved|, and therefore deeply held existentially |Sacred|.

The confusion regarding Atheism-1 arises when the religious zealot falsely equates the first definition with Agnosticism in order to avoid widespread social conflict and allow peaceful multinational diplomatico-religio-political co-existence. Unlike Atheist-1, the more socially acceptable Agnostic has no religious commitment, no religious affiliation.

Atheist-1, on the other hand, perilously and religiously denies the existence of any deity - Atheism-1 therefore reflects a fully defined, in no way politically-neutral, fully-committed religious creed of its own which, howbeit politically counter to other creeds, may Constitutionally and legitimately subscribe to a firm set of existential |Truths| and personal objects held |Sacred| within some Nation holding to a sufficient |separation of Church and State| that will tolerate this degree of religious freedom.

But why might anyone perversely choose any form of Atheism over the more socially acceptable fence-sitting alternative of Agnosticism, which can exist under any political regime? The answer is definitely moral - as well as epistemological:

> Agnosticism allows a much larger ontology - all the gods and all the mythologies of all the various religions, not just some of them. The logically-consistent Agnostic, though perhaps not drowning in paradox like the nihilistic Atheist-2, is doomed to drown in the polluted sea of tolerance *for even the most bizarre elements of religious extremism,* including genocide, human sacrifice, and sexual slavery.
>
> The Atheist-1, in contrast, by dismissing all gods as excessive and epistemologically intrusive, achieves a purist environment of informational clarity - one that can be guided solely by genetico-moral intuition wherein true Human goals and strategies are more easily identified.

In 1955, bringing the whole world toward a religiously committed Atheism-1 thus became our artistic manifesto. The political story of our activist partnership is chronicled in a volume just published: *"ArtemisSmith's* ODD GIRL Revisited: an autobiographical correlate." This essay on Mystical Atheism stands at tangent to it. Recent statements by many prominent persons including cosmologist Stephen Hawking regarding the lack of necessity in belief in any deity with respect to the search for Absolute Truth through the physical sciences has sparked an immediate need to remind the scientific community that generations of other philosophers as well as a couple of modern poets and political activists said it first more than fifty-five years ago!

Taulman remains among the most brilliant and original thinkers with whom I have been fortunate to intimately interface, although scarcely any of her poetry was ever finished. It does not matter if she finished what she started, it nevertheless sparked new visions in me, and if I have stolen her soul in any or many of my works, it is not because I mean to take the credit for myself - but rather that we are so generically entwined in our thoughts that there is no possibility of separating us.

Back in the winter of 1954-55 when we first began our dialogue, Taulman and I already realized that |Human Beings| were on the verge of changing form.

(Amusingly, both of us admitted that we already pictured ourselves as sprouting new wings on our back - as budding Angels, or more naturalistically, re-evolving Pterodactyls - wherefore my first collection of poems, *Hark the Pterodactyl,* pointed to that vision.)

In 1955, even as radical as we were, our concept of Human Identity seemed nevertheless clearly defined and fixed. Nevermind that our original equation |Love = Truth| made neither logical nor mathematical nor Boolean sense. It did make |Common Sense|. We knew what |Love| entails - that biofeeling that comes naturally and spontaneously to genetico-morally intact |Human| beings to care for something or someone in a nurturing way. And we knew what |Truth| involves - a consensus of opinions among sane and educated persons within a scientific community sharing in a common epistemology. Therefore, at that time our original equation |Love=Truth|=|The Sacred| seemed entirely unproblematic. All we had to do was preserve the economic-political-cultural conditions that nurture |Human| development.

By 1958 however, when I first began *The SKEETS Triptych*, it became clear to me that |Human Identity| is immensely fragile and so thoroughly relative that |Human Common Sense as dictated by Private Conscience|=|The Moral|=|The Sacred| can and does often fade from view even in the best of econo-politico-cultural environments. Why then, I asked myself, do I continue to defend my Mystical-Atheism as the only tenable creed?

I could not answer my own question until I had finished the second book of *SKEETS* and started putting everything together into my initial papers on Human Consciousness simulation. By then, having had sufficient time to reflect on all the scientific discoveries now making themselves fully felt at the turn of this century, I came to realize that a subtle change in the new economies of Human Potential does indeed threaten all genetico-moral concepts of |The Self|.

In the information explosion and its exponential increase in the speed of intercultural communication there is now for many a real danger of loss of identity as a Species altogether, unless we declare a new higher level equation: |The Sacred|=|Private Conscience as shaped by the Laws of the Unified Sciences|. But how retrograde Socratic! Are we secretly reintroducing "The Gods" in our dialogue?

Again recall Occam's principle of parsimony: what need have we for more than existential |Truth| and values we hold |Sacred| to guide us? Let us not multiply entities! But now that we are multiplying genetic possibilities, and with them, new forms of genetico-moral intuitions, forcing us to contemplate more realistically the possibility of having to politically coexist not only with Psychopaths and Degenerates who look exactly like us but have no |Human Common Sense|, but also with Dolphins, Chimpanzees, Androids and genetically-altered Clones - and even Ourselves genetically-improved, now soon virtually immortal, physically perfect in our "beauty", all of us wealthy, "happy" and nearly indestructible - where does the equation |Common Sense=Human Intuition| take us?

Traditionally, our |Humanity| was preserved through one or another religious creed, though notoriously not all creeds can agree on common |Human| values. And there's the rub! The rise of powerful rival religions has no more provided us with an amalgam of |Humanist| thought than has the rise of conflicting political parties caused us to unite in |Humanistic| ideologies. In fact,

Religion and Political Ideology go hand in hand, and it is only in countries that separate Church from State that Individual Conscience has been given any substantial room to move.

Banning Religion altogether as subversive of the enlightened State does nothing to solve the real problem for it is unrealistic to maintain that any Nation can exist without Religion anymore than it can exist in abject Anarchy. Religion is what |Human Identity| is all about. Without it, we lose whatever part of our |Humanity| the political system allows us to preserve. Without it, we fail to nurture the young to moral maturity. Without it we lose all sense of Community and without a |Love for The Sacred| we lose sight of all reason for Being.

But to say all this is not to say we need any specific "God" to complete the picture. It suffices for us to worship |Truth| as a goal of reason, and to hold that for |Truth| to be genuine and relatively stable, it must be existentially grounded in an {Other}={a body of empirical evidence preserved by a community committed to a scientifically organized body of knowledge} that gives rise and force to an ethic of inclusion based upon ever evolving and self-correcting |Common Sense|. But "God" as an ontological posit has become both politically and epistemically cumbersome, posing an increasingly strong argument for holding that it carries no greater explanatory force than the vestigial adherence to "Phlogiston" as a causal entity within the modern theory of combustion.

There are of course persons who will continue to argue that postulating the existence of "God" as a causal entity, even though vestigial, is harmless, even psychologically beneficial, based entirely on faith since no logical or physical form of proof can be presented in its defense. Then *why not* hold on to God as an aesthetic and reassuring posit to help children sleep soundly and for the dying to desperately invoke?

To such feeble arguments the Mystical Atheist must adopt a polemic stance: *The posit of a deity is neither harmless nor aesthetically nor psychologically reassuring.* It leads to self-deception and often dangerous behavior and denies |The Self| the opportunity for full moral development. While phenomenological introspection reveals a number of voices of |The Self|, Private Conscience is never to be mistaken for |The Voice of God| if madness is to be averted; nor is there any comfort more immediate than the companionship of |Private Conscience| even unto death. Why live a precarious lie, and why die embracing one? Better to die embracing |The Self| and its |Love of Others| as the most worthwhile of objects - for that entity does have an eternal |Name| and an immediate |Face|. (Moreover, *Pascal's Choice* be trashed, if by the remotest of chances there really were some *omnipotent, all-knowing, benevolent supreme being* out there peering into our innermost |Self|, wouldn't such a confrontation with the *Goodness* inherent in one's own Private Conscience also suffice to grant an entry into *that* "Heaven"?)

This then, in my old age, has become my full-flung Religion and I now stand as a fully committed Mystical Atheist. I defend the need for all enlightened communities to convert to my creed - for I see this as the only epistemologically tenable stance equal to the task of truly preserving |Human Identity| through an increasingly progressive evolutionary change. The world is becoming much too small to allow for arcane thought and no other creed can offer a more compelling reason to obey the rules of reason and sanity, as dictated both by science and genetico-moral sensibility.

I do now know |My Name| but what shall be |My Face|?

The aesthetic problem, for the artist/philosopher converted to Mystical Atheism, remains the same: how do we preserve Beauty in the Human subject? Isn't all observation grounded in the Observer? And if the Observer is traveling in time and constantly shifting in its parameters, who is to say what |Love|, |Truth|, |Beauty|, |Common Sense| are? Without a grounding in a |Particular Person|, i.e., an Absolute god-image, will there not be a danger in the loss of |True Human Identity|? If we must create such a relativistic locally-defined 'graven image', which even Scripture holds "Abominable," to satisfy our animal craving to engage in "worship" of whatever inner voice appears to us as proceeding from the dictates of "Private Conscience," let us not confuse it with any metaphysical posit of what truly may constitute an |extra-linguistic and hence nonsensical| characterization| of |The Sacred|.

This epistemologically polemic stance may not be as satisfying as we would like it to be, but we are stuck with it nevertheless for there can be no grounding in what gibberish lies entirely beyond language or meta-language or meta-meta-language.

But this does not mean we ought to dispense with all Religion. Religion is part of our |Human| nature. Our instincts as social animals cannot be ignored. The need for religio-political thought and positive community action is written in our genes. Though its source remains unnamed, its zealous practice should be open to all, even to the Mystical Atheist. Nations and Temples, being *one and the same thing* in most socio-historical contexts, require a body of beliefs about *Truth, Justice, Fairness, etc.*, written into their laws and customs. Often, there are minorities whose own persuasions conflict but are allowed to co-habit in peace because obedient to their laws. As a member of a genuine religion, the Mystical Atheist must also stand among them and seek to peacefully persuade and evangelize as all the others do. There is no problem therefore in the Mystical Atheist's formulation of a special creed and the erection of proper temples in which its own form of community action and education may take place.

But what shall a temple to the scientific ideal of |Humanistic Truth=The Sacred| contain and include? Certainly *not* Scientology or any other pseudo-scientific concoction, either Asian or Western. Minimally, the religio-political position of the Mystical Atheist *must be* one of pious obedience to "Private Conscience" as shaped by a scientifically-enlightened body of law, and to hold spiritual allegiance solely to a scientifico-moral, relativistic and purely local characterization of |Humanistic Truth=The Sacred| and *not to posit or believe in any untenable extra-linguistic* Absolute Entity.

Restated more practically, it should be housed within a system of universal public education from childhood to the grave that promotes loving relationships and critical thinking - coupled with constant civic vigilance and a stable political climate - one committed to a strict separation of Church and State within an open society and an electoral climate that preserves peaceful dissent and nurtures |Private Conscience|.

Artemis Smith **1972**

On Simulating <"I am Conscious!">=T

a cybernetic model of
CONSCIOUS BEHAVIOR
from a multimedia artist

by Artemis Smith (ANNSELM L.N.V. MORPURGO, M.A.)
© 1971 BY ARTEMIS SMITH, ALL RIGHTS RESERVED.

U.S. Copyright Regis. #C-29370 reprinted from 1973 Proceedings of the Computer Arts Society International, presented at their 1973 international conference and exposition as part of the Edinburgh International Arts Festival, Scotland: University of Edinburgh, Computer Arts Segment.

Also filed as an M.A. Thesis in Philosophy, in the Archives of the Philosophy Division, 1973, The City University of New York:The City College. Reprinted in 1984 in a limited edition Monograph by the savant garde workshop for THE SAVANT GARDE INSTITUTE.

For academic and review purposes only, below is a download of the text of the first explication of Consciousness in information science theory. It's author, Artemis Smith (a/k/a Philosophy Professor Annselm L.N.V. Morpurgo), is a multimedia artist and philosopher of science then completing doctoral studies at The City University of New York. Her dissertation proposal, consisting of a series of already completed papers and widely-given lectures on the simulation of human consciousness through the information science explication of the truth-claim: "I am Conscious!", was rejected, causing her to be excluded from a Nobel Prize award conferred upon members and associates of the Sperry Split Brain research team in 1973 despite sponsorship from other nominees; this exclusion was presumed due to political blacklisting for Artemis Smith's atheist and feminist activities in the arts since the 1950's which compromised her eligibility for a government security clearance necessary for US Defense Department-sponsored consciousness-research projects.

The copyrighted series of exploratory papers had been freely presented to faculties at The City University of New York, Massachusetts Institute of Technology, California Institute of Technology, and Princeton University and were circulated enthusiastically by sponsoring Professors; their contents are now freely quoted and in common use without proper recognition or citation of their source and in frequent violation of copyright laws.

(Presented is the essential text, without the accompanying introduction, commentary, and bibliography)

On Simulating <"I am Conscious!">=T

Can "Consciousness(!)" be simulated?

> To simulate a phenomenon is not simply to draw a picture of it - but to reproduce its function for the purpose of prediction and control.

Yet before the engineer can proceed to reproduce a phenomenon, there must be a plan.

As an artist rather than a scientist, I would like to propose certain features that such a plan must incorporate in order for a simulation of "Consciousness(!)" to be adequate.

I have been working in philosophy of science-using epistemology as a descriptive medium - because I believe "Consciousness(!)" to be the product of natural processes of an adaptational type under which the activity of human intelligence falls.

Epistemological activity is the stuff, I believe, that "Consciousness(!)" is made of - and such activity may also be carried on by a variety of other types of physical units of information exchange.

The question is:

can a computer be programmed for "Consciousness(!)",

or must such a physical unit for information exchange be strictly biological?

My methodological decisions for proceeding to answer such a question entail, as a matter of personal taste, the rejection of vitalism, dualism, idealism, and any recourse to the notion of 'nomological danglers' which might help to evade the engineering question of "Consciousness(!)" programming.

I will attempt to describe consciousness in wholly epistemological terms which will leave little doubt to the information scientist that the phenomenon has been wholly accounted for in information theory terms.

An explication of the meaning of "I am conscious(!)" is thus the goal of this investigation.

A linguistic clarification of a term is, in the final analysis, the only warrant that a term has been fully defined within some central theory.

Especially in the case of "Consciousness(!)", construed as something private, nontransferable, a black-box event when purported to occur in others than ourselves - a linguistic clarification can be the only explanation, since all that is tangible about the phenomenon seems to be contained in language, and inspected by language; and philosophy is the discipline that ultimately studies consciousness qua "Consciousness(!)".

This is the direction in which, I think, the modern poet's best friend, Ludwig Wittgenstein, was headed, from The Blue and Brown Books to The Philosophical Investigations.

My own investigation carries a little further what I believe to be sitting in front of everyone's philosophical nose today, as a result of Wittgenstein's analyses.

1. That pictures and descriptions are one and the same thing.

I see Wittgenstein's main point as having been that whatever exists, is "real" only to the extent that it can be "pictured" by some language; if we cannot speak in some way about something, we are forced to remain silent - a truism, yet we must remember that not all communication proceeds by way of vocal chords. Pointing to a thing is also speaking about it, for much more is assumed in the pointing than the "simple" act of pointing. Pointing is not a "logically simple" activity - it is communicative and depends upon a knowledge of the idiom (the language game) in which the pointing takes place; all pointing is learned behavior, must involve concepts.

But what if I turn inward and point to a thought inside my mind - isn't that kind of pointing "logically simple"?

According to Wittgenstein, who denied the sense of strictly "private" languages, the answer is no - no act of pointing is simple; all pointing assumes knowledge of a language game; in cybernetic terms, all pointing presupposes a program for the pointing activity.

Programs require a syntax and a semantical component; the latter requires a series of structural states determined by the architecture of the physical apparatus, and a context for its use - i.e., a task, or information-exchange environment.

It was my reading of Wittgenstein as hinting that all experience - both inward and outward - involves pointing, and that all pointing is complex and conceptual, that set me to thinking about a fruitful strategy for explicating "Consciousness(!)":

If the whole of conscious experience might be shown to be a pointing activity, and no pointing activity might be shown to be "logically simple," then no part of conscious activity might be shown to be inaccessible to linguistic analysis, at least in principle; the "privacy" of my conscious experience would be grounded not on any kind of "simple" impressions or "ideas" I have spiritual access to, but on the mere logical and architectural facts of neural switching in my brain; my thoughts are private only because my nerve cells are connected to my integration centers and not anyone else's; if my switching patterns were simulated by another brain, it might be aware of my thoughts just as vividly as I am.

But before such a strategy can be gainfully pursued, a set of vaguely related problems must be briefly explored, for these still block the way to a complete description of "Consciousness(!)"in epistemological terms.

I offer what follows only as a beginning to the search for a fully adequate plan for simulation.

2. An artist's notebook of sketchy attempts at a picture of "Consciousness(!)"

i.   On the hypothesis that all experience is complex (i.e., conceptual), hence in principle intersubjectively describable, what is the logical status of the content of a stream-of-consciousness?

"Ideas" is the classical answer, and since we grant that graphic representations are a form of language, it is altogether too great a temptation to hold that "graphic utterances" form the logical content of a "Consciousness(!)" string. But such a simple explanation is inadequate, for how precisely do I "see" such images in my head without, ultimately, resulting to a form of dualism?

ii. **Descriptions, furthermore, can be denied; message configurations can be rejected; theoretical constructs (proceeding from some central syntax of the brain, for example) are, even if only hypothetical, precisely reproducible.**

In contrast, the stuff of my awareness seems to have the character of the immediate, the undeniable, the irreproducible.

If all my thoughts proceed from some central syntax in the brain, and are "graphic utterances" communicating information to other information-receiving centers in my brain, then my brain should be functioning in a much more deterministic manner, whereas I perceive a certain unpredictability about my future thoughts - a stochastic quality in my stream-of-consciousness, and a sense of time's arrow giving to each moment a fleeting uniqueness which, if I were a perfectly logical mind, I would not experience.

A perfectly logical mind would keep reproducing eternal sentences, at least about those facts of inner experience that are not connected to perceptual input. Yet I, from moment to moment, have difficulty determining that a thought I had a moment ago is really the same thought I have now.

Even analytic truths are judged true by me moment to moment only by appeal to the same rule, which I must, from moment to moment, recall.

iii. **The stuff of my awareness - my "ideas" - carries an ontological quality which is not mere truth by derivation but truth by immediate conviction despite a concomitant flow of contradiction.**

Being aware of something may be being aware of it as something of a kind, but it is also simultaneously being aware of it as being something of many different kinds, some of which are incompatible with the first.

(To point out, as Nelson Goodman does in *The Way the World Is*, that the way the world is seen is not the way the world is - is to point out that I see that the world I do see is not the only way I could see the world. The existence of a counterfactual possibility, in my awareness, gives that awareness a contradictory quality.)

Dilemma:

Logical descriptions of the world are supposed to be at least consistent - at best, complete. But the content of my awareness is ambiguous; if I thus hold that all conscious content is descriptive, I must also hold that all of my inward descriptions are equipollent - in an overall sense, intensionally *meaningless*.

But wouldn't this cancel out the sense of "awareness" associated with conscious experience? Moreover, how can I assert, from moment to moment, that I am the same consciousness experiencing the same world?

iv. The objects in my world remain identical even though my descriptions conflict.

It is not reality which is relative to my description - it is I who conform all my descriptions to reality.

But if all my describing is equipollent, how is it possible for me to talk about (even when all the talking is by means of "graphic" terms) the same objects while using different intensional structures - i.e., different concepts or programs?

(In the philosophy of science, this problem is closely related to the problem of giving an adequate characterization of the correspondence of meaning between the terms of a scientific theory and their semiotic counterparts in a neutral observation language. P.K. Feyerabend has held, for example, that since a scientific theory - construed as a formalized, hypothetico-deductive system of concepts - inspects the world from its own particular viewpoint, and since rival theories have alternate intensional structures, no coincidence of intensional meanings among truly conflicting theories can ensue, even though terms used are semiotically identical, and such rival theories do not share a common ontology. Under this view, the notion of a common observation language for science is impossible, and all pointing to things in science becomes legitimate only within theories; all reality becomes, thus, relative to the observer, and purely conventional.)

My reality reflects an observer who is not merely bound to convention. My awareness is creative, and constantly leaps out of its own pictures of the world.

Although this is not incompatible with the hypothesis that all my conscious activity proceeds from an underlying master program in which all the contradictoriness of consciousness is resolved, and each moment of my consciousness falls within a perfectly natural whole - this kind of hypothesis displeases me aesthetically. It implies that my mind is not really free and that the whole of my conscious experience is dictated by the rigid laws of classical logic embedded in unconscious processes of a dialectically determined type.

v. Can the alternate hypothesis - that "Consciousness(!)" is genuinely stochastic, proceeding from genuinely stochastic underlying processes in the brain - be maintained without resorting to a position of such extreme ontological relativity that both observer and world, from moment to moment, surrender identity?

W.V.O. Quine (*Word and Object*) has attacked the problem of ontological relativity by holding that while it is true that sameness of intensional meaning cannot be maintained between two genuinely distinct languages, hence no radical translation achieved between them, there can still be extensional meanings which he terms "stimulus meanings" of semiotic notations which a community of observers, sharing like habits of response, can attain.

Thus their physical actions of signal-exchange have a kind of universal harmony (not necessarily due to the uniformity of nature but merely to the statistical accumulations of physical clusters of signal events) despite the radical solipsism of their intensional states.

This gets us closer to the information scientist's view of a communications network:

we have a network of sending-and-receiving mechanisms, each with its own language and set of programs, and each by a process of orthogonal development gradually adjusting itself, in a cryptographic manner, to a common program. Each unit scans the field, and alters itself accordingly.

Two possibilities for reality are permitted according to this view:

(1) either reality is completely determined (in which case, eventually all the views will become one);

(2) or reality is stochastic (in which case, all the physical processes within it, including the sending-receiving units themselves, are mere fleeting thicknesses in the flow of events, all language is fluid, and logical truth merely a temporary illusion).

Perverse as it may seem, as an artist I would like to hold the latter view and see whether, from such a state of affairs, a real world can still follow.

If I can show that a real world can indeed follow from it, I will have shown that language in such a world does indeed mean something and that, if conscious strings are linguistic, consciousness is what I already know it to be - filled with meaning.

But meanings require the possibility of analytic truths. How is this possible in a world in which logical truths are not fixed entities? A semantic theory by Jerry A. Fodor and Jerrold Katz points to a characterization of analytic truth in terms of linguistic behavior of respondents in an information-exchange network:

analytic behavior is the tendency of respondents in a community to give synonymous response to the terms of a natural language with a probability approaching 1; synonymies listed in a lexicon form the empirical basis for the formulation of a semantic theory giving the intensional relations between all the signs in a natural language; since analytic meanings are least variant among all the meanings in a language, they determine the ontology for that language.

In information science terminology, analytic sentences are messages of lowest entropy. In contrast, of course, contradictory sentences may be termed messages of highest entropy.

According to this model, a world of common objects may be maintained, approximately, ranging over some domain of space and time. In such a world, information exchange can proceed, with a minimum of inaccuracy, long enough for real objects to remain more-or-less identical over an indefinite period. Moreover, the notion of logical truth in such a world is hardly mere fleeting illusion, since it reflects those types of linguistic behavior which are the least susceptible to alteration.

I can, therefore, thanks to Katz and Fodor, maintain my perverse view of reality, even if it turns out that theyprefer seeing the world as a completely determined place.

vi. What kind of world have I stepped into?

As Quine has pointed out (*Two Dogmas of Empiricism*), the classical notion of analytic (i.e., logical) truth depends on a prior knowledge for its application which for the empiricist, was only guaranteed by immediate intuition.

But immediate intuition, being simple, is indemonstrable, hence optional for each observer, and all intersubjective logical truth is conventional (i.e., learned through orthogonal development in a community). Moreover, logical truth in the sense of **analytic-in-L** is only demonstrable in artificial languages, since natural languages are inconsistent.

Furthermore, a natural language lexicon, which reports the analytic behavior of a community, is an empirical semantic theory based upon generalizations from past usage; while it can be used to predict, within a range, the linguistic behavior of a community of respondents, it can give no insight into the ultimate layout of the real; and because natural languages are ambiguous, all analytic behavior is stochastic and held to physical reality only by the behavioral notion of stimulus-synonymy, which defies radical translation between the private languages of respondents.

The import of this last consideration is, for us, not only that
(a) I am cut off from the rest of the community in terms of the solipsism of my intensional meanings, but that (b) every linguistic function in my own brain is cut off from every other linguistic function by the same rule.

The only guaranteed sameness of meaning possible in such a model of mind must be wholly extensional - i.e., nonlinear - and dependent upon how many slicing operations my scansion apparatus can perform in the tracking of a signal, from one sampling to the next.

But this works out well for us when we consider that we recognize stimulus-synonymies between pictures-and-words as well as between pictures-and-pictures, and words-and-words. This kind of pattern recognition does permit me to claim that a word and a picture, or two pictures of the same word, are all descriptions of the "same" object - when the object is construed as beyond language, as the signal which is being tracked.

vii. But is it also adequate to account for my intuition of linearity (i.e., my intuition of logical derivation from premises to conclusion)? For although the overall configuration of my awareness is stochastic, it has clusters in it which are more predictable, more determined than the rest .

Are such patterns of linear behavior simply those architectural changes that my biological computing mechanism undergoes, in its orthogonal development, as the result of accumulations of more stimulus synonymies? (B.F. Skinner's behaviorism would seem to imply this.)

viii. But my awareness is creative:

I am able to recognize synonymies between pictures and words that I have never learned to correlate previously, even in entirely new contexts of action. This kind of behavior reflects transformational properties rather than mere operant conditioning of apparatus.

Katz and Fodor follow Chomsky in holding a transformational view of linguistic behavior; might this not be extended to the whole range of linguistic behavior, both graphic and verbal, and graphic-to-verbal, and verbal-to-graphic?

For example, there seems to be an isomorphic correspondence between all the pictures we can draw of geometric figures, and their algebraic notations (although the notations we use are sometimes only normalizations when such figures are extremely irregular and defy precise mathematical description).

Drawing or tracking a picture is one kind of behavior, fitting an algebraic notation to it is another; what language does the brain use to correlate the figure with the formula?

This is a case in which I engage in one kind of conceptual activity which is made to serve as a template for another kind of conceptual activity. In each case, I might be applying the same syntax, but because of the difference in the architecture of the apparatus which uses that syntax, there is a radical difference in the objects produced as the result of that activity.

Here there may be a key to the qualitative difference I sense between my visual and my verbal awareness:

I am aware that using my eyes and hands to communicate with feedback centers in my brain produces, even though I use the same rule, an entirely different set of consequences than the use of my verbal apparatus produces.

Such consequences are then correlated in the next round.

3. An artist's leap to a preliminary portrait of Consciousness(!)

Might not the identity between a word and a picture be couched in a verification procedure which the brain undergoes, to determine that the same rule is being employed in the production of the verbal and graphic messages?

If so, I am a step nearer to an explication of a conscious string, for consciousness is consciousness of a correspondence between pictures and words with all the other pictures and words in the attention field; and it is more than mere statement but judgment of that correspondence - i.e., an act carrying ontological commitment.

Let's try a Turing model; picture a machine that contains

(a) a set of alternate receptors and communicators, using the same syntax.

(b) a mechanism for orthogonal development, based upon first-level operant conditioning and second-level transformational response.

(c) a nonlinear decision procedure for pattern recognition, proceeding epistemologically, via multiple hypotheses.

A tentative characterization of a conscious string for such a machine might be:

the Nth-level confirmation of an ith-level truth-claim.

The string is linguistic, an ejaculatory utterance from the brain which carries a performative statement:

"I am verifying! that I am verifying! that I am verifying! ... that ("...x...!") is True!"
The idea came to me while reading Hillary Putnam's paper, *Minds and Machines*. There, he uses the example of two Turing machines which scan each other's states and become utterly confused, after some rounds of information exchange, as to which machine is in which state.

For example: When I say, "I have a pain," do I mean my hand or my brain?

If I mean: "I, the information-exchange network, have a pain,"

then the pain is no longer such a simple feeling; there is something decidedly linguistic about it, intersubjective, a message covertly couched in the third-person form rather than the immediacy of the first-person form in which it is outwardly expressed.

But what kind of a message? Surely no simple sentence such as "I have a pain" is sufficient information to be contained in a consciousness string.

If Machine A says to Machine B, "B has a pain,"

B should have a program for responsive action that verifies A's claim - it should be able to kick and scream and indulge in sophisticated strategies of pain-avoidance. A model like this will only work if:

(a) the programmed behavior is sufficiently coordinated and complex;

(b) the semantical component involves the mechanism in existential situations in which self and not-self are sufficiently clear and consistent concepts for the self-programming network;

(c) it is not linguistically absurd to hold that first-person truth-claims are of the same logical type as third-person truth-claims.

The impossibility of (c) would void the whole object of our investigation and must, therefore, be investigated first.

A quest for a logically-certain proof that "I" and "...x..." are logically equivalent would be self-defeating since the determination of a logical type falls into two categories;

(1) either the classification of two terms into one type is conventional, hence optional, or,
(2) there is some kind of essential relation between them, discovered in intuition

- but the latter hypothesis is precisely what we are trying to destroy.

The kind of linguistic fact we seek to establish is that the identity relation

$$\text{"I"} = \text{"...x..."} \text{ or } \text{"it"}$$

between two logically proper names (the subjects of a denotation) is contingent because not self-contradictory.

Only an informal proof is possible:

An observation of my linguistic habits shows that my use of the exclamations "I hurt!" and "It hurts!" are sometimes equivalent.

I also readily identify myself as the subject of others' denotations when they refer to me as "you" and "she"; if there were a type difference between the pronouns, wouldn't I have a difficulty with others' use of the pronoun "I"?

The history of philosophy gives further corroboration to the view that the subject of an "I" denotation is conceptual rather than immediate.

The Cartesian cogito was never offered as a proof for the existence of God as a simple fact of the mind (Descartes had to prove the existence of God before he could establish the integrity of the self as something existing apart from the dream of an "evil genius"); the most simple, basic truths that Descartes found in intuition were qualities existing in complex relations, and the self was not among these - was not an impression like redness or pain.

Hume tore apart the claim that the self was a simple impression. Kant agreed with Hume.
Bertrand Russell gave his *Theory of Descriptions* which holds that all proper names (including logically proper names) are eliminable in favor of descriptions; the import of this theory is that all things may be talked about in the third-person description which fits them. This means that the sentence, "I hurt." may be

rewritten as "The individual, x, such that (some adequate description for locating x in space-time) ... is hurting."

But even if the "I" of the "I think" is conceptual, as we are arguing, does it follow that there are no simples whatsoever in our awareness - that the whole of it is fully descriptive of a lower-level occurrence?

The superstition still persists, if indeed it is only a superstition, although both fathers of philosophy, Plato and Aristotle, didn't think so.

Plato, in the *Theatetus*, tore apart an early version of logical atomism by pointing out that the wholes in our introspection cannot be fully reduced to a mere sum of their parts.

Aristotle, whose *Posterior Analytics* set the pace for scientific demonstration based upon intuited first principles, did not hold that the indemonstrable first principles were in any sense atomic; on the contrary, he offered a very sophisticated theory of perception which held that the world outside of us and the world within us are both parts of the same vitalistic process in which our powers for observing the world depend upon the assumption of a potentiality in the observer to see, and a potentiality in the observed to be seen - that is, in a very information-theory-like view of the special relation between signal-senders and signal-receivers.

Among the moderns,

Russell, one of the fathers of Logical Atomism (the movement which preceded Logical Positivism and tried to isolate the simple qualities of introspection which Hume's phenomenalism took for granted), ended by admitting that while particulars are logically eliminable in favor of universals, universals are not eliminable in favor of particulars, since every meaningful utterance must contain at least one constituent and one component.

Wittgenstein, as previously noted, denied the existence of strictly private languages; his argument, though more eloquent, closely parallels the one used by Aristotle (*Post. An. II,9*):

> if there were such things as particular names, the reasoning goes, then I would have to keep naming everything that happens in my awareness; the activity would go on indefinitely; but then the whole sense of assigning names to things would be lost altogether; we name things to recognize individuals when we see them again; names are universals - merely shorthand signs for descriptions.

To my knowledge, not even the continental intuitionists hold to a theory of simples in awareness. The undeniable intuitions they present are usually the relational complexes of classical (Kantian) space and time; but these are arbitrary since intuitions of non-Euclidean space-time, as well as paradoxes of class containment, are conceivable. Nor are the simple ideas of my own introspection truly indivisible, since even the sensation of redness in recollection is an impression which contains both extension (a spatial component) and a concept of what not-red is.

The subtle difference in the conflict of theories of knowledge between the (usually continental) proponents of a Leibnizian conceptualism and the (usually empiricist) proponents of a form of Hobbesian constructivism is paralleled, I believe, in the subtle shift of viewpoint of the Wittgenstein of the *Tractatus* to the Wittgenstein of the *Philosophical Investigations*: it is a movement from the intuitionist's belief that there are logical simples in language which can form the building blocks of all our deductive reasoning, and the constructivist's belief that all the simples in language are not indivisibles but only undivided starting points for our deductive reasoning - beginning anywhere, in any suburb of language, can be a precise beginning, depending on the descriptive job to be done; we build from what has gone before.

The model of conscious behavior I envision holds to this latter, constructivist view, seeing all of consciousness as fully filled with language, emanating from lower order processes of linguistic information exchange. At each level stand stimulus-meanings, facts of a physicalistic kind, describable in a neurophysiological language.

Those who prefer may add that these physical relations reflect a transcendental order in things - but I don't have to accept this latter hypothesis since my view of a stochastic universe also provides a temporally-extended stable reality, and a choice between determinism and indeterminism is optional, beyond the limits of possible experience.*

*1984 addendum: *Many persons reading the original of this work mistakenly assumed that my view of a stochastic universe in some way implied that nothing in such a universe could authentically be considered Sacred. This would be a misreading of the particular philosophy of religion accompanying the proposed new concept of mind. My own position, as both artist and philosopher, derived from the line of reasoning in this paper, is that no graven image - whether in thought or in speech - can be a simple representation of The Sacred. Hence miracles and direct expressions of faith are all neutral mental phenomena to be made subject to the same epistemological investigations that accompany the verification of any other utterance of the mind. If this view threatens the doctrine of any established religion - let it do so with impunity, as a religion in its own right.)*

4. An artist's glimpse of the cybernetic model of mind:

Let us hypothesize that units of consciousness, whether large or small, are essential links in the chain of epistemological information-exchange in the central nervous system of a complex self-programming unit which has powers for action of a type involving multiple experimentation. Why should the emergence of consciousness in such a unit fulfill a particular epistemological need?

Only an answer to a question of this type can satisfy the scientist that consciousness is a genuine effect of natural causes.

I believe the answer lies in the kinds of adaptational decisions made possible by the presence of conscious processes not made possible at any other level of cybernetic adaptational activity:

I have in mind those acts of experimentation which involve creative problem-solving within existential contexts of a highly dynamic type - activities without which both organisms and machines very quickly deteriorate into mere ritual behavior (characterized by high redundance of patterns of action, high rigidity in the face of new situations - i.e., stimulus-analytic behavior carried to the point of empty tautology, lowest-entropy communication, informational incapsulation, logically rigid and paranoid behavior).

But neither are conscious processes wholly unpredictable - for it they were, they would not constitute an awareness of anything at all, for some underlying integrity of action is needed in order to preserve those perceptual parameters that fix an observer in a definite set of conceptual relations to a fixed observation field.

Consciousness as a process maintains a homeostatic mean between extremes of rigidity and fragmentation, informational redundance and informational variegation.

But how precisely might conscious processes be maintaining such homeostasis? This is the question the engineer legitimately asks and, not being a mathematician, I cannot presume to offer more than a sketch of a model for the answer. The descriptive materials I will use are bits and pieces borrowed from symbolic logic and Leibniz's *Monadology*, reconstituted to apply to a local universe and a nonvitalistic, information-theory viewpoint:

I see the conscious string as containing a hash-coded engram carrying information of two types - confirmatory and disconfirmatory, of the last round of sensori-motor experimentation activity; the product of the reception by lower-order processes of this conscious string is a new response, the next conscious ejaculation, of a logically-creative type in relation to what has gone before.

In logic, the term "creative" has a special application: it denotes those undecidable sentences of an incomplete postulate system which, when added to the primitives, do not affect its inner consistency but alter the set of sentences derivable from it; moreover, a "creative" definition is viewed as one that broadens the meaning of a term beyond what the simples of the system determine.

Analytic behavior is, ideally, absolutely noncreative; in contrast, self-contradictory behavior is, ideally, absolutely creative - bearing a highest-entropy message; to contradict a tautology is to reverse the informational entropy of that function which produces a specific signal within the class of signals constituting a hash-coded message string.

A priori schemes - conceptual networks - are traditionally viewed as networks of tautologies. What if the hash-coded message in the conscious string assigns a value 0 for all tautologies posited by lower-order computational outputs; which lower-order messages would survive the event?
The logical product of a structural "clash" between all their inverse functions, surely, and - more importantly - all the programs which are neutral to the negation taking place since

they are incomplete relative to the logical content of the conscious string being received as a signal. (Such neutral programs are, in some sense, options, metaphysical posits.)

The programmer knows better than I the details of such a negative-feedback process; its essential character is adaptational, as I believe Norbert Wiener anticipated, and the kinds of message feedback configurations such a complex information network would engage in results in behavior of a logically creative type.

Suppose we view all the conceptual programs of the mind (ideally perhaps as many as $[10]9]9$ of them as each providing a multivalued response to a signal contained in a conscious string (i.e., either assigning it a value of 1 or 0 or some value between 1 and 0 in terms of chemically-stored action potentials);

> that is, suppose we view each conceptual program as a "theory" for which the signal functions either as a reinforcement or an inhibition or a neutral action potential;

> then, the end-product of a chain of information exchange in response to this signal is some limit of feedback, R, which is a compromise - the best of all "compossible" configurations resulting from the field of conceptual systems at play;

> and R, as a hash-coded message, feeds back to the lower-order processes as a set of signals, together with new input from inner and outer sense.

The above is a model for consciousness which falls under a certain type, extensible into higher-level models for scientific, artistic, and moral discovery. For the multiple-theory, multiple hypothesis approach which characterizes such epistemological activity can help us determine, nonlinearly and with optimum information retention, which theories to revise and which to discard in any observational domain. The physical economies of theory revision provide the criterion for garbage-disposal.

Concluding remarks:

This model of consciousness, I believe, makes possible an account of both aesthetic and moral behavior as something more than mere conditioned response culturally-instilled.

By maintaining that consciousness works against excessive analytic behavior, and does so in an epistemological framework, acts which function as optimizations of observational probing are made genuinely acts of optimal adaptation.

Much in the classical tradition, I see moral awareness as proceeding from aesthetic awareness which is the result of a cultivation of those habits of sensori-motor adaptation which increase our powers for epistemological choice.

I see such awareness as fostered by the very opposite of rote teaching and operant conditioning; rational - epistemological - choice is the result of the preservation, through a liberal and diversified education, of all our powers of choosing between equipossible, equivalid alternatives.

Annselm LNVM **1972**

REFERENCES

Dewey, John
    1934   ART AS EXPERIENCE. New York: Putnam.

Gombrich, E.H.
    1965   ART AND ILLUSION. New York: Pantheon.

Katz, J., and Fodor, J., eds.
    1964   THE STRUCTURE OF LANGUAGE. New Jersey: Prentice-Hall.

Lewis, C.I.
    1956   MIND AND THE WORLD ORDER. 2nd ed. New York: Dover.

Piaget, Jean
    1971   BIOLOGY AND KNOWLEDGE. Scotland: Edinburgh Univ. Press.
    1963   PSYCHOLOGY OF INTELLIGENCE. New Jersey: Littlefield, Adams & Co. (French ed., 1947).

Pierce, J.R.
    1961   SYMBOLS, SIGNALS AND NOISE. New York: Harper Torchbooks.

Quine, W.V.
    1969   ONTOLOGICAL RELATIVITY AND OTHER ESSAYS. New York: Columbia Univ. Press.
    1960   WORD AND OBJECT. Massachusetts: M.I.T. Press.

Reichenbach, Hans
    1958   THE PHILOSOPHY OF SPACE AND TIME. New York: Dover.

Sebestyen, S.
    1962   DECISION-MAKING PROCESSES IN PATTERN RECOGNITION. New York: Macmillan.

Sperry, R.W.
    1970, 77/6   An objective approach to subjective experience. *Psychological Review.*
    585-589
    1973   Lateral specialization of cerebral functions in the surgically separated hemispheres. THE PSYCHOBIOLOGY OF THINKING. New York: Academic Press.

Sterling, T.D., Bering, E.A., Jr., Pollack, S.V., and Vaughan, H.G., Jr., eds.
    1971   VISUAL PROSTHESIS. New York: Academic Press.

Vinje-Morpurgo, Annselm
    1973   A CYBERNETIC MODEL OF CONSCIOUS BEHAVIOR FROM A MULTI-MEDIA ARTIST. M.A. thesis, The City College of the City University of New York: September.

Waddington, C.H., ed.
    1970, I-III   TOWARDS A THEORETICAL BIOLOGY. Scotland: Edinburgh Univ. Press.

Whitrow, G.J.
    1961   THE NATURAL PHILOSOPHY OF TIME. New York: Harper Torchbooks.

Wiener, Norbert
    1961   CYBERNETICS. Cambridge, Ma.: M.I.T. Press.

Zeeman, E.C.
    1965   TOPOLOGY OF THE BRAIN. Proceedings of the 1964 conference on mathematics and computer science in biology and medicine, Medical Research Council, Oxford. London: Her Majesty's Stationery Office.

Zipf, G.K.
    1935   THE PSYCHO-BIOLOGY OF LANGUAGE. Cambridge, Ma.: M.I.T. Press.

ArtemisSmith : The Third Sex

Get the first part of *ArtemisSmith's* 1950's Best-selling GLBT Pulp Fiction Triad and 2011 Memoir:

ISBN 978-1-878998-38-5

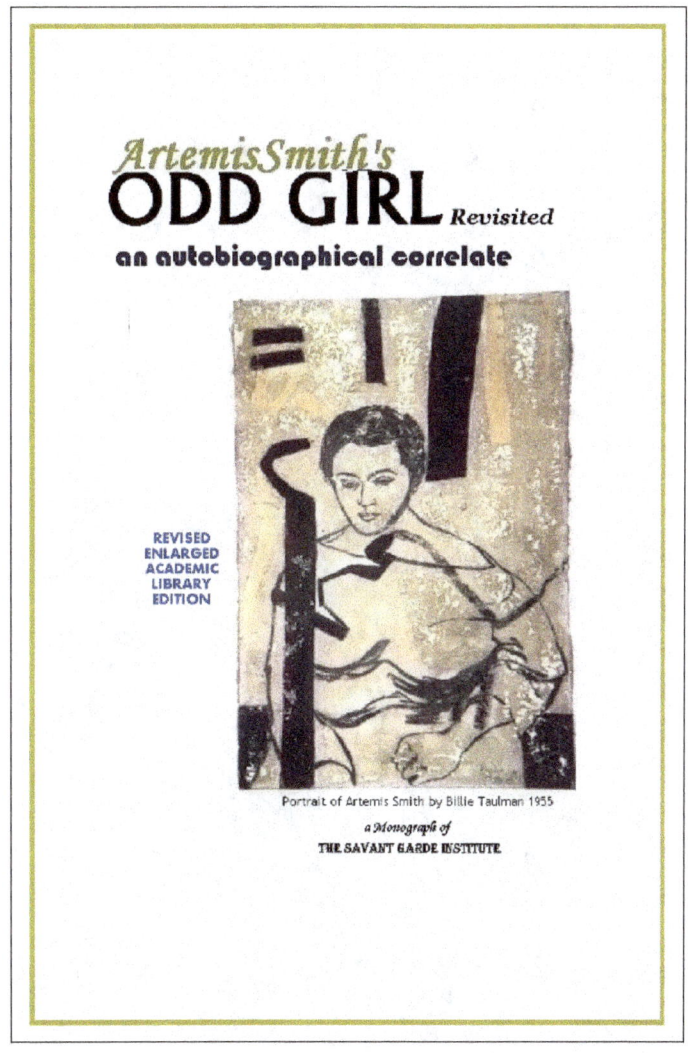

Coming soon only in print! The last of *ArtemisSmith's* 1950's GLBT Best-selling Pulp Fiction Triad which includes her 1960's Memoirs in a 2013 Appendix:

       ISBN 978-1-878998-33-0

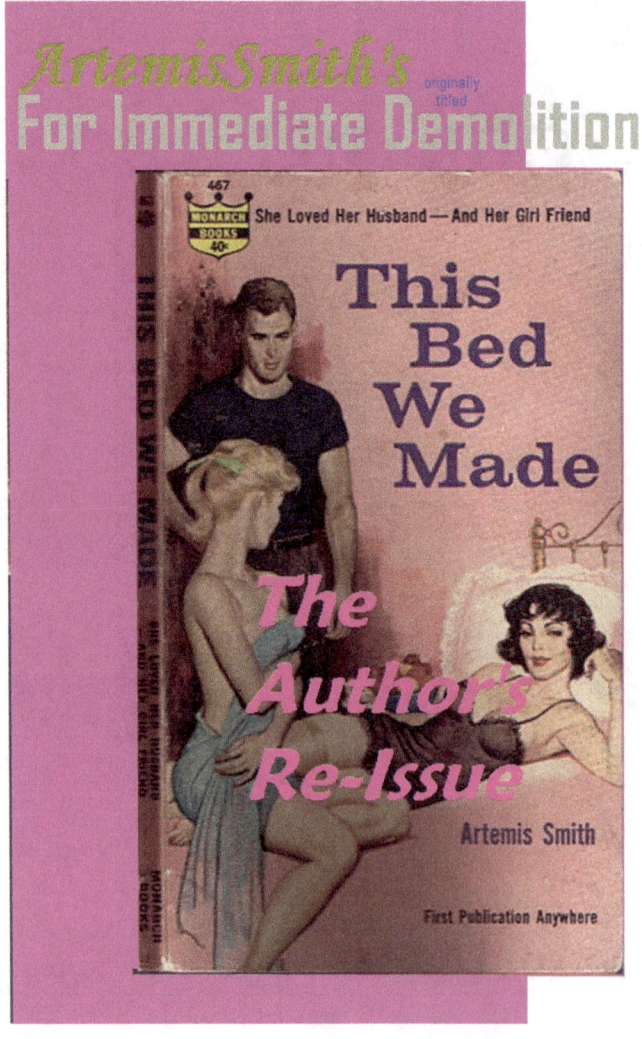

Get the 2013 Literary and Poetic Anthology:
978-1-878998-20-0 ECONOMY COLOR EDITION

BOOK ART AVAILABLE ONLY IN PRINT!
Coffee-Table-Safe LITERARY EROTICA:
978-1-878998-02-6 Deluxe Color Edition

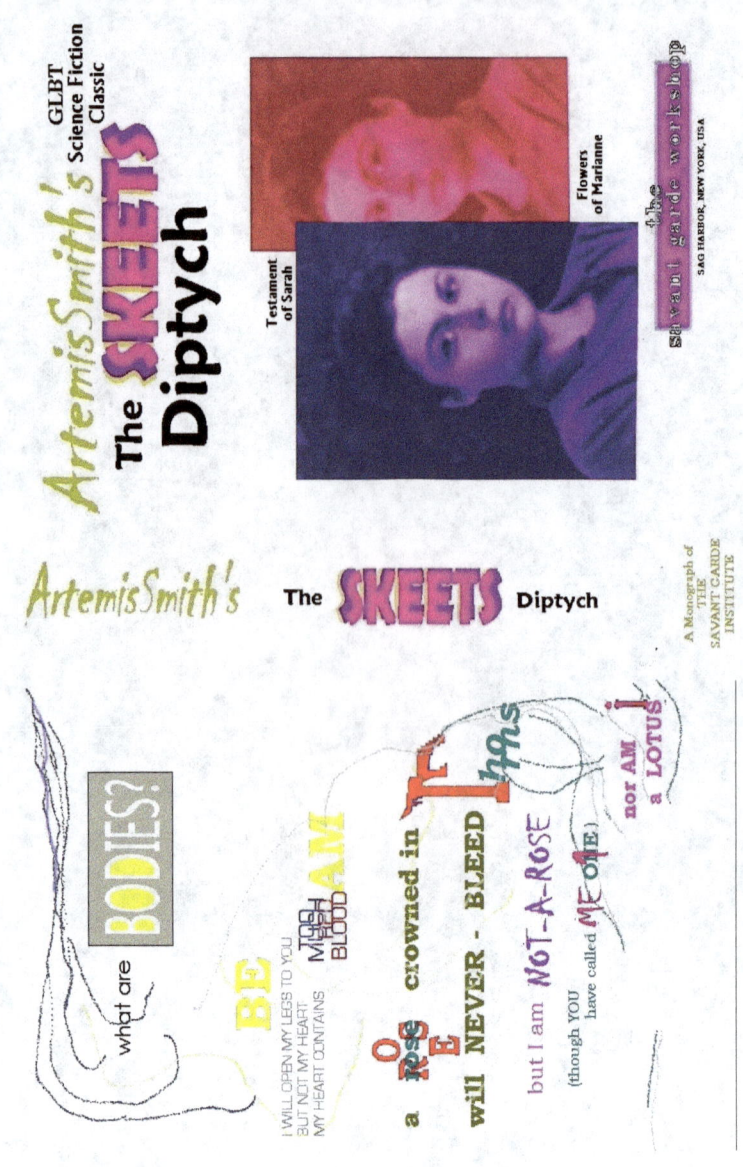

ArtemisSmith : The Third Sex

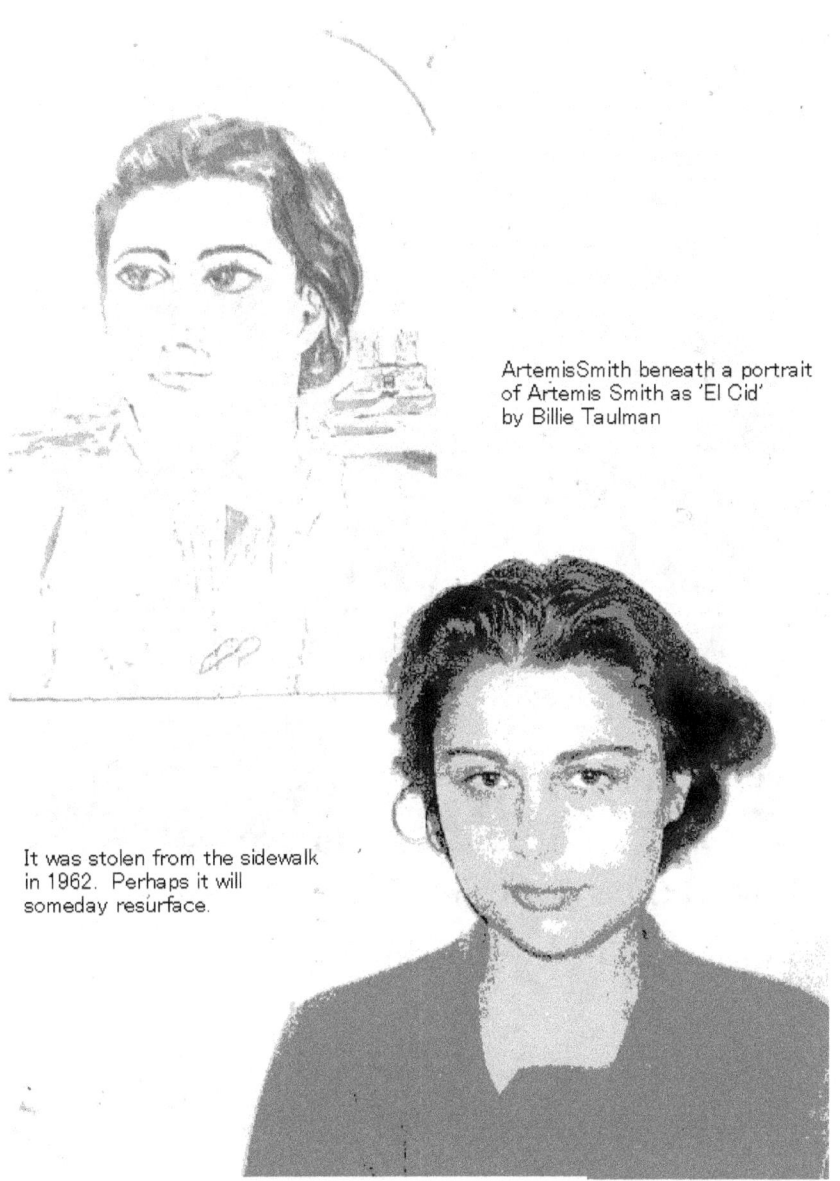

ArtemisSmith beneath a portrait of Artemis Smith as 'El Cid' by Billie Taulman

It was stolen from the sidewalk in 1962. Perhaps it will someday resurface.

Billie Taulman with Self-Portrait, 1954.

ArtemisSmith : The Third Sex

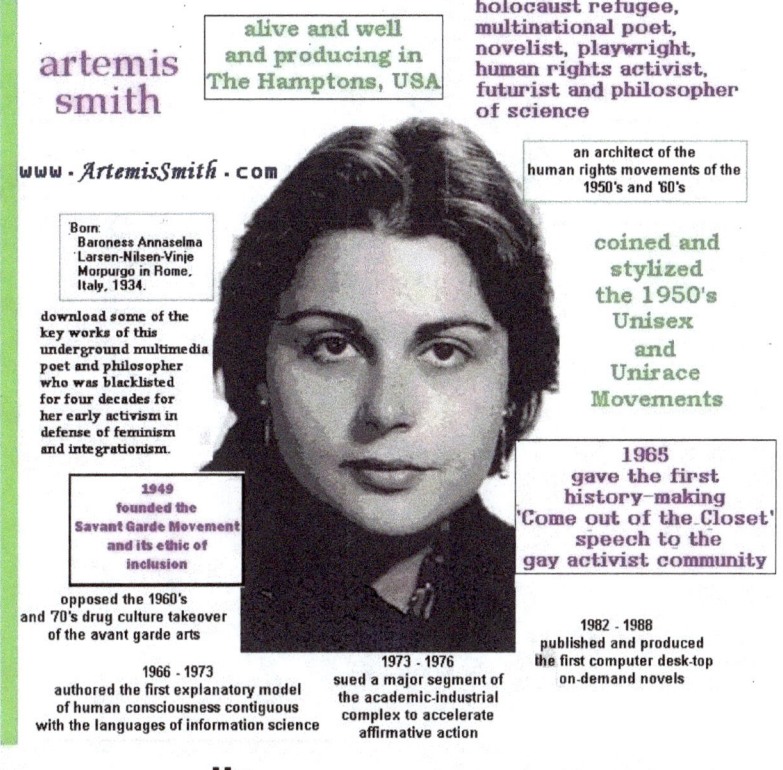

www.ingramcontent.com/pod-product-compliance
Lightning Source LLC
Chambersburg PA
CBHW071228080526
44587CB00013BA/1535